HARVARD SERIES OF LEGAL BIBLIOGRAPHIES

EDITED BY

ELDON R. JAMES

LIBRARIAN OF THE HARVARD LAW SCHOOL

III

A BIBLIOGRAPHY OF
THE WRITINGS OF ROSCOE POUND

LONDON : HUMPHREY MILFORD
OXFORD UNIVERSITY PRESS

Photo by White Studio

Roscoe Pound

A BIBLIOGRAPHY OF

THE WRITINGS OF
ROSCOE POUND

BY

FRANKLYN C. SETARO

CAMBRIDGE, MASSACHUSETTS

HARVARD UNIVERSITY PRESS

1942

PRINTED AT THE HARVARD UNIVERSITY PRESS
CAMBRIDGE, MASSACHUSETTS, U.S.A.

PREFACE

It is a pleasant task to acknowledge gratitude to the many who have aided in the preparation of this volume. I am indeed indebted to a veritable host, both here and abroad, for kindnesses of one sort or another. It is a matter of deep regret that formal limitations make it impossible to mention them separately. They are too numerous. However, it is my earnest hope that this general recognition of indebtedness will be deemed a sufficient expression of my warmest and most sincere gratitude.

More particular acknowledgment is due to the following for their valuable and extensive contributions to this undertaking: Miss Clara L. Craig, Reference Librarian, University of Nebraska, and her assistant, Miss Ruby C. Wilder; the late Mr. J. Hugo Tatsch, Director of Education and Librarian, and Miss Muriel A. Davis, Assistant Librarian, Grand Lodge A. F. and A. M. of Massachusetts; Professor Frederick C. Hicks, Law Librarian, and his secretary, Miss Ruth A. Hazelton, Yale University; Mr. Miles O. Price, Law Librarian, and Miss Margaret E. Hall, Reference Law Librarian, Columbia University; Mr. Dennis A. Dooley, Librarian, Massachusetts State Library; and Miss Hilda F. Harris of the Farlow Reference Library of Cryptogamic Botany, and Miss Ruth D. Sanderson of the Gray Herbarium, both in Harvard University. To the authorities of the following institutions, I am indebted for a cordial welcome and many courtesies: the Association of the Bar of the City of New York, the Harvard Club of New York City, the Grand Lodge Library, F. and A. M. of New York, Columbia University, the New York Public Library, the University of Chicago, and the Elbert H. Gary Library, the library of the Northwestern University Law School. I am also indebted to various members of the staff of the Harvard Law School Library, particularly to Mr. George R. Arthur for checking the manuscript and to Miss Helen Sherman for typing it.

The following have placed me under an extraordinarily deep obligation. They have contributed much to the making of this bibliography.

Miss May M. McCarthy, secretary to Professor Roscoe Pound,

has liberally allowed me to make use of her bibliographical materials. Every page of this volume bears the imprint of her cordiality, enthusiasm, and many kindnesses.

Mr. Francis X. Dwyer, Assistant Librarian, Harvard Law School Library, has carefully checked and greatly expanded my original manuscript to include many items which were not available to me, particularly the Chinese and Japanese translations. His devoted efforts are deeply appreciated.

I desire to acknowledge the courtesy and consideration extended to me by the Syndics of the Harvard University Press. I also wish to thank the editor of the Harvard Series of Legal Bibliographies, Professor Eldon R. James, Librarian of the Harvard Law School, who has devoted much effort and time to the perfecting of this work. Also, I wish to thank the Committee on Publications of the Harvard Law School for their approval of the manuscript and their recommendation of it for publication.

Notwithstanding all this contributed labor and cooperation, I must take the burden of responsibility for the volume's imperfections and trust that they may be viewed with charity. I have endeavored to include all of Professor Pound's writings published before July 1, 1940. The bibliography is numbered chronologically in the various sections according to the date of the appearance of the print.

Finally, to Professor Roscoe Pound I must confess a debt of gratitude which almost transcends expression. In executing this work, I have had the advantage of his constant and discriminating assistance. He has given generously of his time and has opened to me many matters which I could not have found in any other way and has been kind enough to read and criticize the original draft of the manuscript. Without his encouragement, it would have been difficult, if not impossible, to proceed. For all this, and for the rare privilege of sitting under him some years ago, which, I might say, is the *primum mobile* of this production, this volume stands as a modest tribute of admiration, reverence, and sincere appreciation — *hoc erat in votis.*

F. C. S.

NEW YORK CITY
January, 1941

CONTENTS

I. LAW AND LEGAL EDUCATION 3
    Section 1 Books and Major Papers 3
    Section 2 Shorter Papers, Addresses, and Reports . . 56
    Section 3 Articles and Reports Written with Others . . 77

II. JUDICIAL WRITINGS 82
    Section 1 Nebraska Reports 82
    Section 2 Nebraska Unofficial Reports 101
    Section 3 American and British Claims Arbitration . . 119
    Section 4 Report as Special Examiner in Administrative
    Hearing 121

III. NON-LEGAL BOOKS AND PAPERS 122
    Section 1 Botany 122
    Section 2 Freemasonry 127
    Section 3 Miscellaneous 133

APPENDICES 137
    A. WRITINGS ABOUT ROSCOE POUND 139
      1. Principal Papers 139
      2. Brief Articles and Notices 142

    B. REVIEWS OF BOOKS AND PAPERS OF ROSCOE POUND . . 145
TABLE OF CASES 153

INDEX 163

BIBLIOGRAPHY OF ROSCOE POUND

BIBLIOGRAPHY OF ROSCOE POUND

PART I

LAW AND LEGAL EDUCATION

SECTION I. BOOKS AND MAJOR PAPERS

1896

1. *The Influence of the Civil Law in America*
   Nebraska Legal News, vol. 4, no. 7. January 4, 1896.
2. *Actions on Penal Statutes*
   42 Central Law Journal 135–139. February 14, 1896.
3. *Dogs and the Law*
   8 Green Bag 172–174. April, 1896.
   31 Irish Law Times 163–164. April 10, 1897.
4. *The Study of Roman Law*
   Nebraska Legal News, vol. 4, no. 36. July 25, 1896.
5. *Are Judgments Quasi Negotiable*
   43 Central Law Journal 440–444. November 27, 1896.

1897

6. *Wig and Gown*
   Nebraska Legal News, vol. 5, no. 37. July 31, 1897.
7. *Something about Reporters*
   Nebraska Legal News, vol. 5, no. 41, p. 1.[1] August 28, 1897.

[1] Possibly continued, but continuation not located.

1899

8. *Professor Thayer on the Law of Evidence*
   Nebraska Legal News, vol. 7, no. 40, p. 1. August 5, 1899.
9. *Legal Education*
   Nebraska Legal News, vol. 7, no. 51, p. 1.[1] September 2, 1899.

[1] Possibly continued, but continuation not located.

1901

10. *King Alfred in Legal History* [1]
Nebraska Legal News, vol. 10, no. 9, p. 1. November 2, 1901.

[1] Address delivered at the Anniversary Services at Memorial Hall, Lincoln, Nebraska, October 28, 1901.

1903

11. *The Decadence of Equity* [1]
Proceedings of the Nebraska State Bar Association, vol. 1, p. 152–166. 1903.
5 Columbia Law Review 20–35.[2] January, 1905.

[1] Paper read by "Mr. Commissioner Pound" at the second annual meeting of the Nebraska State Bar Association, January 9 and 10, 1902, held in Court Room Number 1 in the Court House at Omaha. The published text carries fifty-two bibliographical footnotes.

[2] *Corrigendum:* p. 20, n. 1, "Read before the third annual meeting" should read "Read before the second annual meeting." *Op. cit.* p. 39.

12. *The Evolution of Legal Education* [1]
Lincoln, Neb., Jacob North & Co., 1903. 20 p.

[1] Inaugural lecture, as Dean of the Faculty of Law in the University of Nebraska, delivered September 19, 1903.

13. OUTLINES OF LECTURES ON JURISPRUDENCE CHIEFLY FROM THE ANALYTICAL STANDPOINT
Lincoln, Neb., Jacob North & Co., 1903. 67 p.
Under title: OUTLINES OF LECTURES ON JURISPRUDENCE
2d ed. Cambridge, Mass., The University Press, 1914. 99 p.[1]
3d ed. Cambridge, Mass., The University Press, 1920. iv, 136 p.
4th ed. Cambridge, Mass., The University Press, 1928. vi, 156 p.

[1] See title no. 55 *infra.*

1904

14. *A New School of Jurists*
University Studies,[1] vol. 4, no. 3, p. 249–266. July, 1904.
Reprint: n.p., n.d. 18 p.

[1] University of Nebraska, Lincoln, Nebraska. See title no. 52 *infra.*

15. CASES ON PRACTICE: SELECT CASES AND OTHER AUTHORITIES ON PROCEDURE IN CIVIL CAUSES WITH REFERENCES TO THE CODE AND DECISIONS OF NEBRASKA, VOL. 1.[1]
Lincoln, Neb., Jacob North & Co., 1904. 461 p.

[1] No more published.

16. *Code Pleading: Outline and Practical Exercises*
Lincoln, Neb., Jacob North & Co., 1904. 16 p.

17. READINGS ON THE HISTORY AND SYSTEM OF THE COMMON LAW
Lincoln, Neb., Jacob North & Co., 1904. 404 p.
2d ed. Boston, Mass., The Boston Book Company, 1913.
xix, 625 p.
3d ed.[1] Rochester, N. Y., The Lawyers Cooperative Publishing Company, 1927. xx, 731 p.

[1] With Theodore F. T. Plucknett.

1905

18. *Do We Need a Philosophy of Law?*
5 Columbia Law Review 339–353. May, 1905.
Reprint: n.p., n.d. 339–353 p.

1906

19. *The Spirit of the Common Law*
18 Green Bag 17–25. January, 1906.
Proceedings of the Nebraska State Bar Association, vol. 2,
p. 262–276.[1] 1909.
Reprint: Boston, Mass., n.d. 16 p.

[1] Paper read at the sixth annual meeting of the Nebraska State Bar Association, held in Edward Creighton Hall in the City of Omaha, November 22, 23, 1905. Mr. Pound's paper was published with bibliographical notes.
It remains to be stated that a considerable part of this address is taken from *Do We Need a Philosophy of Law?* See title no. 18 *supra*.

20. *The Causes of Popular Dissatisfaction with the Administration of Justice* [1]
Report of the 29th Annual Meeting of the American Bar Association [vol. 29], part 1, p. 395–417. 1906.
Reprint: n.p., n.d. 23 p.
40 American Law Review 729–749. September–October, 1906.
14 American Lawyer 445–451. October, 1906.
20 Journal of the American Judicature Society[2] 178–187.
February, 1937.

[1] Mr. Pound's initial Address, August 29, 1906, before the American Bar Association. The meeting was held at the Capitol Building, St. Paul, Minnesota.
[2] This reprint included an introduction written by John H. Wigmore entitled *Roscoe Pound's St. Paul Address of 1906; The Spark that Kindled the White Flame of Progress.*

72 United States Law Review [3] 28–42. January, 1938.
6 Lawyers' Journal [4] 638–643. July 31, 1938.
C. C. H. Legal Periodical Digest, 1938 ed., p. 4027–4028.

[3] This reprint bears a significant editorial headnote: "An Analysis of Fundamentals Published in the American Law Review Thirty Years Ago, but Strikingly Appropriate To-Day."
[4] Manila, P. I.

21. READINGS IN ROMAN LAW
Lincoln, Neb., Jacob North & Co., 1906. 234 p.
Under title: READINGS IN ROMAN LAW AND THE CIVIL LAW AND MODERN CODES AS DEVELOPMENTS THEREOF; AN INTRODUCTION TO COMPARATIVE LAW
2d ed. Part I. Cambridge, Mass., Harvard University Press, 1914. vii, 159 p.
[Part II.] [1] Cambridge, Mass. Issued privately, 1916. 352 sheets, multigraphed.

[1] Portions of Part II were reissued in multigraphed form by Professor Frederick de Sloovere for use only in the course in Roman Law at New York University. 1934.

1907

22. *Executive Justice*
55 American Law Register [1] 137–146. March, 1907.
Reprint: n.p., n.d. 137–146 p.

[1] 46 New Series.

23. *Spurious Interpretation*
7 Columbia Law Review 379–386. June, 1907.

24. *The Need of a Sociological Jurisprudence*
19 Green Bag 607–615. October, 1907.
Reprint: n.p., n.d. 11 p.
Report of the 30th Annual Meeting [1] of the American Bar Association [vol. 31], 911–926. 1907.

[1] Held in the City Hall, Portland, Maine, August 26–28, 1907. This was the "Chairman's Address," Section of Legal Education.

1908

25. *Common Law and Legislation*
21 Harvard Law Review 383–407. April, 1908.
26. *Legacies on Impossible or Illegal Conditions Precedent*
3 Illinois Law Review 1–23. May, 1908.
Reprint: n.p., n.d. 24 p.

27. *The German Movement for Reform in Legal Administration and Procedure*

American Bar Association. Comparative Law Bureau. Annual Bulletin. No. 1, p. 31–36. July, 1908.

28. *Enforcement of Law*

20 Green Bag 401–410. August, 1908.

125 Law Times 493–496. September 26, 1908.

Proceedings of the Illinois State Bar Association, 32nd Annual Meeting,[1] part 2, p. 81–100. 1908.

Reprint: n.p., n.d. 20 p.

[1] Chicago, Illinois, June 25, 26, 1908. This was one of several "Special Addresses." Portrait facing p. 81.

29. *Mechanical Jurisprudence*

8 Columbia Law Review 605–623. December, 1908.

Reprint: n.p., n.d. 19 p.

Proceedings of the North Dakota Bar Association [1] for the years 1906–1907 and 1907–1908, p. 151–163. 1909.

[1] Meeting held in Valley City, North Dakota, September 25, 1908. Portrait facing p. 150.

None of the reports of Mr. Pound's many appearances before our various state bar associations is more delightful than that of the Valley City, N. D., meeting. In a sense, it stands as a fine tribute to the spirit which animated the formative years in the history of the several state bar organizations of our nation.

30. *Inherent and Acquired Difficulties in the Administration of Punitive Justice* [1]

Proceedings of the American Political Science Association, vol. 4, p. 222–239. 1908.

[1] Paper presented at the fourth annual meeting of the American Political Science Association, held at Madison, Wisconsin, December 27–31, 1907.

1909

31. *The Influence of French Law in America*

3 Illinois Law Review 354–363. January, 1909.

Reprint: n.p., n.d. 11 p.

Étude sur l'Influence du Droit Français en Amérique [1]

44 Bulletin de la Société de Législation Comparée 390–401. October–December, 1915.

[1] Translated by M. Jules Valery.

32. *Liberty of Contract*

18 Yale Law Journal 454–487. May, 1909.

Reprint: New Haven, Conn., S. Z. Field, n.d. 34 p.

Reprinted in: Selected Essays in Constitutional Law,[1] bk. 2, p. 208–237. 1938.

[1] Compiled and edited by a Committee of the Association of American Law Schools. 5 bks. in 4 v. Chicago, The Foundation Press, Inc., 1938.

33. *Uniformidad de las leyes en Todo el Continente Americano*
Trabajos del Cuarto Congreso Científico (1° Pan-Americano),[1] vol. 20, p. 240–254. 1909.

Uniformity of Commercial Law on the American Continent [2]
8 Michigan Law Review 91–107. December, 1909.

Reprint: n.p., n.d. 17 p.

21 American Legal News 22–30. January, 1910.

[1] Held December 25, 1908–January 5, 1909, at Santiago de Chile.

[2] The English version of the paper read before the Pan-American Scientific Congress at Santiago de Chile, on December 30, 1908. The subject was chosen at the suggestion of the American Delegation commissioned to the Congress.

34. *Law in Books and Law in Action*
Report of the 14th Annual Meeting of the Maryland State Bar Association,[1] p. 298–323. 1909.

42 Chicago Legal News 59–60.[2] October 2, 1909.

44 American Law Review 12–36. January–February, 1910.

[1] Held at Old Point Comfort, Virginia, July 7–9, 1909; the address was delivered on July 9th.

[2] A short summary of the Maryland Bar paper.

1910

35. *Some Principles of Procedural Reform* [1]
4 Illinois Law Review 388–407; 491–508. January–February, 1910.

Reprint: n.p., n.d. 39 p.

Grundsätze der Prozessreform [2]
2 Rheinische Zeitschrift für Zivil- und Prozessrecht 498–547. July, 1910.

[1] Paper read before the Chicago Law Club on December 3, 1909.

[2] Translated by A. Mendelssohn Bartholdy.

36. *A Practical Program of Procedural Reform*
42 Chicago Legal News 370–371.[1] June 25, 1910.

22 Green Bag 438–456. August, 1910.

[1] A short summary of the Illinois Bar address.

Reprint: n.p., n.d. 438–456 p.

Proceedings of the Illinois State Bar Association, 34th Annual Meeting,[2] p. 373–404. 1910.

Reprint: [3] n.p., n.d. 32 p.

[2] Held at Chicago, Illinois, June 23, 24, 1910; paper presented on the 23rd. Portrait facing p. 373.

[3] Subtitle: "Being the subject for discussion at the annual meeting of the Illinois State Bar Association at Hotel La Salle, Chicago, June 23, 1910." Bibliographical notes, p. 29–32.

37. *The Law and the People* [1]

43 Chicago Legal News 42–44, 46. September 17, 1910.

3 University of Chicago Magazine 1–16.[2] November, 1910.

Reprint: Chicago, Ill., n.d. 16 p.

[1] Address delivered on the occasion of the Seventy-Sixth Convocation of the University of Chicago, held in the Leon Mandel Assembly Hall, September 2, 1910.

[2] Portrait.

38. *Principles of Practice Reform*

71 Central Law Journal 221–228.[1] September 30, 1910.

22 Green Bag 643–644.[2] November, 1910.

[1] The editor's comment reads, "This splendid article was prepared by Mr. Pound for the benefit of the Special Committee of the American Bar Association, appointed to suggest remedies and formulate proposed laws to prevent delay and unnecessary cost in litigation. . . ."

[2] Extracts from the Central Law Journal.

39. *Discussion of "A Practical Program of Procedural Reform"* [1]

Proceedings of the Illinois State Bar Association, 34th Annual Meeting, p. 124–136. 1910.

[1] Part of a discussion of "A Practical Program of Procedural Reform" participated in by Mr. Pound and thirteen others. See title no. 36, *supra.*

40. *The Etiquette of Justice*

Proceedings of the Nebraska State Bar Association, vol. 3, p. 231–251.[1] 1910.

Reprint: Omaha, Neb., n.d. [5]–25 p.

[1] The meeting, November 23, 24, 1908, was held at the House of Representatives in the State Capitol, Lincoln, Neb.

41. *Outline of a Course in the Law of Irrigation*

[Chicago, Ill.], 1910. 10 p.

2d ed. [Cambridge, Mass.], 1912. 10 p.

42. *Puritanism and the Common Law*
    Bar Association of the State of Kansas, Proceedings, 27th
    Annual Meeting,[1] p. 45–58. 1910.
    45 American Law Review 811–829. November–December,
    1911.

[1] The meeting of the Association was held in the Supreme Court Room,
Topeka, Kan., January 27–28, 1910. The paper was read on the 27th. See
titles no. 65 and 107.

1911

43. *The Scope and Purpose of Sociological Jurisprudence* [1]
    24 Harvard Law Review 591–619; 25 *ibid.* 140–168; 489–
    516. June, December, 1911; April, 1912.
    Reprint: Cambridge, Mass., 1912. 591–619, 140–168, 489–
    516 p.
    社會法理學論略 *She-hui fa di-hsüeh lun lüch.* Shanghai,[2]
    Commercial Press, Ltd., November, 1926. 112 p.
    2d ed. Shanghai, Commercial Press, Ltd., November, 1930.
    [3d ed.] Shanghai, Commercial Press, Ltd., 1935.
    *La Extensión y Propósito de la Escuela Sociológica de Juris-
    prudencia* [3]
    2 Revista Jurídica de la Universidad de Puerto Rico 265–304.
    February–March, 1933.

[1] Published in the Harvard Law Review in three instalments, *viz.*: I.
Schools of Jurists and Methods of Jurisprudence. II. [The Social-Philosophi-
cal Jurists in Their Relation to Sociological Jurisprudence]. III. Sociological
Jurisprudence.
[2] Translated by Ting-K'ueh Lu. "Political Science Series."
[3] Translated by José López Baralt. "*Con permiso de* Harvard Law Review.
*Este es el primero de tres artículos que forman este trabajo. . . . El primero
que ahora se traduce, se publicó originalmente en* 1911, *en* 24 Harvard Law
Review, 591."

44. *Law and Equity in Federal Courts — Abolishing the Distinc-
    tion and Other Reforms* [1]
    73 Central Law Journal 204–210. September 22, 1911.

[1] "This article is an argument prepared by Prof. Pound at the request
of the Committee of the American Bar Association to Prevent Delay and
Unnecessary Cost in Litigation."

45. *Irrigation Law*
    In: American Law and Procedure,[1] vol. 5, p. 363–416. 1911.
    Reprint: Chicago, Ill., 1913. 363–416 p.

[1] Published by La Salle Extension University, 1914.

46. *Outline of a Course on Mining Law*
[Chicago, Ill.], 1911. 34 p.

1912

47. *Democracy and the Common Law*
18 Case and Comment 447–451. January, 1912.

48. *Cardinal Principles to be Observed in Reforming Procedure*
75 Central Law Journal 150–153. August 23, 1912.

49. *Social Problems and the Courts* [1]
18 American Journal of Sociology 331–341. November, 1912.
Reprint: n.p., n.d. 331–341 p.
Proceedings of the National Conference of Charities and Correction, 39th Annual Session, p. 176–184. 1912.
Reprint: n.p., n.d. 11 p.

[1] Address made before the National Conference of Charities and Correction at its June 12–19, 1912, meeting held in Cleveland, Ohio.

50. *Taught Law* [1]
3 American Law School Review 164–173. November, 1912.
Report of the 35th Annual Meeting of the American Bar Association [vol. 37], 975–996. 1912.

[1] The "President's Address" delivered at the twelfth annual meeting of the Association of American Law Schools. Published in the Report of meeting of the American Bar Association, August 27–29, 1912, at Milwaukee, Wisconsin.

51. *Social Justice and Legal Justice* [1]
75 Central Law Journal [2] 455–463. December 20, 1912.
Publications, Allegheny County Bar Association. 1912. 21 p.
Proceedings of the 30th Annual Meeting [3] of the Missouri Bar Association, p. 110–125. 1913.

[1] Address delivered before the Allegheny County Bar Association (Pennsylvania) at its meeting held at Pittsburgh, April 5, 1912.
[2] Reprinted with some minor omissions.
[3] Meeting held at St. Louis, Missouri, September 26–28, 1912. Portrait facing p. 110.

52. *Theories of Law* [1]
22 Yale Law Journal 114–150. December, 1912.
Reprint: New Haven, Conn., S. Z. Field, n.d. 37 p.

[1] The general idea, and some parts of the argument, presented in this article were previously set forth in the paper, *A New School of Jurists.* See title no. 14 *supra.*

53. *Courts and Legislation* [1]
    Proceedings of the 31st Annual Meeting [2] of the Bar Association of Tennessee, p. 74–91. 1912.
    7 American Political Science Review 361–383. August, 1913.
    Reprint: Baltimore, Md., n.d. 361–383 p.
    77 Central Law Journal 219–231. September 26, 1913.
    Reprinted in: Science of Legal Method,[3] ch. 7,[4] p. 202–228.
    1917.

[1] Paper originally presented before the American Political Science Association, December 28, 1911, at its eighth annual meeting (December 27–30) held at Buffalo, New York, but not published in the Association's volume of proceedings for 1911.
[2] Meeting held at Knoxville, Tennessee, July 9–11, 1912; the paper being delivered on the 10th.
[3] Select essays by various authors. Modern Legal Philosophy Series: Vol. 9. Boston, Mass., Boston Book Co., 1917. lxxxvi, 593 p.
[4] Reprinted from the American Political Science Review with some additions to the notes. *Corrigendum:* p. 202, n. 1, "Reprinted . . . August 1915" should read "Reprinted . . . August 1913."

54. *Introduction to Study of Law*
    In: Library of American Law and Practice,[1] vol. 1, p. 1–59.
    1912.
    Reprints: [2] Chicago, Ill., [1912], [1920], [1924], [1928].
    59, 2 p.
    法學緒言   *Fa hsüeh i-yen.*[3] Shanghai, Commercial Press, Ltd., July, 1928.
    2d ed.[4] Shanghai, Commercial Press, Ltd., November, 1930.
    1, 2, 2, 106 p.
    [3d ed.] [5] Shanghai, Commercial Press, Ltd., 1934. 1, 2, 104 p.

[1] Published by the American School of Correspondence.
[2] Issued with subtitle "Instruction paper" and with an examination paper added.
[3] Translated by Peh Hung Lei.
[4] "Political Science Library."
[5] "Social Science Small Library."

55. *Outline of a Course on the Theory of Law and Legislation* [1]
    Part I. [Cambridge, Mass.], 1912. 26 p.
    Part II. [Cambridge, Mass.], 1913. 12 p.

[1] These two parts were later incorporated, with slight changes, in the second edition of OUTLINES OF LECTURES ON JURISPRUDENCE. See title no. 13 *supra*.

1913

56. *The Organization of Courts* [1]
    70 Legal Intelligencer 86–88. February 7, 1913.
    Publications, Law Association of Philadelphia, 1913. 22 p.
    Proceedings, Minnesota State Bar Association,[2] 14th Annual
    Session, p. 169–189. 1914.
    American Judicature Society, Bulletin 6, p. 1–28. 1914.
    11 Journal of the American Judicature Society 69–83.[3] October, 1927.
    C. C. H. Legal Periodical Digest, 1928 ed., p. 111–113.
    February, 1928.

[1] Address delivered on January 31, 1913, before the Law Association of Philadelphia. It was thereafter issued in pamphlet form by the Association.
[2] In substantially the same form the paper was presented at the St. Paul meeting of the Minnesota State Bar Association, held on August 22, 1914.
[3] "Republished from Bulletin 6, American Judicature Society."

57. *The Administration of Justice in the Modern City*
    26 Harvard Law Review 302–328. February, 1913.
    Reprint: Cambridge, Mass., 1913. 302–328 p.

58. *Legislation as a Social Function* [1]
    18 American Journal of Sociology 755–768.[2] May, 1913.
    7 Papers and Proceedings of the American Sociological Society 148–161. 1913.
    Reprint: n.p., n.d. 148–161 p.

[1] Paper presented at the seventh annual meeting of the American Sociological Society held at Boston, Massachusetts, December 28, 30, 31, 1912.
[2] "Reprinted from the Publications of Proceedings of the American Sociological Society."

59. *The Philosophy of Law in America*
    24 International Journal of Ethics 70–73.[1] October, 1913.
    In: Proceedings of the Conference on Legal and Social
    Philosophy,[2] p. 1–4. 1913.

[1] An extract, which follows the text of the Conference's publication. The extract is divided into three main headings: 1. How did there come to be so complete a separation of jurisprudence and philosophy in Anglo-American juristic thought? 2. The present situation with respect to philosophy of law in America. 3. The problems of philosophical jurisprudence in America.
[2] Conference held at the College of the City of New York on April 25, 1913; and at Columbia University on April 26, 1913.

7 Archiv für Rechts- und Wirtschaftsphilosophie [3] 213–
223; 385–400. January, April, 1914.
Reprint: Berlin, n.d. 26 p.

[3] Bibliographical notes, p. 223, 400.

60. *Justice According to Law* [1]
13 Columbia Law Review 696–713; 14 *ibid.* 1–26; 103–121.
December, 1913; January, February, 1914.
Reprint: New York Evening Post Job Printing Co., 1914.
61 p.
Part 4, Executive Justice,[2] *reprinted in:* Selected Essays on
Constitutional Law, bk. 4,[3] p. 63–75. 1938.

[1] In five parts: I. Justice Without Law; II. Justice According to Law;
III. Legislative Justice; IV. Executive Justice; V. Judicial Justice.
[2] Reprinted from 14 Columbia Law Review, pages 12 to 26.
[3] Bk. 4 "Administrative Law."

61. *Judicial Justice*
Report, Colorado Bar Association, 16th Annual Meeting,[1]
vol. 16, p. 252–282. 1913.
South Carolina Bar Association, Transactions of the 21st
Annual Meeting,[2] p. 105–132. 1914.

[1] The "Annual Address" at Colorado Springs, July 10–12, 1913. Portrait
facing p. 252. Bibliographical notes.
[2] Held at Columbia, South Carolina, January 15–16, 1914. Portrait facing
p. 105. Published without the bibliographical notes.

62. *The Place of Judge Story in the Making of American Law* [1]
Proceedings of the Cambridge Historical Society, p. 33–50.
1913.
Reprint: Cambridge, Mass., 1914. 33–50 p.
48 American Law Review 676–697.[2] September–October,
1914.
1 Massachusetts Law Quarterly [3] 121–140. May, 1916.

[1] Paper read at the twenty-fourth meeting of the Cambridge Historical
Society, at Cambridge, Massachusetts, January 23, 1912.
[2] "Reprinted by permission of the Cambridge Historical Society."
[3] Reprinted with the subtitle, "An address delivered before the Cambridge
Historical Society and reprinted by permission."

63. *Political and Economic Interpretations of Jurisprudence* [1]
9 Proceedings of the American Political Science Association
94–105. 1913.
Reprint: n.p., n.d. 94–105.

[1] Paper presented before the American Political Science Association, its ninth annual meeting, held at Boston, and Cambridge, Massachusetts, December 28–31, 1912.

1914

64. *The End of Law as Developed in Legal Rules and Doctrines*
27 Harvard Law Review 195–234. January, 1914.
Reprint: Cambridge, Mass., 1914. 195–234 p.

65. *The Socialization of the Common Law* [1]
Boston Transcript. February 3, 1914, p. 12:1–2; February 6, p. 13:1–2; February 10, p. 12:1–2; February 13, p. 12:1–2; February 17, p. 16:1–3; February 20, p. 13:1–2; February 24, p. 12:1–2; February 27, p. 11:1–2.
26 Green Bag 166–170.[2] April, 1914.

[1] A course of eight lectures delivered under the auspices of the Lowell Institute of Boston. The topics of the lectures were: 1. Feudal Law (see title no. 68 *infra*). 2. Puritanism and the Law (see title no. 42 *supra*). 3. The Courts and the Crown (see title no. 70 *infra*). 4. The Rights of Englishmen and the Rights of Man. 5. The Pioneers and the Common Law (see title no. 100 *infra*). 6. Philosophy of Law in the Nineteenth Century. 7. Judicial Empiricism. 8. Legal Reason and the New Justice. Summaries of these lectures were published in the Boston Transcript.

[2] Subtitle: "Professor Pound's Lowell Institute Lectures." The article in the Green Bag is an epitome of the summaries of the lectures as reported in the Boston Transcript.

See the preface to THE SPIRIT OF THE COMMON LAW, title no. 107 *infra*.

66. *The End of Law as Developed in Juristic Thought*
27 Harvard Law Review 605–628; 30 *ibid.* 201–225. May, 1914; January, 1917.

67. *The Lay Tradition as to the Lawyer*
12 Michigan Law Review 627–638. June, 1914.
Report of the 16th Annual Meeting [1] of the Rhode Island Bar Association, p. 16–33. 1914.
Reprint: n.p., n.d. 12 p.
Publications, Bar Association of the County of Middlesex.[2] 1916. 18 p.

[1] Meeting held at Providence, Rhode Island, December 1, 1913.
[2] Address made at Boston, Massachusetts, April 8, 1916, to the Bar Association of the County of Middlesex, Massachusetts. Imprint: Boston, Mass., 1916.

68. *A Feudal Principle in Modern Law* [1]
     25 International Journal of Ethics 1–24. October, 1914.
     Reprint: n.p., n.d. 24 p.

   [1] The introductory lecture of the "Lowell Institute Lectures" upon the
   Spirit of the Common Law, delivered February 2, 1914. See title 65, note 1,
   and title 107.

69. *Codification*
     In: Cyclopedia of American Government,[1] vol. 1, p. 302–
     305. 1914.

   [1] New York, D. Appleton and Co. 3v. Edited by Andrew C. McLaughlin
   and Albert Bushnell Hart. Bibliographical "references," p. 305.

70. *The Judicial Office in the United States* [1]
     Proceedings of the 20th Annual Session [2] of the Iowa State
     Bar Association, p. 96–113. 1914.
     Publications, Worcester County Bar Association. 1914. 21 p.

   [1] Address to the Worcester County Bar Association at the Court House,
   Worcester, Massachusetts, Tuesday, March 10, 1914. Issued in pamphlet
   form by the Association; cover title, p. 3–18. Bibliographical notes, p. 19–21.
   [2] Meeting held at Burlington, Iowa, June 25, 26, 1914. Lacks the bibliographical notes. See titles no. 65 and 107.

1915

71. *Interests of Personality*
     28 Harvard Law Review 343–365; 445–456. February,
     March, 1915.
     Reprint: Cambridge, Mass., 1915. 343–365, 445–456 p.
     Reprinted in: Selected Essays on the Law of Torts,[1] p. 87–
     121. 1924.

   [1] Cambridge, Mass., Harvard Law Review Association (Plimpton Press,
   Norwood, Mass.). vii, 770 p.

72. *Making Law and Finding Law*
     60 Ohio Law Bulletin 341–351. August 16, 1915.
     13 Ohio Law Reporter 283–300. August 23, 1915.
     The Ohio State Bar Association, Proceedings of the 36th
     Annual Session,[1] vol. 36, p. 94–111. 1915.
     82 Central Law Journal 351–359. May 19, 1916.

   [1] Held at Cedar Point, Ohio, July 6–8, 1915; address delivered on the 7th.

73. *Legal Rights*
     26 International Journal of Ethics 92–116. October, 1915.
     Reprint: [Chicago, Ill.], 1915. 92–116 p.

74. *Regulation of Judicial Procedure by Rules of Court* [1]
    10 Illinois Law Review 163–177. October, 1915.

[1] By virtue of Laws of Ohio, 1914, p. 190 (Act of February 17, 1914) a
commission was created "to investigate the causes of delay and expense in
the administration of justice in civil and criminal actions in the courts of
Ohio." This paper was prepared at the request and for the use of this
commission.

75. CASES ON EQUITABLE RELIEF AGAINST DEFAMATION AND
    OTHER INJURIES BY WRITING OR SPEAKING [1]
    Cambridge, Mass., Issued privately, 1915. 43 sheets, multi-
    graphed.
    CASES ON EQUITABLE PROTECTION OF PERSONALITY AND OF
    SOCIAL AND POLITICAL RELATIONS [1]
    Cambridge, Mass., Issued privately, 1915. 74 sheets, mul-
    tigraphed.
    CASES ON EQUITABLE RELIEF AGAINST DEFAMATION AND
    INJURIES TO PERSONALITY [1]
    Cambridge, Mass., Published by the Editor, 1916. 77 p. [2]
    Corrected Reprint: [1] Cambridge, Mass., Published by the
    Editor, 1916. 77 p.
    2d ed. [3] Langdell Hall, Cambridge, Mass., Published by
    Z. Chafee Jr., 1930. viii, 147 p.

[1] "Supplementary to Ames's Cases in Equity Jurisdiction, vol. 1."
[2] This volume includes the contents of both the multigraphed pamphlets
listed above.
[3] "Supplementary to Chafee's Cases on Equitable Relief against Torts."
Also issued with the latter in one volume under title: CASES ON EQUITABLE
RELIEF AGAINST TORTS INCLUDING DEFAMATION AND INJURIES TO PERSONALITY
by Zechariah Chafee Jr. and Roscoe Pound. Langdell Hall, Cambridge,
Mass., Published by Z. Chafee Jr., 1933.

76. *Law and Morals*
    Proceedings of the 31st Annual Meeting [1] of the West Vir-
    ginia Bar Association, 187–201. 1915.
    Reprint: n.p., n.d. 15 p.
    New Jersey State Bar Association, Year Book, 1916–1917,
    p. 45–62. 1916. [2]

[1] Held at Clarksburg, West Virginia, December 29, 30, 1915. Portrait facing
p. 186.
[2] Address delivered at the annual meeting held in the Hotel Traymore,
Atlantic City, New Jersey, June 16, 1916.

77. *Report upon Uniformity of Laws Governing the Establishment and Regulation of Corporations and Joint Stock Companies in the American Republics* [1]
    Washington, D. C., Government Printing Office, 1915. 13 p.

[1] Submitted to the International High Commission, Pan-American Financial Conference, 1915.

1916

78. *Individual Interests in the Domestic Relations* [1]
    14 Michigan Law Review 177–196. January, 1916.
    Reprint: n.p., n.d. 20 p.

[1] The theory of interests and the manner of subject treatment follow the pattern of the earlier paper, *Interests of Personality.* See title no. 71 *supra.*

79. *Vesting in the Courts the Power to Make Rules Relating to Pleading and Practice* [1]
    2 American Bar Association Journal 46–55. January, 1916.

[1] Extracts from a debate held at the twenty-sixth annual meeting of the Ohio State Bar Association, Cedar Point, Ohio, July 6–8, 1915.

80. *Equitable Relief against Defamation and Injuries to Personality*
    29 Harvard Law Review 640–682. April, 1916.
    Reprint: Cambridge, Mass., 1916. 640–682 p.

81. *Bibliography and Readings on Modern Juristic Thought and Its Significance for America*
    Cambridge, Mass., Harvard University Press, 1916. 10 p.

82. *The Limits of Effective Legal Action*
    Report of the 22nd Annual Meeting [1] of the Pennsylvania Bar Association [vol. 22], p. 221–239. 1916.
    Reprint: n.p., n.d. 19 p.
    3 American Bar Association Journal 55–70. January, 1917.
    27 International Journal of Ethics 150–167. January, 1917.
    62 Ohio Law Bulletin 81–88. February 12, 1917.

[1] Meeting held at Bedford Springs, Pennsylvania, June 27–29, 1916; Mr. Pound made his address on the 27th. Portrait facing p. 221.

1917

83. *A Bibliography of Procedural Reform, Including Organization of Courts* [1]

    11 Illinois Law Review 451–463. February, 1917.

    Reprints: Chicago, Ill.,[2] 1917. 451–463 p.

    73 Annals of the American Academy of Political and Social Science [3] 90–103. September, 1917.

    5 Massachusetts Law Quarterly [4] 332–345. May, 1920.

[1] Originally prepared for the use of the California Bar Association, and presented at the August, 1916, meeting as part of the report of the Committee appointed to investigate and report upon the advisability of having matters of procedure and practice governed by rules of court in place of statutory direction. It is to be noted that Mr. Pound divided his bibliography into two parts, and only the first was published in the report of the Committee. Both parts, however, were subsequently printed in the San Francisco Recorder. Its appearance in the Illinois Law Review brought the bibliography down to 1917.

[2] Two pamphlet reprints, differing somewhat in size, were issued by the Northwestern University Press.

[3] Reprinted from the Illinois Law Review as "Exhibit B" to the Report of the "Committee of Nine" of the Phi Delta Phi Club of New York, entitled The Simplification of the Machinery of Justice with a View to its Greater Efficiency, p. 1 *et seq.*

[4] A reprint from the Illinois Law Review together with a "Supplementary Bibliography," p. 344–345, to the year 1920.

84. *Juristic Problems of National Progress* [1]

    22 American Journal of Sociology 721–733. May, 1917.

    Reprint: n.p., n.d. 721–733 p.

[1] Paper presented on the occasion of the twenty-fifth anniversary of the University of Chicago, June 5, 1916, to the Conference of the Departments of History, Sociology, Political Economy, Political Science, and Philosophy.

85. *Commerce and Legal Progress* [1]

    22 Bulletin, Commercial Law League of America 600–608. September, 1917.

    28 American Legal News 19–27. October, 1917.

[1] The "Annual Address" delivered at the twenty-third annual convention of the Commercial Law League of America, held at Saratoga Springs, New York, July 23–26, 1917. Portrait p. 497.

86. *Our Lady, the Common Law* [1]

    Proceedings, Seventh Annual Convention,[2] California Bar Association, p. 247–261. 1917.

[1] Address at Annual Banquet, August 19, 1916.

[2] Held at Del Monte, California, August 17, 18, 19, 1916.

87. *Procedure in Common Law* [1]
    Proceedings, Seventh Annual Convention, California Bar
    Association, p. 86–112. 1917.

[1] Annual address delivered on Friday, August 18, 1916.

88. *Remarks on Report of Special Section on Reformation of
    Practice* [1]
    Proceedings, Seventh Annual Convention, California Bar
    Association, p. 129–138, 139. 1917.

[1] Remarks delivered on Friday, August 18, 1916.

89. *The Revival of Personal Government*
    Proceedings of the Nebraska State Bar Association, vol. 9,
    1916, p. 105–124.[1] [1917].
    Proceedings of the Bar Association of the State of New
    Hampshire, 1917 [vol. 4],[2] p. 13–35. 1917.
    Reprint: n.p., n.d. 23 p.
    Report of the 37th Annual Session of the Georgia Bar Asso-
    ciation,[3] p. 118–141. 1920.
    Reprint: n.p., n.d. 24 p.
    Proceedings of the twenty-third Annual Session of the Bar
    Association of Arkansas, 1920, p. 118–140.[4] [1920].

[1] Seventeenth Annual Meeting held at Omaha, Hotel Fontenelle, December 29, 30, 1916. Address delivered on the 30th.
[2] Old Series, vol. 9.
[3] Tybee Island, Georgia, May 27–29, 1920; the "Annual Address" delivered
on the 28th. Portrait with facsimile signature facing p. 118.
[4] Meeting held in Hot Springs, June 2, 3, 1920. The address was delivered
on the 3rd.

90. A SELECTION OF CASES ON THE LAW OF TORTS. James Barr
    Ames and Jeremiah Smith. New edition by Roscoe Pound.
    Cambridge, Mass.,[1] Harvard University Press, 1917.
    x, 1025 p.
    Reprinted: [2] Cambridge, Mass., Harvard University Press,
    1919. 1028 p.

[1] "This edition was first published in four parts. Part I (pp. 1–167) appeared September 25, 1916; part II (pp. 168–368), December 1, 1916; part
III (pp. 369–618), February 20, 1917; and part IV (pp. 619–1008), April 23,
1917."
[2] With "a few recent decisions" added to the notes.

1918

91. *Juristic Science and Law*
    31 Harvard Law Review 1047–1063. June, 1918.
    2 Current Legal Thought 314–317.[1] December, 1935.
    [1] An abstract of 31 Harvard Law Review 1047.

92. *Judicial Organization*
    Texas Bar Association, Proceedings of the 37th Annual Session,[1] p. 69–90. 1918.
    In: Discussion of proposed amendment of Judiciary Articles of Constitution of Texas, and Address of Dr. Roscoe Pound of Harvard University, Address of Gov. Emmet O'Neal of Alabama on Judicial Organization, p. 115–135. Houston, Texas, n.d.
    [1] Held at Wichita Falls, Texas, on July 3–5, 1918. Portrait facing p. 69.

93. *The Lay Idea of the Lawyer* [1]
    Texas Bar Association, Proceedings of the 37th Annual Session, p. 332–336. 1918.
    [1] Subtitle: "Response to a Toast by Dr. Roscoe Pound."

94. *Reform in Court Organization*
    Texas Bar Association, Proceedings of the 37th Annual Session, p. 205–216. 1918.

1919

95. *Consideration in Equity*
    13 Illinois Law Review 667–692.[1] April, 1919.
    In: Wigmore Celebration Legal Essays, p. 435–460.[2] 1919.
    Reprint: Chicago, Ill., 1919. 435–460 p.
    [1] Numbers 3–9 of volume 13 were issued in four installments as a "Festival Publication in Honor of John H. Wigmore to Mark the Twenty-fifth Year of His Service as a Professor of Law in Northwestern University."
    [2] This volume is a reprint, with some additions, of the material in 13 Illinois Law Review.

96. *The Administrative Application of Legal Standards* [1]
    Report of the 42nd Annual Meeting of the American Bar Association [vol. 44], p. 445–465. 1919.
    Reprinted in: Selected Essays on Constitutional Law, bk. 4, p. 76–92. 1938.
    [1] Address made before the Section of Public Utility Law of the American Bar Association, at Boston, Massachusetts, during the September 1919 meeting.

97. *Outline of a Course on the History and System of the Common Law* (*Introduction to American Law*)[1]
Cambridge, Mass., 1919. 48 p.
Under title: *An Introduction to American Law* [2]
Dunster House Papers, No. 3. Cambridge, Mass., Dunster House Bookshop, 1920; 1924. 44 p.

[1] At head of title: Trade Union College under the Auspices of the Boston Central Labor Union, Spring Term, 1919.
There are five main divisions: I. Fundamental Conceptions, p. 3–8; II. History of the Common Law, p. 8–21; III. The Common Law in America, p. 21–22; IV. Sources and Forms of Law, p. 23–28; V. System of the Common Law, p. 28–48.
Contains bibliographies.
[2] Subtitle: An Outline of a Course Delivered at the Trade Union College under the Auspices of the Boston Central Labor Union, Spring Term, 1919.

1920

98. *The Progress of the Law, 1918–1919: Equity* [1]
33 Harvard Law Review 420–441; 813–837; 929–955. January, April, May, 1920.
Reprint: Cambridge, Mass., 1933, 1936. 420–441, 813–837, 929–955 p.

[1] In three parts: I. Nature of Equity Jurisdiction and Equitable Rights; II. Recovery of Specific Chattels; III. Specific Performance.

99. *Anachronisms in Law* [1]
3 Journal of the American Judicature Society 142–148. February, 1920.

[1] Address delivered before the Conference of Bar Association Delegates at the meeting of the American Bar Association held at Saratoga, New York, September 3, 1917. The address was not published in the Association's volume for 1917; such addresses were not so published at that date.

100. *The Pioneers and the Common Law*
27 West Virginia Law Quarterly *and* The Bar 1–19. November, 1920.
Proceedings of the 22nd Annual Session [1] of the North Carolina Bar Association,[2] p. 188–206. 1920.
Reprint: n.p., n.d. 1–19 p.

[1] Meeting held at Asheville, North Carolina, June 29, 30, and July 1, 1920; address delivered on the 1st. Portrait with facsimile signature facing p. 188.
[2] A considerable part of this address is taken from the Lowell Institute lecture, "The Pioneers and the Common Law." See titles no. 65 and 107.

101. *The Future of Legal Education*
In: Indiana University 1820–1920, Centennial Memorial Volume, p. 259–272.[1] 1920.
Indiana University Bulletin. Official Series, vol. 19, no. 2, February, 1921.

[1] A biographical sketch of Mr. Pound is contained on page 257.

102. *The Future of the Criminal Law* [1]
1920 Proceedings of the Annual Congress of the American Prison Association, p. 68–83.[2] 1920.
21 Columbia Law Review 1–16.[3] January, 1921.
Reprint: New York, 1921. 16 p.

[1] Paper read before the semi-centennial session of the American Prison Congress, at Columbus, Ohio, October 15, 1920.
[2] Published without the footnotes.
[3] Contains the bibliographical notes.

103. *The Law School and the Common Law* [1]
In: Two Addresses Delivered before the Alumni of the Harvard Law School,[2] p. 1–20. 1920.
Separate issue: [3] n.p., n.d. 26 p.

[1] Cambridge, Massachusetts, June 21, 1920; delivered on the occasion of the celebration of the Centennial of the Harvard Law School (1817–1917).
[2] Boston, Mass., Harvard Law School Association, n.d., 34 p. The other address, entitled *Some Observations on Legal Education and Democratic Progress*, p. 21–34, was given by Charles Evans Hughes.
[3] Cover title: The Law School and the Common Law, Address by Dean Roscoe Pound, Delivered on the Occasion of the Centennial Celebration of the Harvard Law School.

1921

104. *Judge Holmes's Contributions to the Science of Law*
34 Harvard Law Review 449–453. March, 1921.

105. *The Maxims of Equity — I* [1]
34 Harvard Law Review 809–836. June, 1921.
Reprint: Cambridge, Mass., 1921. 809–836 p.

[1] Of Maxims Generally . . . 1. Proverbs and Maxims . . . 2. Maxims in Roman Law . . . 3. Maxims in the Canon Law . . . 4. Maxims in the Civil Law . . . 5. Maxims in Germanic Law . . . 6. Maxims in the Common Law . . .
Though the note "To be continued" appears at the end, no other parts have been published.

106. *Criminal Justice in the American City*[1]
    47 Survey 149–155; 332–337, 345, 346. October, November, 1921.

[1] An early draft of title no. 110 *infra*.

107. THE SPIRIT OF THE COMMON LAW[1]
    Boston, Mass., Marshall Jones Co., 1921. xv, 224 p.
    Reprinted: October, 1922; July, 1925; November, 1931.
    英米法の精神 *Ei-Bei hô no seishin.* Tokyo,[2] 1925. 5, 7, 2, 1, 127 p.
    2d ed. Tokyo,[2] 1932. 5, 7, 2, 1, 4, 127 p.

[1] Half-title: Dartmouth Alumni Lectureships on the Gurnsey Center Moore Foundation . . . 1921. See titles no. 42, 65, 68, 70, 100. "All these materials have been used freely, but all have been revised and much has been wholly rewritten." — Preface.
[2] Translated by Takazo Yamaguchi.

108. *A Theory of Social Interests*[1]
    15 Papers and Proceedings of the American Sociological Society 16–45. 1921.
    Reprint: n.p., n.d. 16–45 p.
    Reprinted in part in: Readings in Jurisprudence.[2] Jerome Hall. p. 238–246. 1938.

[1] Paper presented at the fifteenth annual meeting of the American Sociological Society, held in Washington, D. C., December 27–29, 1920.
[2] Indianapolis, Ind., The Bobbs-Merrill Co., 1938. xix, 1183 p.

1922

109. *La Filosofia nel Diritto Costituzionale Americano*
    Rivista Internazionale di Filosofia del Diritto,[1] anno 2, fascicolo 1, p. 1–13. January–March, 1922.
    Reprint: Genova, 1922. 1–13 p.

[1] Mr. Pound's paper is dated, "Roma, 8 dicembre 1921." Contains bibliographical notes.

110. CRIMINAL JUSTICE IN THE AMERICAN CITY — A SUMMARY[1]
    Cleveland, Ohio, Cleveland Foundation, 1922. viii, 94 p.

[1] "Cleveland Foundation Survey of Criminal Justice in Cleveland, Part 7." A revision of title no. 106 *supra*.
"This is a summary section of the report of the Cleveland Foundation Survey of Criminal Justice in Cleveland. The survey was directed and the reports edited by Roscoe Pound who is the author of this report, and Felix Frankfurter. . . . The sections are published first in separate form . . . and are to be consolidated in a single volume entitled 'Criminal Justice in Cleveland.' " — Preface.

Reprinted in: Criminal Justice in Cleveland,[2] pt. 8,[3] p. 559–652. 1922.

[2] Cleveland, Ohio, Cleveland Foundation, 1922. Directed and edited by Roscoe Pound and Felix Frankfurter. xxvii, 729 p.

[3] The work of Mr. Pound, originally appearing as Part 7 of the Survey, is reprinted as Part 8 thereof.

111. AN INTRODUCTION TO THE PHILOSOPHY OF LAW [1]
New Haven, Conn.,[2] Yale University Press [etc., etc.]; 1922. 307 p.
Reprinted: May, 1922; December, 1924; May, 1925; April, 1930; September, 1937.

[1] Half-title: William L. Storrs Lecture Series, 1921–1922. Delivered before the Law School of Yale University.

[2] Bibliography, p. 285–307.

1923

112. *Projet for a Professorship of Criminal Law*
25 Harvard Alumni Bulletin 498–502. January 25, 1923.
Reprinted in: The Harvard Law School, p. 28–32. 1923.[1]

[1] Reprinted from the Harvard Alumni Bulletin, January 25, 1923.

113. *The Theory of Judicial Decision* [1]
36 Harvard Law Review 641–662; 802–825; 940–959. April, May, June, 1923.
Reprint: Cambridge, Mass., 1923. 641–662; 802–825; 940–959 p.
2 Canadian Bar Review 263–280; 335–355; 443–460. April, May, September, 1924.
Reprinted in: 4 Lectures on Legal Topics [2] [1922–1923] 93–167. 1928.
34 Case and Comment, Law School ed.,[3] no. 1, p. 7–11. January–March, 1928.

[1] A series of three lectures delivered before the members of the Association of the Bar of the City of New York, in the month of January, 1923.

The lectures were published in the Harvard Law Review in three installments: I. The Materials of Judicial Decision. . . . II. Nineteenth-Century Theories of Judicial Finding of Law. . . . III. A Theory of Judicial Decision for To-day. . . .

Part I, The Materials of Judicial Decision . . . , was reprinted in part in Readings on the History and System of the Common Law, 3d ed., 1927, p. 16–24. See title no. 17 *supra.*

[2] New York, 1928, The Association of the Bar of the City of New York.

[3] A short summary of the lecture.

114. *[Law and Morals]* [1]
    1 Journal of Social Forces 350–359, 528–537. May, September, 1923.

[1] In two parts: I. The Historical View; II. The Analytical View. See title no. 123 *infra.*

115. *Preventive Justice and Social Work*
    Proceedings of the National Conference of Social Work (50th Anniversary Session),[1] p. 151–163. May, 1923.
    Reprint: n.p., n.d. 151–163 p.

[1] Held at Washington, D. C., May 18–23, 1923.

116. *The Work of the American Law School* [1]
    30 West Virginia Law Quarterly *and* The Bar 1–17. November, 1923.
    Reprint: n.p., n.d. 17 p.
    30 Case and Comment, Pocket ed., 71–75.[2] May–July, 1924.

[1] Address delivered at the Dedication Exercises for the College of Law Building, West Virginia University, at Morgantown, West Virginia, on November 17, 1923.
[2] Extracts from the address reprinted by permission of the West Virginia Law Quarterly *and* The Bar.

117. *The Growth of Administrative Justice* [1]
    Proceedings of the Wisconsin State Bar Association [vol. 14, 1922–23], p. 191–208. 1923.
    2 Wisconsin Law Review 321–339.[2] January, 1924.

[1] Address delivered at the annual meeting at Janesville and Beloit, Wisconsin, June 26, 27, 28, 1923.
[2] The editorial note to the article states, "This address was given by Dean Pound extemporaneously: the manuscript having been left at Janesville, while the address was given at Beloit. It is printed as it was given orally; and not as prepared in manuscript."

118. INTERPRETATIONS OF LEGAL HISTORY [1]
    Cambridge, Eng., The University Press, 1923. xvii, 171 p.

[1] Half-title: Cambridge Studies in English Legal History. Edited by Harold Dexter Hazeltine.
    In the preface it is said that "These lectures are printed as they were delivered at Trinity College, Cambridge, in Lent Term, 1922, with addition of some notes partly by way of illustration and partly to assist any who may be interested in pursuing the subject more deeply." — p. xv.

New York, The Macmillan Company, 1923. xvii, 171 p.
Reprinted: Cambridge, Eng., The University Press, 1930.
法律史觀 *Fa-lü shih kuan.* Shanghai,[2] Min Chih.
法律史觀 *Hôritsu shi kan.* Tokyo,[3] 1931. 4, 18, 5, 349 p.

[2] Translated by Ch'ü Huang.
[3] Translated by Kenzo Takayanagi.

119. *Philosophical Theory and International Law* [1]
   In: 1 Bibliotheca Visseriana Dissertationvm ivs Internationale Illvstrantivm 71–90. 1923.
   哲學的理論と國際法 *Tetsugaku-teki riron to kokusai hô* [2]
   In: 國際法の基本問題 *Kokusaihô no kihon mondai,*[3] p.
   113–159. Tokyo, 1931.

[1] Lecture delivered in the University of Leiden.
[2] Translated by Sho Osawa and On Nomiyama.
[3] Fundamental Problems of International Law.

1924

120. *Preliminary Report on Classification of the Law* [1]
   Publications, American Law Institute,[2] [Philadelphia,] 47 p.
   February, 1924.
   In: Proceedings of the American Law Institute, vol. 2,
   p. 379–425. 1924.

[1] At head of title: Report No. 2; Preliminary Report to the Council on
Classification of the Law.
   Verso: To the Members of the Institute — This report and its recommenda-
tions and inquiries will be the subject of discussion at the Second Annual
Meeting of the Institute on Saturday, February 23, 1924, at Washington,
D. C. . . .
[2] The Report of Mr. Pound comprehends six major phases; *viz.:* I. The
Purpose of Classification. . . . II. Theories of the Basis of Classification. . . .
III. History of Classification. . . . IV. Classification in the Civil Law. . . .
V. Classification in the Common Law. . . . VI. Suggestions for the Classifica-
tion of Anglo-American Law. . . . *Cf.* title no. 122, note 1 *infra.* See title
no. 121, note 1 *infra.*

121. *Classification of Law* [1]
   5 American Law School Review 269–278. March, 1924.

[1] Address delivered on December 28, 1923, before the Association of American Law Schools at its twenty-first annual meeting, Chicago, Illinois.
   This title and the one which follows have been erroneously cited and in-
dexed as one and the same.

122. *Classification of Law* [1]

   37 Harvard Law Review 933–969. June, 1924.

   Reprint: Cambridge, Mass., 1924. 933–969 p.

   Reprinted in part in: Readings in Jurisprudence. Jerome
   Hall. p. 603–615. 1938.

[1] This paper is divided into the following sections: I. Classification and
Logic. . . . II. The Purpose of Classification of Law. . . . III. Theories of
the Basis of Classification. . . . IV. History of Classification. . . . V. Classification in the Civil Law. . . .
This paper is "based upon the preliminary report on classification of law
presented to the Council of the American Law Institute. . . ." See title
no. 120 *supra.*
Though the note "To be continued" appears at the end, no further parts
have been published.

123. LAW AND MORALS [1]

   Chapel Hill, N. C., The University of North Carolina Press;
   [etc., etc.], 1924.[2] iii, 156 p.

   2d ed. Chapel Hill, N. C., The University of North Carolina Press; [etc., etc.],[3] 1926. x, 144 p.

   法律と道徳 *Hôritsu to dôtoku.*[4] Tokyo, 1928. 263 p.

   法と道徳 *Hô to dôtoku.*[5] Tokyo, 1929. 232 p.

[1] Half-title: The John Calvin McNair Lectures, 1923. Delivered at the
University of North Carolina, Chapel Hill, North Carolina. Text of chapters
1 and 2 identical with that of 1 Journal of Social Forces 350–359, 528–537.
See title no. 114 *supra.*
[2] Bibliography, p. 125–153.
[3] Bibliography, p. 117–140.
[4] Translated by Mitsuo Maebara.
[5] Translated by Kenzo Takayanagi and Shin Iwata. Bibliography, p. 147–
193.

124. *Some Parallels from Legal History*

   10 American Bar Association Journal 547–553, 564. August, 1924.

   Reports of the 47th Annual Meeting of the American Bar
   Association,[1] [vol. 49], p. 204–223. 1924.

   Reprint: n.p., 1924. 20 p.

[1] Philadelphia, Pennsylvania, July 8–10, 1924; delivered on the 8th. Reported in the New York Times, July 9, 1924, 21:1.

1925

125. *Address on the Law* [1]
   27 Harvard Alumni Bulletin 1073–1081. June 18, 1925.
[1] Delivered before the Harvard Law School Association, at its annual meeting on April 14, 1925, at the Harvard Club of New York City. Mr. Pound was the special guest of the occasion.
The address appears, in the Harvard Alumni Bulletin, in *Two Addresses on the Law*, p. 1071–1081. The other address referred to was delivered by Judge Learned Hand, p. 1071, 1072. Reported in the New York Times, April 15, 1925, 12:1.

126. *Grotius in the Science of Law*
   19 American Journal of International Law 685–688. October, 1925.
   Reprint: n.p., n.d. 685–688 p.

127. *Dedicatory Address* [1]
   24 George Washington University Bulletin 15–26. November, 1925.
[1] Delivered at the proceedings incident to the dedication of Stockton Hall of the George Washington University Law School, on November 14, 1925, at Washington, D. C.

128. *The Law School and the Professional Tradition* [1]
   24 Michigan Law Review 156–165. December, 1925.
   Reprinted in: The Lawyers' Club Dedication Papers, n.p., n.d. p. 1–32.
[1] One of the "Dedication Papers" read at the dedicatory exercises for the Lawyers' Club of the University of Michigan Law School.

129. *The Common Law* [1]
   Vermont Bar Association,[2] Report of the Proceedings of the Forty-seventh Annual Meeting, vol. 18, p. 76–88. 1925.
   New York County Lawyers' Association, Year Book, 1925 [vol. 17], p. 175–186.[3] 1925.
   Proceedings of the 18th Annual Session of the Florida State Bar Association,[4] p. 112–124. 1925.
[1] The address, though essentially the same on all three occasions, was considerably revised for both the later meetings.
[2] Address delivered on January 6, 1925.
[3] Address delivered at the Annual Bar Dinner, February 28, 1925.
[4] Gainesville, Florida, March 20–21, 1925.

130. *Jurisprudence*
   In: The History and Prospects of the Social Sciences, chapter 9, p. 444–479.[1] 1925.
   Reprint: [2] n.p., 1925. 444–479 p.
   Právni Věda Našeho Času Ve Svých Význačných Rysech A Problémech.[3] Bratislava, Czechoslovakia, 1927. 14 p.

   [1] By various authors. Edited, with an introduction, by Harry Elmer Barnes. New York, Alfred A. Knopf, 1925. xxi, 534 p.
   The main divisions of Mr. Pound's paper: I. History of Jurisprudence. . . . II. Characteristics of Recent Legal Science. . . . III. The Problems of Jurisprudence To-Day. . . . Contains bibliographical notes, and a list of "Selected References" on pages 478–479.
   [2] Cover title: Reprinted from the History and Prospects of the Social Sciences.
   [3] Translated by Dr. Joseph Schutzner. Reprinted from Právny Obzor. Rŏc. 10.

131. *Law*
   In: Immanuel Kant, 1724–1924, p. 75–82.[1] 1925.

   [1] New Haven, Yale University Press. 88 p. Edited by E. C. Wilm.

132. *[The Lay Tradition of the Lawyer]* [1]
   Bar Association of the State of Kansas, Proceedings, 43rd Annual Meeting,[2] p. 263–272. 1925.
   12 American Bar Association Journal 153–155. March, 1926.

   [1] This paper is substantially the same as the one presented before the Rhode Island Bar Association in December, 1913, entitled *The Lay Tradition as to the Lawyer.* See title no. 67 *supra.*
   [2] Delivered at the annual banquet, November 24, 1925, at Emporia, Kansas.

133. *The Legal Profession and the Law* [1]
   Proceedings of the Eighteenth Annual Meeting [2] of the Oklahoma State Bar Association, p. 179–205. 1925.

   [1] Address delivered December 30, 1924.
   [2] Held at Oklahoma City, December 29 and 30, 1924.

134. *The Problem of the Lawyer*
   Bar Association of the State of Kansas, Proceedings, 43rd Annual Meeting,[1] p. 150–172. 1925.
   Under title: *The Problem of Law*
   12 American Bar Association Journal 81–87. February, 1926.

   [1] At Emporia, Kansas, November 23, 1925.

135. *Soziologische Jurisprudenz in Amerika*
    1 Jahrbuch für Soziologie, Eine Internationale Sammlung 88–100.[1] 1925.
    Reprint: n.p., n.d. 88–100 p.
[1] Bibliographical notes, p. 99–100.

1926

136. *The Crisis in American Law* [1]
    152 Harper's Monthly Magazine 152–158. January, 1926.
    10 Journal of the American Judicature Society 5–10, 26.[2]
    June, 1926.

[1] Mr. Pound presents "in broad perspective the present crisis in American law, and reveals a general condition of which our crime wave and the notorious congestion of our courts may be merely symptoms." Reported in the New York Times, Dec. 22, 1925, 20:8.
[2] Republished from Harper's Monthly Magazine.

137. *The Task of the American Lawyer* [1]
    20 Illinois Law Review 439–454. January, 1926.
    Reprint: n.p., n.d. 439–454 p.

[1] Address to the Chicago Bar Association, at Chicago, Illinois, on November 12, 1925.

138. *The Sesquicentennial of the [Virginia] Bill of Rights*
    67 Congressional Record 11541–11544.[1] June, 1926.
    Reprinted in: The Virginia Convention of 1776 and George Mason; Speech of Hon. R. Walton Moore. Washington, D. C., p. 6–16. 1926.
    32 Case and Comment, Pocket ed., 131–134.[2] November–December, 1926.

[1] Proceedings and Debates of the 1st Session, 69th Congress.
    In the House of Representatives, Friday, June 18, 1926: " 'The Virginia Convention of 1776 and George Mason.' Mr. Moore of Virginia. Mr. Speaker, I wish to make some slight reference to an anniversary celebration held a few days ago, in which a joint committee of Congress participated. . . . I have risen mainly for the purpose of asking leave to extend my remarks by printing the [address] delivered at Williamsburg on June 12 by . . . Dr. Roscoe Pound, dean of the law school of Harvard University." —p. 11540.
[2] Contains extracts from the address.

139. *Canons of Procedural Reform*
    12 American Bar Association Journal 541–545.[1] August, 1926.

[1] Portrait facing p. 541.

Reprint: n.p., n.d. 14 p.
Report of the 49th Annual Meeting of the American Bar
Association [vol. 51],[2] p. 290–303. 1926.
[2] Meeting at Denver, Colorado, July 14–16, 1926; address made on the
15th. Reported in the New York Times, July 16, 1926, 4:2.

140. *The Rule-Making Power of the Courts* [1]
12 American Bar Association Journal 599–603. September,
1926.
10 Journal of the American Judicature Society 113–120.
December, 1926.
163 Law Times 144–146.[2] February 12, 1927.
21 Massachusetts Law Quarterly 70–80. July, 1936.

[1] Address delivered, July 13, 1926, at the meeting of the Conference of
Bar Association Delegates, as part of the annual meeting of the American
Bar Association, Denver, Colorado, July, 1926.
[2] "From the American Bar Association Journal."

141. *The Problem of Criminal Justice* [1]
Los Angeles, Cal.,[2] The Chimes Press, 1926. 32 p.
Le Problème de la Justice Criminelle [3]
7 Revue de Droit Pénal et de Criminologie 715–737. July,
1927.
Reprint: Louvain, July, 1927. 23 p.

[1] Lecture No. 1, July 6, 1926. The first of two lectures delivered at the
July, 1926, sessions of the Los Angeles Institute of Public Affairs; held at
the University of California, Southern Branch. See title no. 146 *infra* for
second lecture.
[2] "Handy Book" series.
[3] Translated by Mlle. Ada Sand and M. Paul Cornil.

142. *Enforcement of Law* [1]
Publications, Lackawanna Bar Association. 1926. 21 p.

[1] Address before the Lackawanna Bar Association, at its meeting of January 9, 1926, at Scranton, Pennsylvania.

143. *Interstate Commerce Under the Constitution*
In: Publications, Lawyers Club of New York City, John
Marshall Anniversary,[1] p. 9–22. 1926.

[1] A pamphlet publication of the proceedings at the Dinner on January 20,
1926, to commemorate the One Hundred and Twenty-fifth Anniversary of
the appointment of John Marshall as Chief Justice of the United States
Supreme Court. Reported in the New York Times, Jan. 21, 1926, 23:3.

144. *Law and the Christian Code*
 In: An Outline of Christianity; [1] The Story of Our Civilization, vol. 5, p. 106–114. 1926.

[1] New York, Bethlehem Publishers, Inc., Dodd, Mead & Company, Distributors, 1926. 5 v. Vol. 5: Christianity Today and Tomorrow.

145. *On Certain Maxims of Equity.*
 In: Cambridge Legal Essays,[1] written in honour of and presented to Doctor Bond, Professor Buckland, and Professor Kenny, p. 259–277. 1926.

[1] Cambridge, Eng., W. Heffer and Sons, Ltd., 1926. viii, 331 p. Bibliographical notes.

146. *Criminal Justice in Nineteenth-Century America* [1]
 Los Angeles, Cal.,[2] The Chimes Press, 1926. 32 p.

[1] Lecture No. 2, July 7, 1926. Los Angeles Institute of Public Affairs. Mr. Pound's concluding lecture before the Institute. See title no. 141 *supra.*
[2] "Handy Book" series.

147. *The Work of the American Appellate Court* [1]
 Report of the 49th Annual Meeting of the American Bar Association, [vol. 51], p. 764–777. 1926.

[1] Paper presented at the proceedings of the Judicial Section of the American Bar Association, at Denver, Colorado. A summary of this address was printed in 12 American Bar Association Journal 648, September, 1926.

1927

148. *What Can Law Schools Do for Criminal Justice?* [1]
 12 Iowa Law Review 105–113. February, 1927.
 Reprint: Iowa City, Iowa, 1927. 105–113 p.
 6 American Law School Review 127–132.[2] May, 1927.

[1] Paper presented at a Round Table meeting of the Association of American Law Schools at its Chicago meeting, December 29, 1926.
[2] "Reprinted from the Iowa Law Review, February, 1927."

149. *Regulating Procedural Details by Rules of Court*
 13 American Bar Association Journal, pt. 2,[1] p. 12–14. March, 1927.
 4 State Bar Journal [2] 261–265. June, 1930.

[1] Supplement to the March issue, entitled "The Rule-Making Power of the Courts."
[2] Official organ of the State Bar of California.

150. *Unsettled Problems in American Law* [1]

     3 Docket [2] 3052–3057. March–April, 1927.

[1] Excerpts from an address delivered before the Chicago Bar Association.
[2] Full title: West Publishing Co.'s Docket. St. Paul, Minn.

151. *The Law of the Land*

     1 Dakota Law Review 99–109. October, 1927.

     Reprint: [1] Fargo, N. D., 1927. 11 p.

     Proceedings of the 23rd Annual Session, 1927, and the 24th
     Annual Session, 1928,[2] of the State Bar Association of
     Utah 56–75. 1928.

     Reprint: n.p., 1928. 24 p.

     4 Bar Briefs [3] 167–180.[4] January, 1928.

     62 American Law Review 174–192. March–April, 1928.

     6 Tennessee Law Review [5] 206–224. April, 1928.

     C. C. H. Legal Periodical Digest, 1928 ed., p. 675–677.
     June, 1928.

     166 Law Times 208–211.[6] September 29, 1928.

[1] Caption title: An Address Delivered to the North Dakota Bar Association at Grand Forks, September 8, 1927.
[2] The meeting was held at Ogden, Utah, on July 14, 1927. Remarks, with biographical references, introducing the speaker, p. 54–56.
[3] A publication of the Bar Association of North Dakota.
[4] The Annual Meeting Number. The issue contains the minutes of the proceedings held at Grand Forks, North Dakota, September 6–7, 1927. Portrait facing p. 166.
[5] "Reprinted with permission of the Dakota Law Review."
[6] Reprinted from 62 American Law Review 174.

152. *Law and Laws* [1]

     University of Missouri Bulletin, vol. 28, no. 47,[2] p. 25–39.
     December 1, 1927.

     C. C. H. Legal Periodical Digest, 1928 ed., p. 492. May,
     1928.

[1] Delivered at the dedication exercises for the Lee H. Tate Memorial Law Building, University of Missouri, October 1, 1927.
[2] Law Series 37. Cover title: Dedication of Lee H. Tate Hall, Memorial Law Building, University of Missouri. 39 p.

153. *Law and Social Work* [1]

     3 Indiana Law Journal 183–195. December, 1927.

     C. C. H. Legal Periodical Digest, 1928 ed., p. 108–109.
     February, 1928.

[1] Address before the Indiana Conference on Social Work held at Elkhart, Indiana, on October 4–18, 1927.

154. *The Progress of the Law — Analytical Jurisprudence, 1914–1927* [1]

    41 Harvard Law Review 174–199. December, 1927.

    C. C. H. Legal Periodical Digest, 1928 ed., p. 94–95. February, 1928.

    Reprinted in part in: Readings in Jurisprudence. Jerome Hall. p. 534–537. 1938.

[1] Mr. Pound wrote in an introductory footnote to the article, "The starting point [1914] is chosen in order to go on from my paper, *The Scope and Purpose of Sociological Jurisprudence.* [See title no. 43 *supra.*] There is something to be said for 1914 as a natural starting point. The war and the decade since the war may turn out to make a new period in juristic thought."
Though the note "To be continued" appears at the end, no further parts have been published.

155. *The American Attitude Toward the Trial Judge*

    Report of the Proceedings of the 45th Annual Meeting [1] of the Missouri Bar Association, p. 138–149. 1927.

    Report of the 28th Annual Meeting [2] of the South Dakota Bar Association, p. 103–116. 1927.

    Reprint: n.t.p. 14 p.

    2 Dakota Law Review [3] 5–16. February, 1928.

    Reprint: n.p., 1927. 14 p.

[1] The "Annual Address," September 30, 1927, at Columbia, Missouri.
The other address by Mr. Pound, *Dedication Address — Law and Laws,* recited in the agenda was not published in the report of the proceedings. See title no. 152 *supra.*
[2] Meeting held at Huron, South Dakota, on September 9–10, 1927; address delivered on the 9th.
[3] "An Address. . . . Published in the Report of the 28th Meeting of the South Dakota Bar Association."

156. *Law, Politics, and Religion*
    In: Religion and Modern Life,[1] p. 323–342. 1927.

[1] Half-title: Lectures Given for the Phillips Brooks House Association, Harvard University. New York, Charles Scribner's Sons. x, 370 p.

157. *The Part of Philosophy in International Law* [1]
    In: Proceedings of the Sixth International Congress of Philosophy,[2] p. 372–381. 1927.

[1] Paper read at the meeting of the Philosophical Congress held at Harvard University, September 13–17, 1926. Reported in the New York Times, September 17, 1926, 18:1.
[2] New York, Longmans, Green and Co., 1927. lxxxvii, 716 p. Edited by Edgar Sheffield Brightman.

158. *Sociology and Law*
   In: The Social Sciences and Their Interrelations,[1] ch. 26,
   p. 319–328.[2] 1927.

[1] Boston, New York, [etc.], Houghton Mifflin Company. viii, 506 p. Edited by William Fielding Ogburn and Alexander Goldenweiser.
[2] "Selected References," p. 327–328.

1928

159. *Social and Economic Problems of the Law*
   136 Annals, American Academy of Political and Social
   Science, no. 225,[1] p. 1–9. March, 1928.
   Reprint: [2] Philadelphia, Pa., n.d. 9 p.
   C. C. H. Legal Periodical Digest, 1928 ed., p. 1000–1001.

[1] This issue entitled *Progress in the Law* is devoted to "a discussion of some of the tendencies of the law and the administration of justice tending constantly to adapt law to the changing conditions of our modern social and economic life."
[2] Caption title: Reprinted from The Annals of the American Academy of Political and Social Science. Philadelphia, March, 1928, Publication No. 2119.

160. *The Future of the Common Law* [1]
   7 Nebraska Law Bulletin 107–122. July, 1928.
   Proceedings of the Nebraska State Bar Association, vol. 18,
   1927, p. 107–122. [1928].

[1] Address to the Nebraska State Bar Association, at its twenty-eighth annual meeting, held at Omaha, Nebraska, December 28–29, 1927.

161. *Science and Legal Procedure* [1]
   8 American Journal of Psychiatry [2] 33–51. July, 1928.
   Reprint: n.p., n.d. 33–51 p.

[1] The "Annual Address" at the eighty-fourth meeting of the American Psychiatric Association, held in Minneapolis, Minnesota, on June 5–8, 1928.
[2] Old Series 85.

162. *A Foreword to the Pageant of Magna Carta* [1]
   14 American Bar Association Journal 526–529. October,
   1928.
   Report of the 51st Annual Meeting of the American Bar
   Association [vol. 53], p. 282–291. 1928.
   8 Oregon Law Review [2] 61–69. December, 1928.

[1] This paper was "written to be read in connection with the presentation of 'Magna Carta: A Pageant-Drama' at the Semi-Centennial Meeting of the American Bar Association."
[2] "Reprinted by permission of the American Bar Association Journal."

C. C. H. Legal Periodical Digest, 1928 ed., p. 1079–1080.
Reprinted in: Magna Carta; A Pageant Drama (by Thomas
Wood Stevens), p. 11–20. 1930.

163. *Comparative Law in the Formation of American Common
Law*
In: Actorum Academiae Universalis Iurisprudentiae Comparativae, vol. 1 [1] — Mémoires de L'Académie Internationale de Droit Comparé, vol. 1, p. 183–197.[2] 1928.[3]
Reprint: Berlin, Paris, [etc.], 1928. 183–197 p.

[1] *Quod illius auspiciis curavit* Elemér Balogh.
[2] *Publié sous sa direction par M. Le Professeur* Elemér Balogh.
[3] Contains bibliographical notes and portrait.

164. *Opening Statement [On the Codification of the Law of Nations] at the First Meeting of the Advisory Committee.*[1]
1928. 5 sheets, multigraphed.

[1] Delivered at the opening organizational meeting of the Research in
International Law, Harvard Law School, in 1928.

165. *A Task for the University Law School*[1]
In: Address of Dean Roscoe Pound [2] . . . and Exercises at
the Dedication of Richardson Hall, 10 November, 1928.
1928. 12 p.

[1] Address made at the exercises of dedication for Richardson Hall, Brooklyn Law School, N. Y., in honor of Dean William Payson Richardson, November 10, 1928.
[2] At head of title: St. Lawrence University, The Brooklyn Law School.

1929

166. *Types of Legal Periodical*[1]
14 Iowa Law Review 257–265. April, 1929.
Reprint: Iowa City, 1929. 257–265 p.
C. C. H. Legal Periodical Digest, 1929 ed., p. 1746–1747.
June, 1929.

[1] Paper read at a Round Table meeting of the Association of American
Law Schools on December 27, 1928, at Chicago, Illinois.

167. *The Judicial Office in America*[1]

Proceedings of the 40th Annual Meeting,[2] The Virginia State
Bar Association, p. 406–421. 1929.

Reprint: Richmond, Va., 1929. 16 p.

10 Boston University Law Review 125–137. April, 1930.

[1] This address was originally delivered before the Bigelow Association of
Masters of Law (the Alumni Association of the Graduate School, Boston
University School of Law) at its November 14, 1928, meeting held in the
rooms of the Bar Association of the City of Boston. The summer following,
July 31, 1929, the paper was presented at the annual meeting of the Virginia
Bar Association, at the Homestead, Hot Springs, Virginia.

[2] Reported in volume 61 of the Virginia Bar Reports. Portrait facing p. 406.

168. *Jurisprudence*

In: Research in the Social Sciences, Its Fundamental Methods and Objectives,[1] p. 181–206. 1929.

法學史 *Fa hsüeh shih.*[2] Shanghai, Commercial Press, n.d.
1, 4, 96 p.

[1] At head of title: Institute for Research in the Social Sciences, The University of Virginia. A series of lectures delivered at the Institute. Edited by
Wilson Gee. Cf. Introduction. New York, The Macmillan Company, 1929.
x, 3–305 p.

[2] Translated by Binnan P. Louis. "Social Science Library," published by
V. W. Wong.

1930

169. *Pound Traces the Law*[1]

2 New York State Bar Association Bulletin 263–271. May,
1930.

[1] Editorial subtitle: Harvard Dean Praises Law Institute as the Promoter
of Certainty. Portrait p. 263.

170. *The New Feudal System*

35 Commercial Law Journal 397–403. August, 1930.

C. C. H. Legal Periodical Digest, 1930 ed., p. 860–861.
September, 1930.

19 Kentucky Law Journal 1–15. November, 1930.

Reprint:[1] n.p., n.d. 15 p.

Proceedings of the 29th Annual Meeting of the Kentucky
State Bar Association,[2] p. 88–107. 1930.

Reprint: n.p., n.d. 16 p.

Reprinted in: Selected Essays on Constitutional Law, bk. 2,
p. 82–94.[3] 1938.

[1] Cover title: The New Feudalism.

[2] At Paducah, Kentucky, April 10, 11, 1930. Introductory remarks, p. 88;
the address, p. 89–107.   [3] "Reprinted from the Kentucky Law Journal."

Under title: *The New Feudalism*
16 American Bar Association Journal 553–558. September, 1930.

171. *Cooperation in Enforcement of Law*
Los Angeles Daily Journal, p. 8:3. September 19, 1930.
Proceedings of the 3rd Annual Meeting,[1] The State Bar of California, p. 63–77. 1930.
17 American Bar Association Journal 9–14, 63, 64. January, 1931.
C. C. H. Legal Periodical Digest, 1931 ed., p. 4506–4507.
Under title: *Dean Pound's Address at Pasadena* [2]
2 The Summons 6–7. Winter, 1930/31.

[1] The "Alexander F. Morrison Foundation" lecture delivered under the auspices of The State Bar of California at Pasadena, September 18, 1930.
[2] A condensation of the address as reported in the Los Angeles Daily Journal.

172. CRIMINAL JUSTICE IN AMERICA [1]
New York, Henry Holt and Co., 1930. xiv, 226 p.
[1] Half-title: Brown University. The Colver Lectures, 1924.

173. *The Individualization of Justice*
National Probation Association, Year Book, 1930,[1] p. 104–112. 1930.
[1] The record of the twenty-fourth Annual Conference held at Boston, Massachusetts, June 6–10, 1930. Mr. Pound's paper is a contribution to Part II — Crime Treatment.

174. *The Law School, 1817–1929*
In: The Development of Harvard University Since the Inauguration of President Eliot, 1869–1929,[1] ch. 30, p. 472–507.[2] 1930.
[1] Cambridge, Mass., Harvard University Press, 1930. xc, 660 p. *Half-title:* The Tercentennial History of Harvard College and University 1636–1936. Edited by Samuel Eliot Morison.
[2] Mr. Pound's account is divided into: Periods and Principles in the History of the School, 1817–1929, p. 472; The Faculty, p. 477; Teaching, p. 488; Graduate Instruction and Research, p. 495; The Student Body, p. 498; The Library, p. 500; Student Activities, p. 502; Administration, p. 504; Endowment and Buildings, p. 506.
The illustrations accompanying the article: 1. Christopher Columbus Langdell (*from the portrait by Frederick P. Vinton*) facing p. 478; 2. John Chipman Gray (*from an etching by Otto J. Schneider*) facing p. 479; 3. James Bradley Thayer (*from an etching by Sidney L. Smith*) facing p. 504; and 4. James Barr Ames (*from an etching by Otto J. Schneider*) facing p. 505.

Reprint: n.p., n.d. 472–507 p.

Under title: *Sketch of the History of the Harvard Law School*[3]

In: Harvard Law School Year Book . . . ,[4] vol. 1, p. 25–48. 1937.

[3] An abridgment by Mr. Pound, with permission of the Harvard University Press, of his account in "The Development of Harvard University," *supra.*

[4] Published by the Year Book Committee of Phillips Brooks House Association of Harvard University, Cambridge, Mass.

175. *Public Opinion and Social Control*

Proceedings of the National Conference of Social Work, 57th Annual Session,[1] p. 607–623. 1930.

Reprint: n.p., n.d. 607–623 p.

[1] Held in Boston, Massachusetts, June 8–14, 1930. Reported in the New York Times, June 15, 1930, 2:5.

176. *The Revival of Comparative Law*

5 Tulane Law Review 1–16. December, 1930.

Reprint: New Orleans, La., 1930. 1–16 p.

Report of the Louisiana State Bar Association for 1930,[1] vol. 30, p. 91–109. 1930.

C. C. H. Legal Periodical Digest, 1931 ed., p. 4008–4009.

[1] The annual meeting was held in Monroe, April 25, 26, 1930. Address delivered at the April 26th session.

177. *The School of Law*

In: Higher Education in America,[1] ch. 9, p. 262–283.[2] 1930.

[1] New York, Ginn & Co., 1930. x, 689 p. Edited by Raymond A. Kent.
[2] "Selected References," p. 283.

1931

178. *The Call for a Realist Jurisprudence*

44 Harvard Law Review 697–711. March, 1931.

C. C. H. Legal Periodical Digest, 1931 ed., p. 4030–4031.

179. *Crime and the Law*[1]

49 Medical Times *and* Long Island Medical Journal 117, 118–122. March, 1931.

Publications, Society of Medical Jurisprudence.[2] 1931. 21 p.[3]

[1] The paper, as published, is a stenographic report of the address delivered as part of the proceedings of the 391st regular meeting of the Society of Medical Jurisprudence, New York City, October 13, 1930, at the New York Academy of Medicine.
[2] A reprint from the Medical Times *and* Long Island Medical Journal.
[3] Introductory remarks p. 3–8; the address, p. 8–21.

180. *The Ideal Element in American Judicial Decision*
    45 Harvard Law Review 136–148. November, 1931.
    C. C. H. Legal Periodical Digest, 1932 ed., p. 4001.
    Reprinted in part in: Readings in Jurisprudence. Jerome
    Hall. p. 326–332. 1938.

181. *The Opportunities for Developing Research in the Field of Jurisprudence*
    Journal of Proceedings and Addresses of the 33rd Annual
    Conference,[1] Association of American Universities, p. 119–
    134. November, 1931.

[1] Meeting held at the University of North Carolina, November 12–14, 1931.

182. *Common Law*
    In: Encyclopaedia of the Social Sciences,[1] vol. 4, p. 50–56.
    1931.

[1] New York, Macmillan. 15 v., 1930–1935. Reissued 15 v. in 8, 1935.

183. *Contract — Legal Doctrine and History*
    In: Encyclopaedia of the Social Sciences, vol. 4, p. 323–
    329, 339.[1] 1931.

[1] List of references to be consulted, p. 339. The second part of the article,
Contract — Institutional Aspects, p. 329–339, was written by K. N. Llewellyn.

1932

184. *Education and the Legal Order* [1]
    2 Harvard Teachers Record 68–73. April, 1932.

[1] Paper presented at the forty-first annual meeting of the Harvard Teachers
Association held in Cambridge, Massachusetts, March 19, 1932.

185. *Jurisprudence: Science or Superstition*
    18 American Bar Association Journal 312–314. May, 1932.

186. *The Problem of an Ordered Society* [1]
    11 Tennessee Law Review 1–13. December, 1932.
    C. C. H. Legal Periodical Digest, 1933 ed., p. 4010–4011.

[1] Paper read before the Institute of Justice, University of Chattanooga,
April 29, 1932.

187. *The Ideal Element in Law*
    Proceedings of the 38th Annual Session [1] of the Iowa State
    Bar Association, p. 223–237. 1932.
    10 Dicta 225–238.[2] June, 1933.[3]

[1] Held at Burlington, Iowa, June 9 and 10, 1932.
[2] A publication of the Denver Bar Association.
[3] Delivered at "Annual Banquet" of the Denver Bar Association.

188. *Jurisprudence*
   In: Encyclopaedia of the Social Sciences, vol. 8, p. 477–492.[1] 1932.

[1] An extensive bibliography on jurisprudence and its schools is appended to the article.

189. *Jury — England and the United States*
   In: Encyclopaedia of the Social Sciences, vol. 8, p. 492–498, 501.[1] 1932.

[1] List of references to be consulted, p. 501. The Jury in Other Countries, p. 498–501, was written by William Seagle.

190. *Men and Rules* [1]
   Bound in: Addresses, Lectures, etc., v. 3.[2] 13 sheets, type-written.

[1] Address made before the members of the Association of the Bar of the City of New York, December 18, 1931.
[2] Association of the Bar of the City of New York, volume of unpublished addresses, lectures, etc., for 1930–1932.

1933

191. *What Use Can Be Made of Judicial Statistics* [1]
   12 Oregon Law Review 89–95. February, 1933.
   Reprint: n.p., n.d. 89–95 p.
   C. C. H. Legal Periodical Digest, 1933 ed., p. 4521.

[1] Address made before the Judicial Section at the 53rd annual meeting of the American Bar Association, October 11, 1932.

192. *Training for the Bar* [1]
   2 Bar Examiner [2] 123–128. March, 1933.
   Law Series I, Lecture No. 2. University of Chicago Press, 1933. 11 p.

[1] A radio address, February 19, 1933; the second in a series of fifteen broadcasts, entitled The Lawyer and the Public, sponsored by the National Advisory Council on Radio in Education, Inc., and presented by the American Bar Association, February to May, 1933. Each address was subsequently published separately by the University of Chicago Press, 1933.
[2] Reprinted by permission of the National Advisory Council on Radio in Education and the University of Chicago Press.

193. *The Ideal and the Actual in Law — Forty Years After* [1]
89 New York Law Journal 2119–2120. April 10, 1933.
1 George Washington Law Review 431–447. May, 1933.
C. C. H. Legal Periodical Digest, 1933 ed., p. 4036–4037.

[1] Address at the Association of the Bar of the City of New York on March 29, 1933.

The editorial headnote in the New York Law Journal states: "No recent address before the Association of the Bar of the City of New York created more interest than the address delivered by Dean Pound . . . [he] compared the views expressed by the late James C. Carter in his celebrated essay 'The Ideal and the Actual in the Law,' which was written some forty years ago, with ideas current to-day. The seats in the large auditorium of the Association were unable to accommodate the audience and many who wished to stand were turned away. . . ."

194. *Hierarchy of Sources and Forms in Different Systems of Law* [1]
7 Tulane Law Review 475–487. June, 1933.
Reprint: New Orleans, La., 1933. 475–487 p.
C. C. H. Legal Periodical Digest, 1933 ed., p. 4039–4040.
Reprinted in part in: Readings in Jurisprudence. Jerome Hall. p. 661–666. 1938.
Printed as: *Rapport Général de M. Roscoe Pound*
In: Actorum Academiae Universalis Jurisprudentiae Comparativae,[2] vol. 2, part 2 — Mémoires de L'Académie Internationale de Droit Comparé, vol. 2, part 2, p. 9–21. 1934.
Reprint: Paris, n.d. 9–21 p.

[1] The General Report by Mr. Pound to the International Congress of Comparative Law, held at the Peace Palace, The Hague, August 2–6, 1932. Title variants in the American and Continental printings are noted; both texts are in English.

[2] *Librarie du Recueil Sirey*, Paris, 1934.

195. *A Comparison of Ideals of Law*
47 Harvard Law Review 1–17. November, 1933.
Reprint: Cambridge, Mass. 1933. 17 p.
C. C. H. Legal Periodical Digest, 1934 ed., p. 4001–4002.
In: Actorum Academiae Universalis Jurisprudentiae Comparativae,[1] vol. 2, part 4 — Mémoires de L'Académie In-

[1] *Librarie du Recueil Sirey*, Paris, 1935.

ternationale de Droit Comparé, vol. 2, part 4, p. 200–215.
1935.
Reprint: Paris, n.d. 200–215 p.

196. *The Future of the Common Law* [1]
7 University of Cincinnati Law Review 343–361. November,
1933.
Reprint: n.p., 1933. 18 p.
C. C. H. Legal Periodical Digest, 1934 ed., p. 4006–4007.

[1] Delivered at the Centennial Celebration of the University of Cincinnati
Law School, June 9, 1933.

197. *What is a Good Legal Education?* [1]
19 American Bar Association Journal 627–631. November,
1933.
7 American Law School Review 887–894. December, 1933.
C. C. H. Legal Periodical Digest, 1933 ed., p. 4549.

[1] Address before the Section of Legal Education and Admissions to the
Bar, August 29, 1933, at Grand Rapids, Michigan.

198. *Recent Developments in the Law of Equity of Interest to
Practicing Lawyers*
In: Lectures before the Institute of the Cleveland Bar Asso-
ciation,[1] p. 3–51. 1933.

[1] Published by the Cleveland Bar Association, Cleveland, Ohio, 1933.

1934

199. *Law and the Science of Law in Recent Theories*
43 Yale Law Journal 525–536. February, 1934.
Reprint: n.p., n.d. 525–536 p.
7 American Law School Review 1057–1063.[1] April, 1934.
C. C. H. Legal Periodical Digest, 1934 ed., p. 4014–4015.
Reprinted in: Handbook of the Association of American Law
Schools,[2] p. 93–100. n.d.

[1] Abridgment read as part of the symposium "Modern Trends in Jurisprudence," at the 31st annual meeting of the Association of American Law
Schools, Chicago, Illinois, December 30, 1933.
[2] "And Proceedings of the Thirty-First Annual Meeting, December 28–30,
1933."

200. *The Place of Comparative Law in the American Law School
Curriculum*
8 Tulane Law Review 161–170. February, 1934.
C. C. H. Legal Periodical Digest, 1934 ed., p. 4507–4508.

201. *Legal Interrogation of Persons Accused or Suspected of Crime*[1]

24 Journal of the American Institute of Criminal Law and Criminology 1014–1018. March–April, 1934.

Reprint: n.p., n.d. 1014–1018 p.

12 The Panel 15–16.[2] March–April, 1934.

Pittsburgh Legal Journal. June 30, 1934.[3]

C. C. H. Legal Periodical Digest, 1934 ed., p. 2516–2517.

[1] Paper read before a Round Table Conference of the Association of American Law Schools at Chicago, Illinois, December 30, 1933.
[2] Bulletin of the Association of Grand Jurors, New York County, New York.
[3] Vol. 82, no. 26, supplement to daily edition, p. 17–19.
Under title: *Legal Interrogation of Persons Accused or Suspected.*

202. *New Possibilities of Old Materials of American Legal History*[1]

40 West Virginia Law Quarterly *and* The Bar 205–211. April, 1934.

Reprint: Morgantown, W. Va., n.d. 205–211 p.

[1] Paper presented at the Round Table on Jurisprudence and Legal History, the annual meeting of the Association of American Law Schools held at Chicago, Illinois, December 28–30, 1933.

203. *The American Constitution in the Light of Today*[1]

68 United States Law Review 304–308. June, 1934.

Reprint: New York, Crusaders Inc., n.d. 6 p.

[1] The full text of a radio address over the Columbia Broadcasting System originating in Boston, Massachusetts.
Extracts from this paper appeared in an editorial of the New York Law Journal for June 22, 1934. This editorial was reprinted in the Pittsburgh Legal Journal for July 28, 1934, vol. 82, no. 30, supplement to daily edition, p. 8–9; under title: *Dean Pound's Address.*

204. *The New Deal in the Courts: A Changing Ideal of Justice*

New York Times, Sept. 9, 1934,[1] VIII, 3:6.

Under title: *New Conceptions of Justice Being Formed*
Pittsburgh Legal Journal. October 6, 1934.[2]

[1] Portrait.
[2] Vol. 82, no. 42, supplement to daily edition, p. 19–22.
Reprinted from the New York Times.

205. *Unification of Law* [1]
   20 American Bar Association Journal 695–696. November,
   1934.
   Under title: *Unification through the Common Law* [2]
   9 State Bar Journal 285, 298, 299. November, 1934.

   [1] Paper presented before the joint meeting of the Judicial Section and the National Conference of Judicial Councils. Meeting held at Milwaukee, Wisconsin, on Wednesday, August 29, 1934.
   [2] Publication of State Bar of California. "From an address delivered at Milwaukee [August, 1934] during the Convention of the American Bar Association."

206. *Fundamental Law in the Society of Today*
   13 Tennessee Law Review 1–13.[1] December, 1934.
   1 Current Legal Thought 5–8.[2] March, 1935.
   C. C. H. Legal Periodical Digest, 1935 ed., p. 4003.

   [1] See the Chattanooga [Tenn.] Times, April 28, 1934.
   [2] An abstract of the article in 13 Tennessee Law Review.

207. *Outlines of a Course on Legislation*
   Cambridge, Mass. viii, 59 p. 1934.

208. *Rule of Law*
   In: Encyclopaedia of the Social Sciences, vol. 13, p. 463–
   466. 1934.

209. *Twentieth-Century Ideas as to the End of Law*
   In: Harvard Legal Essays,[1] written in honor of and presented to Joseph Henry Beale and Samuel Williston, p.
   357–375. 1934.
   Reprint: Cambridge, Mass., Harvard University Press, 1934,
   p. 357–375.

   [1] Cambridge, Mass., Harvard University Press. xviii, 553 p. Edited by Roscoe Pound. Preface by the editor.

1935

210. *Needed Reforms in Criminal Procedure* [1]
   13 Tennessee Law Review 113–118. February, 1935.
   Law Series II, Lecture No. 11. n.p., n.d. 6 sheets, multigraphed.

   [1] Radio address, December 15, 1934; the eleventh in a series of twelve lectures entitled The Lawyer and the Public, October to December, 1934, arranged by the American Bar Association and sponsored by the National Advisory Council in Education. Reported in the New York Times, December 16, 1934, II, 4:6.

211. *Trends of Current Legal Philosophy* [1]
92 Legal Intelligencer [2] 1, 28–29. March 22, 1935.
22 District and County Reports,[3] appendix, p. vi–xiv. 1935.

[1] Address delivered before the Law Academy of Philadelphia, March 19, 1935.
[2] Philadelphia, Pa.
[3] Contains, for temporary use, advance sheets of the cases decided in the various judicial districts of the Commonwealth of Pennsylvania. Philadelphia, Pa., published by the Legal Intelligencer. 22 District and County Reports, reprinted from 92 Legal Intelligencer.

212. *Toward a Better Criminal Law*
21 American Bar Association Journal 499–504.[1] August, 1935.
Report of the 58th Annual Meeting of the American Bar Association, p. 322–336.[2] 1935.
5 Lawyers' Journal 531–535.[3] 1937.
C. C. H. Legal Periodical Digest, 1935 ed., p. 2544–2545.

[1] Contribution to *National Bar Program Addresses on the Criminal Law and its Enforcement*, p. 495–511.
[2] Los Angeles, California, July 16–19, 1935.
[3] Manila, P. I.

213. *The Bar Examinations in Retrospect and Prospect* [1]
8 American Law School Review 305–314. December, 1935.
Under title: *The Bar Examination in Retrospect and Prospect* [1]
4 Bar Examiner 455–464.[2] September, 1935.

[1] Address made before the National Conference of Bar Examiners at its fifth annual meeting held at Los Angeles, California, July 16, 1935.
[2] An abbreviated version of the address.

214. [*The Constitution in This Day and in Respect to Social and Legislative Trends*]
10th Annual Meeting of the Federation of Bar Associations of Western New York,[1] p. 66–82. (Multigraphed.) [2] 1935.

[1] Held at Norton Hall, University of Buffalo, at the City of Buffalo, on Saturday, June 29, 1935.
[2] Reported by John J. Sly, Law Stenographer, Buffalo, N. Y.

215. *Law and Laws in the Twentieth Century* [1]
   In: Dedicatory Exercises of the Law Quadrangle [2]. . . . University of Michigan Law School, June 15th, 1934, p. 25–46. 1935.
   Reprint: [3] Ann Arbor, Mich., n.d. 25–46 p.

   [1] Address delivered on the occasion of the dedication of the Law Quadrangle of the University of Michigan.
   [2] Published by the University of Michigan Law School. Illustrations.
   Portrait — a group picture, reading from left to right — Henry M. Bates, Tappan Professor of Law and Dean of the Law School of the University of Michigan; Marvin M. Rosenberry, Chief Justice of the Supreme Court of Wisconsin; Roscoe Pound; Harlan F. Stone, Associate Justice of the Supreme Court of the United States; and Newton D. Baker, Secretary of War, 1916–1921 — facing p. 10.
   [3] Reprinted from Dedicatory Exercises of the Law Quadrangle.

216. *More About the Nature of Law*
   In: Legal Essays in Tribute to Orrin Kip McMurray,[1] p. 513–535. 1935.
   Reprint: n.p., 1935. 513–535 p.

   [1] Berkeley, Cal., University of California Press, 1935. x, 694 p. Edited by Max Radin and A. M. Kidd.

217. *Some Constitutional Aspects of the Oil Problem* [1]
   Transactions of the American Institute of Mining and Metallurgical Engineers, vol. 114, p. 207–219. 1935.
   Reprint: n.p., n.d. 15–27 p.

   [1] Paper contributed to a symposium on stabilization of the oil industry, held by the Petroleum Division Stabilization Committee, A. I. M. E., on February 22, 1934, in New York City. The paper was published in the 1935 volume of proceedings.

1936

218. *Visitatorial Jurisdiction over Corporations in Equity*
   49 Harvard Law Review 369–395. January, 1936.
   2 Current Legal Thought 345–351.[1] January, 1936.
   C. C. H. Legal Periodical Digest, 1936 ed., p. 3022–3024.

   [1] An abstract.

219. *What May We Expect from Comparative Law?* [1]
   22 American Bar Association Journal 56–60. January, 1936.

   [1] Address at the Annual Dinner of the Section of International and Comparative Law, July 16, 1935, at Los Angeles, California.
   See Proceedings of the Second Annual Meeting of the Section *in* Report of the 58th Annual Meeting of the American Bar Association [vol. 60], 611–614, at p. 611.

220. *How Far Are We Attaining a New Measure of Values in Twentieth-Century Juristic Thought?* [1]

> 42 West Virginia Law Quarterly *and* The Bar 81–95. February, 1936.
>
> C. C. H. Legal Periodical Digest, 1936 ed., p. 4019–4020.

[1] Paper read before the Round Table on Jurisprudence and Legal History at the annual meeting of the Association of American Law Schools, at New Orleans, Louisiana, December 28, 1935.

221. *Present Tendencies in Legal Education*

> 15 Nebraska Law Bulletin 207–218.[1] November, 1936.
>
> *In:* Annual Review of Legal Education for 1935,[2] p. 1–12. 1936.

[1] "Reprinted from the Annual Review of Legal Education for 1935."
[2] Published by the Section of Legal Education and Admissions to the Bar of the American Bar Association. Chicago, Ill., 1935. 70 p. Excerpts from this article appear in 22 American Bar Association Journal 293–294, May, 1936.

222. *Modern Organization and an Old Profession* [1]

> 22 American Bar Association Journal 767–769. November, 1936.
>
> Annual Report of the American Bar Association, vol. 61, p. 397–403. 1936.

[1] Delivered at the Annual Dinner of the Conference of Bar Association Delegates. Boston, Massachusetts, August 24, 1936.

1937

223. *What is the Common Law?* [1]

> 4 University of Chicago Law Review 176–189. February, 1937.
>
> *In:* The Future of the Common Law,[2] p. 3–23. 1937.
>
> *Reprint:* Cambridge, Mass., 1937. 21 p.
>
> C. C. H. Legal Periodical Digest, 1937 ed., p. 4015–4016.

[1] Address delivered at the Conference on the Future of the Common Law, as part of the Harvard University Tercentenary Celebration (1636–1936), held at the Harvard Law School on August 19–21, 1936.

For a discussion, see *Attacks on the Common Law Discussed by Dean Pound*, Pittsburgh Legal Journal, Aug. 29, 1936, vol. 84, no. 35, p. 25; also supplement to daily edition, Aug. 26, 1936.

[2] Cambridge, Mass., Harvard University Press, 1937. x, 247 p.

Half-title: Harvard Tercentenary Publications; The Future of the Common Law.

224. *Fifty Years of Jurisprudence* [1]
     50 Harvard Law Review 557–582; 51 *ibid.* 444–472; 777–
     812. February, 1937; January, March, 1938.
     Reprint: Cambridge, Mass., 1938. 557–582; 444–472; 777–
     812.
     C. C. H. Legal Periodical Digest, 1937 ed., p. 4019–4021;
     1938 ed., p. 4015–4016, 4036–4038.

[1] In six parts: I. Jurisprudence in the last decades of the nineteenth century; II. Progress in the nineteenth-century methods in fifty years; III. The rise of the twentieth-century schools; IV. Realist schools; V. Sociological jurisprudence; VI. Conclusion.
See title no. 229 *infra.*

225. *The Prospect for American Law*
     16 Nebraska Law Bulletin 97–108. July, 1937.
     Proceedings of the Nebraska State Bar Association,[1] vol. 27,
     p. 97–108. 1936.

[1] 37th Annual Meeting held at Omaha, Nebraska, December 29–30, 1936.

226. *The Constitution: Its Development, Adaptability and Future* [1]
     23 American Bar Association Journal 739–745. October,
     1937.
     C. C. H. Legal Periodical Digest, 1937 ed., p. 4058–4059.

[1] Address delivered before the Chicago Bar Association at its sesquicentennial meeting, September 16, 1937.

227. *The Future of Law* [1]
     47 Yale Law Journal 1–13.[2] November, 1937.
     Publications, Tokyo Imperial University. 1937. 20 p.
     C. C. H. Legal Periodical Digest, 1937 ed., p. 4057–4058.
     4 Current Legal Thought 93–99.[3] November, 1937.
     法の將來 *Hô no Shirai.*[4] Publications, Tokyo Imperial
     University. 1937. 23 p.

[1] An address delivered at the Tokyo Imperial University on February 20th, 1937, before an audience of "more than one thousand."
Mr. Kenzo Takayanagi, presently occupying the Chair of English Law at Tokyo Imperial University and Director of its Library, writes to say that Mr. Pound's lecture "was also printed in the April, 1937, number of the *Hogaku Kyokai Zasshi* (Journal of the Juridical Society [published by the Law Faculty of the University]). The translation thereof was published in the April, 1937, number of the *Nippon Hyôron,* a magazine somewhat along the lines of the Atlantic Monthly."
[2] The last paragraph in the Tokyo publication has been omitted in the Yale reprint.   [3] An abstract.   [4] Translated by Professor Kenzo Takayanagi.

228. *Fashions in Juristic Thinking* [1]
Publications, Holdsworth Club of the University of Birmingham. 1937. 20 p.

[1] The "Presidential Address" to the Holdsworth Club of the Students of the Faculty of Law in the University of Birmingham, England. Delivered at the University, Edmund Street, Birmingham, on Friday, May 7, 1937, Professor C. E. Smalley-Baker, Dean of the Faculty of Law and Director of Legal Studies, in the Chair.

229. *Fifty Years of Jurisprudence* [1]
1937 Journal of the Society of Public Teachers of Law,[2] p. 17–31.
Reprint: n.t.p. 14 p.

[1] Paper presented at University College, London, before the annual meeting of the Society of Public Teachers of Law, on the afternoon of July 6, 1937.
The published paper, p. 17–30, is supplemented by the discussion from the floor which followed its delivery, p. 30–31.
This is not the same paper as No. 224 *supra.*
[2] Published by Butterworth & Co. Ltd., London.

230. *A Hundred Years of American Law* [1]
In: Law; A Century of Progress 1835–1935,[2] vol. 1, p. 8–26. 1937.

[1] This is the revised text of an address delivered at the forty-ninth reunion dinner of the New York University Law School Alumni Association, February 9, 1935.
[2] Contributions in Celebration of the One-Hundredth Anniversary of the Founding of the Law School of New York University. 3 v. New York University Press, Washington Square, New York, 1937.

1938

231. *Individualization of Justice* [1]
7 Fordham Law Review 153–166. May, 1938.
C. C. H. Legal Periodical Digest, 1938 ed., p. 4045–4047.

[1] Address made at a meeting of the United States Federation of Justice, held at the building of the Association of the Bar of the City of New York, December 3, 1937.

232. *Some Implications of Recent Legislation* [1]
49 United States Investor 1749–1752. November 5, 1938.
5 Vital Speeches of the Day [2] 90–95. November 15, 1938.

[1] Address before the Investment Bankers Association of America at their meeting in White Sulphur Springs, West Virginia, October 29, 1938.
[2] Mr. Pound's address is published with the subtitle, *The Super-Man Administrator.*

45 West Virginia Law Quarterly 205–219. April, 1939.
C. C. H. Legal Periodical Digest, 1939 ed., p. 4035–4036.

233. *The Influence of the Civil Law in America* [1]
1 Louisiana Law Review 1–16. November, 1938.
C. C. H. Legal Periodical Digest, 1939 ed., p. 4003–4005.

[1] Paper read at the symposium on *The Position of the Civil Law in America*,
held in connection with the dedicatory exercises of Leche Hall, law building
of the Louisiana State University Law School, at Baton Rouge, Louisiana,
April 8, 1938.

234. THE FORMATIVE ERA OF AMERICAN LAW [1]
Boston, Mass., Little, Brown and Company, 1938. x, 188 p.
2d printing. Boston, Mass., Little, Brown and Company,
1939.

[1] Preface: "... four lectures ... printed as they were delivered at the
Law School of Tulane University on the occasion of the centennial of the
death of Edward Livingston, October 27–30, 1936 ... some notes intended
for the most part to illustrate or explain the points made [have been added]."
I. Natural Law, p. 3–30; II. Legislation, p. 38–72; III. Judicial Decision,
p. 81–127; IV. Doctrinal Writing, p. 138–167. Bibliographical notes: p. 30–
37; 72–80; 127–137; 167–172. Index: p. 175–188.

235. *La Législation dans la Période de Formation du Droit
Américain* [1]
In: Introduction à l'Étude du Droit Comparé [2] — Recueil
d'Études en l'Honneur d'Edouard Lambert, vol. 1, p. 404–
420. 1938.
Reprint: n.p., n.d. 404–420 p.
[1] Translated by Professor Jacques Lambert.
[2] 3 v. Paris, 1938.

1939

236. *The Recrudescence of Absolutism* [1]
47 Sewanee Review 18–28. January–March, 1939.

[1] The article is editorially described as a "piercing analytical examination
of the threatening forces of the new political absolutism which endanger
established ideas and customs of the American democratic order."

237. *Public Law and Private Law* [1]
24 Cornell Law Quarterly 469–482. June, 1939.
C. C. H. Legal Periodical Digest, 1939 ed., p. 4065–4066.

[1] "A lecture delivered at the Cornell Law School under the Frank Irvine
Lectureship of the Phi Delta Phi Foundation, April twenty-second, nineteen
hundred and thirty-nine." — *Ed.*

238. *The Judicial Office Today* [1]

87 Pittsburgh Legal Journal, No. 29, p. 3–4.[2] July 22, 1939.

25 American Bar Association Journal 731–737, 754. September, 1939.

[1] Address delivered before the Section of Criminal Law, San Francisco, July 11, 1939.

[2] Excerpts.

239. *Property Rights and Liberty; the Law of Property and Recent Juristic Thought* [1]

69 Trusts and Estates [2] 57–62. July, 1939.

Under title: *The Law of Property and Recent Juristic Thought*

25 American Bar Association Journal [3] 993–999. December, 1939.

C. C. H. Legal Periodical Digest, 1940 ed., p. 4003–4004.[4]

[1] An address delivered at the annual dinner of the Section of Real Property, Probate and Trust Law at San Francisco, July 11, 1939.

[2] The text as found in the Trusts and Estates is not complete. It lacks several paragraphs at the beginning and it differs slightly in wording at one or two points.

[3] Portrait, p. 995.

[4] A digest of the address as it appeared in 25 American Bar Association Journal.

240. *The Function and Prospects of Judicial Councils* [1]

23 Journal of the American Judicature Society 53–59. August, 1939.

Under title: *Administrative Absolutism* [2]

Bar Bulletin,[3] No. 152, p. 6–8.

[1] An address delivered at a meeting of the National Conference of Judicial Councils, in Washington, Mar. 11, 1939.

Mr. Pound is Director of Research of the National Conference of Judicial Councils. Portrait, p. 53.

[2] Excerpt.

[3] Published by the Bar Association of the City of Boston.

241. *Judicial Councils vs. Absolutism*

2 Texas Bar Journal 265–266. August, 1939.

242. *Practical Advantages of Rules of Court for Criminal Procedure* [1]

25 American Bar Association Journal 825–827. October, 1939.

[1] Address delivered before the Section of Judicial Administration at its meeting in San Francisco, July 11, 1939.

243. *The Work of a Judicial Council*
    18 Texas Law Review [1] 98–110. October, 1939.
[1] Bar Association Number, Proceedings, Texas Bar Association, vol. 58.

244. *A Generation of Law Teaching*
    38 Michigan Law Review [1] 16–29. November, 1939.
    C. C. H. Legal Periodical Digest, 1939 ed., p. 4077–4078.

[1] "The contributors of this number of the Michigan Law Review join in this tribute in recognition that the occasion is one for congratulation to Dean Bates for a public service so admirably performed. . . ." — Harlan F. Stone.

245. *For the Study of Jewish Law*
    27 Menorah Journal 14–17. Winter, 1939.

246. *American Juristic Thinking in the Twentieth Century*
    In: A Century of Social Thought,[1] p. 143–172. 1939.

[1] "A Series of Lectures delivered at Duke University during the Academic Year 1938–1939 as a part of the Centennial Celebration of that Institution." Durham, N. C., Duke University Press, 1939.

247. *The Church in Legal History*
    In: Jubilee Law Lectures,[1] 1889–1939, School of Law, the Catholic University of America, p. 3–97. 1939.

[1] "As a contribution to the celebration of the Golden Jubilee Year of the Catholic University of America, the School of Law arranged two series of lectures on 'The Church in Legal History' and 'The Function of Law in Society Today.'
    "The University was fortunate in securing the generous services of the eminent scholar Roscoe Pound, Esq., for the four lectures of the series 'The Church in Legal History.'
    "Four noted legal authorities, Daniel J. Lyne, Esq., of Boston, Massachusetts, Grenville Clark, Esq., of New York City, Hector David Castro, Esq., of El Salvador, and John J. Burns, Esq., of Boston, Massachusetts, treated individual aspects of the second series, 'The Function of Law in Society Today'." — Preface.
    The titles of the lectures by Roscoe Pound which form Part I of the book are: 1. The Idea of Universality; 2. The Idea of Authority; 3. The Idea of Good Faith; 4. The Idea of Law.
    Washington, D. C., The Catholic University of America Press, 1939. 182 p.

248. *A General Summary*
    Proceedings of the 50th Annual Meeting of the Virginia State Bar Association, p. 443–456. 1939.
    Reprinted in: A Legal Institute on Modern Federal Administrative Law,[1] p. 79–92. 1939.

[1] Held at Richmond, Va., April 28, 29, 1939.

249. THE HISTORY AND SYSTEM OF THE COMMON LAW [1]
New York,[2] P. F. Collier & Son, 1939. xvii, 347 p.[3]

[1] At head of title: An Encyclopedia of Law for the Modern Reader.

[2] This work is volume one of the set, NATIONAL LAW LIBRARY, 6 v., Roscoe Pound, Supervisory Editor.

[3] General introduction by Roscoe Pound, p. v–viii; notes on citations, abbreviations, and technical language, p. ix–x; contents, p. xi–xvii; text, p. 1–309; bibliography, p. 309–316; index, p. 317–347.

250. *The Idea of Law in International Relations*
Proceedings of the American Society of International Law at 33rd Annual Meeting,[1] p. 10–23. 1939.
Reprint: n.p., n.d. 10–23 p.

[1] The meeting was held at Washington, D. C., April 27–29, 1939.

251. *Modern Administrative Law*
Proceedings of the 50th Annual Meeting of the Virginia State Bar Association, p. 372–388. 1939.
Reprinted in: A Legal Institute on Modern Federal Administrative Law,[1] p. 8–24. 1939.

[1] Held at Richmond, Va., April 28, 29, 1939.

1940

252. *The Economic Interpretation and the Law of Torts* [1]
53 Harvard Law Review 365–385. January, 1940.
Reprint: Cambridge, Mass., 1940. 365–385 p.
6 Current Legal Thought 379–387.[2] April, 1940.
C. C. H. Legal Periodical Digest, 1940 ed., p. 7011–7013.[2]

[1] "One of a series of public lectures under the auspices of the Faculty of the Harvard Law School, delivered November 1, 1939." Editorial Note.

[2] An abstract of the lecture.

253. *Survey of the Conference Problems* [1]
14 University of Cincinnati Law Review 324–342. March, 1940.

[1] Cincinnati Conference on the Status of the Rule of *Stare Decisis*, held February 17, 1940, in the Netherland Plaza Hotel, Cincinnati, Ohio.

254. *Principles and Outline of a Modern Unified Court Organization* [1]
23 Journal of the American Judicature Society 225–233. April, 1940.

[1] A pre-print of the last chapter of ORGANIZATION OF COURTS. See title no. 256.

254a. *Law and Religion* [1]

27 The Rice Institute Pamphlet 109–172. April, 1940.

[1] "Rockwell Lectures on Religious Subjects, delivered at the Rice Institute, April 2, 3, and 4, 1940 . . ."
The titles of the lectures are: I. The Medieval Church and the Law; II. Puritanism and Modern Law; III. Religion and Social Control in the Society of Today.

255. CONTEMPORARY JURISTIC THEORY [1]

[Claremont, California], Pomona College, Scripps College, Claremont Colleges, 1940. (9), 83 p.

[1] "Three lectures delivered at Claremont Colleges, Pomona College, Scripps College. The Lectures were sponsored by fifty-six attorneys of Southern California."

256. ORGANIZATION OF COURTS [1]

Boston, Massachusetts, Little, Brown and Company, 1940. xiii, 322 p.

[1] Published by the National Conference of Judicial Councils in their Judicial Administration Series.

SECTION 2. SHORTER PAPERS, ADDRESSES, AND REPORTS,
INCLUDING ACCOUNTS OF ADDRESSES NOT REPORTED
IN FULL

1907

257. *Illinois Law Review*

Vol. 2, no. 3 — Vol. 4, no. 2. Editor-in-Chief, Roscoe Pound. October, 1907–June, 1909.

1908

258. *Editorial:* Professional Ethics — Proposed Codification by the American Bar Association

2 Illinois Law Review 398–401. January, 1908.

259. *Note:* Contracts — Offer under Seal — Options — "Mutuality"

2 Illinois Law Review 463–467. February, 1908.

260. *Note:* Constructive Service — Name — Error in the Initials of a Middle Name

2 Illinois Law Review 601–602. April, 1908.

261. *Note:* Wills — Probate — Jurisdiction to Probate Will of a Non-Resident
    2 Illinois Law Review 605–607. April, 1908.

262. *Review:* The Laws of England, vol. 2. Ed. The Earl of Halsbury, 1908.
    3 Illinois Law Review 253. November, 1908.

263. *Review:* The Science of Jurisprudence. Hannis Taylor. 1908.
    3 Illinois Law Review 253–254.[1] November, 1908.
    [1] See title no. 257 *infra.*

1909

264. *Editorial:* The Proposed Act in Relation to Courts
    3 Illinois Law Review 365–368. January, 1909.

265. *Editorial:* Public Provision for Criminological Research
    3 Illinois Law Review 364–365. January, 1909.

266. *Editorial:* New Technicalities and Old Principles — The Appeal to "The Wisdom of Our Ancestors"
    3 Illinois Law Review 532–533. March, 1909.

267. *Editorial:* Taylor's Science of Jurisprudence — A Literary Application of the Doctrine of Accession
    3 Illinois Law Review 525–532.[1] March, 1909.
    [1] See title no. 263 *supra.*

268. *Editorial:* Political Nominations for Judicial Office
    3 Illinois Law Review 588–589. April, 1909.

269. *Editorial:* Proposals of the Judges for Reform in Procedure
    3 Illinois Law Review 586–588. April, 1909.

270. *Editorial:* The Revision of the Code of Civil Procedure in Kansas
    4 Illinois Law Review 53–55. May, 1909.

271. *Review:* The Principles of Anthropology and Sociology in Their Relation to Criminal Procedure. Maurice Parmelee, 1908.
    3 American Political Science Review 281–284. May, 1909.

272. *Editorial:* Oral Instructions to Juries
    4 Illinois Law Review 140–143. June, 1909.

273. *Review:* Cases on Criminal Law. William E. Mikell, 1908.
    4 Illinois Law Review 150–151. June, 1909.

274. *Review:* Il Concetto della Natura e il Principio del Diritto Giorgio Del Vecchio, 1908.
     24 Political Science Quarterly 321–323. June, 1909.

275. *Review:* The Law Governing Sales of Goods at Common Law and under the Uniform Sales Act. Samuel Williston, 1909.
     4 Illinois Law Review 150. June, 1909.

276. *Review:* Law; Its Origin, Growth, and Function. James C. Carter, 1907.
     24 Political Science Quarterly 317–320. June, 1909.

277. *Editorial:* American Bar Association — The Detroit Meeting [1]
     4 Illinois Law Review 198–201. October, 1909.
[1] August, 1909.

278. *Editorial:* The American Institute of Criminal Law and Criminology
     4 Illinois Law Review 195–196. October, 1909.

1910

279. *Review:* General Theory of Law. N. M. Korkunov. English translation by W. C. Hastings, 1909.
     10 Columbia Law Review 585–587. June, 1910.

280. *Review:* A Pocket Code of the Rules of Evidence on Trials at Law. John Henry Wigmore. 1910.
     5 Illinois Law Review 190–191. October, 1910.

281. [*Opening Address at the First National Conference on Criminal Law and Criminology*] [1]
     Proceedings of the First National Conference on Criminal Law and Criminology,[2] p. 1–4. 1910.

[1] The Conference was called in celebration of the Fiftieth Anniversary of the Founding of Northwestern University School of Law (Union College of Law). The meetings were held in Northwestern University Building, Chicago, Illinois, June 7 and 8, 1909. Mr. Pound was Chairman of the Committee of Organization of the Conference.
[2] Published for the American Institute of Criminal Law and Criminology. Chicago, Illinois, Northwestern University, 1910. xxviii, 221 p.

1911

282. *Roscoe Pound on Reform in Procedure* [1]
     72 Central Law Journal 158–159. March 3, 1911.

[1] A letter to the editor of the Central Law Journal, published under "Correspondence."

2 Journal of Criminal Law and Criminology 293–294.[2]
July, 1911.

[2] Selections from this letter.

283. *Review:* Trichotomy in Roman Law. Henry Goudy. 1910.
24 Harvard Law Review 683–685. June, 1911.

284. *Review:* Willis and Oliver's Roman Law Examination Guide
for Bar and University (Questions and Answers). 3rd ed. David
T. Oliver and W. Nadler Williams. 1910.
24 Harvard Law Review 687. June, 1911.

285. *Review:* The Special Law Governing Public Service Corporations and All Others Engaged in Public Employment.
Bruce Wyman. 1911.
25 Harvard Law Review 97–99. November, 1911.

286. *Introduction:* The Individualization of Punishment. Ray-
mond Saleilles. English translation by R. S. Jastrow.[1]
Boston, Mass., Little, Brown & Co., 1911. xliv, 322 p.
Introduction, p. xi–xix.

[1] Modern Criminal Science Series: No. 4. Translated from the second
edition of the French, with an introduction by Gabriel Tarde.

287. *Introduction:* Introduction to the Science of Law. Karl
Gareis. English translation by A. Kocourek.[1]
Boston, Mass., Boston Book Company, 1911. xxix, 375 p.
Introduction, p. iii–ix.

[1] Modern Legal Philosophy Series: Vol. I. Translated from the third revised edition of the German.

1912

288. *Review:* Introduction to the Study of Law. Frederic M.
Goadby. 1910.
25 Harvard Law Review 397–398. February, 1912.

289. *Review:* Water Rights in the Western States. Samuel C.
Wiel. 3d ed. 1911.
25 Harvard Law Review 673–674. May, 1912.

290. *Review:* Historical Introduction to the Roman Law. Frederick Parker Walton. 2d ed. 1912.
26 Harvard Law Review 189–190. December, 1912.

291. *Review:* The Underlying Principles of Modern Legislation.
W. Jethro Brown. 1912.
26 Harvard Law Review 186–188. December, 1912.

1913

292. *Reforming Procedure by Rules of Court*
76 Central Law Journal 211–212. March 21, 1913.

293. *Review:* The Distinctions and Anomalies Arising out of the Equitable Doctrine of the Legal Estate. R. M. P. Willoughby. 1912.
26 Harvard Law Review 462–464. March, 1913.

294. *Review:* Das Problem des Natürlichen Rechts. Erich Jung. 1912.
27 Harvard Law Review 191–192. December, 1913.

1914

295. *Response by Professor Pound* [1] *[The Common Law]*
Proceedings of the Twentieth Annual Session of the Iowa State Bar Association, p. 140–146. 1914.

[1] Response to toastmaster at the annual banquet, Thursday, June 25, 1914, at Elks Hall, Burlington, Iowa.

296. *Review:* The Rationale of Punishment. Heinrich Oppenheimer. 1913.
27 Harvard Law Review 293–294. January, 1914.

297. *Review:* Elementary Principles of the Roman Private Law. W. W. Buckland. 1912.
27 Harvard Law Review 501. March, 1914.

298. *Note to:* The New Philosophies of Law. Robert Ludlow Fowler.[1]
27 Harvard Law Review 731–735. June, 1914.

[1] Mr. Fowler's article appears in 24 Harvard Law Review 718–731.

1915

299. *Review:* Conservation of Water by Storage. George F. Swain. 1915.
28 Harvard Law Review 824–825. June, 1915.

300. *Ezra Ripley Thayer*
29 Harvard Law Review 9–12.[1] November, 1915.

[1] The memorial to Ezra Ripley Thayer, 1866–1915, predecessor of Roscoe Pound in the deanship of the Harvard Law School, p. 1–12; the memorial by William H. Dunbar, p. 1–9.

301. *Review:* Evolution of Law. Albert Kocourek and John H. Wigmore. 1915.
29 Harvard Law Review 236–237. December, 1915.

1916

302. *Remarks of Professor Roscoe Pound*
    In: Proceedings at the Meeting of the Bar in the Supreme Judicial Court of Massachusetts in Memory of Ezra Ripley Thayer, July 7, 1916, p. 32–36. 1916.[1]

[1] The memorials presented to the Supreme Judicial Court of Massachusetts by a committee specially appointed by the Bar Association of the City of Boston.
Cambridge, Mass., The Riverside Press, 1916. 42 p.

303. *Address of Acceptance of the Portrait [of Ezra Ripley Thayer] by Dean Pound*
    In: Ezra Ripley Thayer: An Estimate of His Work as Dean of the Harvard Law School, A Sketch of His Life and Reprints of Certain of His Writings, p. 2–4.[1] 1916.

[1] Published by the Harvard Law School Association. Cambridge, Mass., The University Press, 1916. 103 p.

1917

304. *[Annual Report of the Dean of the Harvard Law School to the President of Harvard University, 1915–16]* [1]
    In: Report of the President and the Treasurer of Harvard College, 1915–16. Official Register of Harvard University, vol. 14, no. 12, March 26, 1917, p. 140–153.
    Reprint: Cambridge, Mass., 1917.[2] 14 p.

[1] In his report for each year Mr. Pound considers the work of the School and in addition usually discussess matters of general interest in the field of legal education. In this report he considers One Hundred Years of the Harvard Law School and New Lines of Legal Development, p. 140–144.
[2] Reprinted for distribution to the Graduates of the Law School by the Harvard Law School Association.

305. *Foreword:* Waiver Distributed Among the Departments Election, Estoppel, Contract, Release. John S. Ewart.
    Cambridge, Mass., Harvard University Press, 1917. xx, 304 p. Foreword, p. iii–vi.

1918

306. [*Annual Report of the Dean of the Harvard Law School
to the President of Harvard University*, 1916–17]
> *In:* Report of the President and the Treasurer of Harvard
> College, 1916–17. Official Register of Harvard University,
> vol. 15, no. 6, February 28, 1918, p. 136–141.

307. *Introduction:* Spirit of the Courts. Thomas W. Shelton.
Baltimore, Md., John Murphy Company, 1918. xxxvii,
264 p. Introduction, p. xi–xvii.

1919

308. *Remarks of Mr. Roscoe Pound, Dean of the Harvard Law
School*
> *In:* Exercises in Memory of Judge Charles E. Shattuck; [1]
> Held in the Superior Court at Boston, Saturday, Janu-
> ary 18, 1919, p. 18–19. 1919.

[1] The memorials presented to the Superior Court of Massachusetts, Justice
Charles E. Jenney presiding, by a committee specially appointed by the Bar
Association of the City of Boston.
Boston, Mass., Addison C. Getchell & Son, 1919. 32 p.

309. [*Annual Report of the Dean of the Harvard Law School
to the President of Harvard University*, 1917–18]
> *In:* Report of the President and the Treasurer of Harvard
> College, 1917–18. Official Register of Harvard University,
> vol. 16, no. 10, March 20, 1919, p. 118–123.

310. *Review:* Judicial Tenure in the United States. William S.
Carpenter, 1918.
32 Harvard Law Review 866–868. May, 1919.

311. *Translation:* Laws of France, 1919, Town Planning and
Reparation of Damages Caused by the Events of the War
New York.[1] October, 1919. 51 p.

[1] Publication of the National Civic Federation, New York City, and published "separately as addenda to the Report of Our Foreign Commission on
Industrial Inquiry." Cf. foreword.

312. *Review:* Juridical Reform. John D. Works, 1919.
33 Harvard Law Review 326–327. December, 1919.

313. *The Harvard Law School*[1]
New York. 1919. 24 p.

[1] Cover title: The Harvard Law School by Dean Roscoe Pound. Published by the Harvard Endowment Fund Committee from Funds Furnished by Harvard Law School Association.
Preface dated, New York, 1919. A pamphlet issued in connection with the drive to raise an endowment fund for the Harvard Law School. 1919.

1920

314. [*Annual Report of the Dean of the Harvard Law School to the President of Harvard University*, 1918–19]
In: Report of the President and the Treasurer of Harvard College, 1918–19. Official Register of Harvard University, vol. 17, no. 7, March 8, 1920, p. 121–129.

1921

315. *Foreword:* The Valuation of Property in the Roman Law.[1]
Nathan Matthews.
34 Harvard Law Review 227–228. January, 1921.

[1] Mr. Matthews' article appears in 34 Harvard Law Review 229–259.

316. [*Annual Report of the Dean of the Harvard Law School to the President of Harvard University*, 1919–20]
In: Report of the President and the Treasurer of Harvard College, 1919–20. Official Register of Harvard University, vol. 18, no. 7, March 3, 1921, p. 163–171.

317. *Review:* Text Book of Roman Law from Augustus to Justinian. W. W. Buckland. 1921.
11 Journal of Roman Studies 269–277. 1921.
36 Harvard Law Review 119–124.[1] November, 1922.

[1] The same as the above with some omissions.

1922

318. [*Annual Report of the Dean of the Harvard Law School to the President of Harvard University*, 1920–21]
In: Report of the President and the Treasurer of Harvard College, 1920–21. Official Register of Harvard University, vol. 19, no. 5, February 24, 1922, p. 202–209.

319. *Review:* Outlines of Historical Jurisprudence, vol. 1. Sir Paul Vinogradoff. 1920.
35 Harvard Law Review 774–783. April, 1922.

320. *Review:* Storia del Diritto Italiano. Giuseppe Salvioli. 8th ed. 1921.
   35 Harvard Law Review 891–892. May, 1922.

321. *An Appreciation of Eugen Ehrlich.* 1862–1922.
   36 Harvard Law Review 129–130.[1] December, 1922.

   [1] Mr. Pound's writing is followed by Ehrlich's *The Sociology of Law*, translated by Nathan Isaacs, p. 130–145.

322. [*Legal Position of Women: The United States*] [1]
   In: Encyclopaedia Britannica, 12th ed., vol. 3, supplement, p. 1043–1044. 1922. Encyclopaedia Britannica, 13th ed., vol. 3, supplement, p. 1055–1056. 1926.

   [1] Part 2 of Women, Legal Position of.

323. *A Note upon Legal Entanglement as a Division of Evil*
   In: The Kingdom of Evils.[1] Elmer Ernest Southard and Mary C. Jarrett.[2] p. 563–567. 1922.

   [1] Psychiatric social work presented in one hundred case histories together with a classification of social divisions of evil.
   [2] New York, Macmillan, 1922. xx, 708 p. Bibliographical notes.

324. *Review:* History of Conspiracy and Abuse of Legal Procedure. Percy Henry Winfield. 1922.
   1 Cambridge Law Journal 156–165. 1922.

1923

325. Interview: *Poor Man Has Not Equal Chance With Rich Man in Our Courts of Law*
   Boston Post. February 18, 1923.

326. [*Annual Report of the Dean of the Harvard Law School to the President of Harvard University,* 1921–22]
   In: Report of the President and the Treasurer of Harvard College, 1921–22. Official Register of Harvard University, vol. 20, no. 6, February 26, 1923, p. 157–161.

327. *Review:* Problem of Proof. Albert S. Osborn. 1922.
   36 Harvard Law Review 1042–1044. June, 1923.

328. Letter: *The Harvard Law School* [1]
   26 Harvard Alumni Bulletin 43–44. October 4, 1923.

   [1] A letter to F. W. Grinnell, Esq., on the needs of the Law School, incorporated in Mr. Grinnell's article, The Harvard Law School Association, p. 42 *et seq.*

1924

329. *Review:* Cases and Other Authorities on Equity, vol. 1. Walter Wheeler Cook. 1923.
37 Harvard Law Review 396–399. January, 1924.

330. [*Annual Report of the Dean of the Harvard Law School to the President of Harvard University*, 1922–23]
    In: Report of the President and the Treasurer of Harvard College, 1922–23. Official Register of Harvard University, vol. 21, no. 6, February 29, 1924, p. 188–193.

331. *Review:* La Science Juridique Pure. Ernest Roguin. 1923.
37 Harvard Law Review 525–526. February, 1924.

332. *Address at Dinner to the American Bar Association in the Middle Temple Hall* [1]
    10 American Bar Association Journal 594–595. August, 1924.
    Under title: *American and English Legal Ideals* [2]
    59 Law Journal 517–518. August 9, 1924.

[1] The address was delivered upon the visit of the American Bar Association to England, July, 1924.
[2] Excerpt from the address.

333. *An Address by Dean Pound: Only One Earth and All of Us Want It* [1]
    Boston Globe, December 18, 1924, p. 28:7.

[1] An address delivered at the home of Mrs. Edwin S. Webster, 306 Dartmouth Street, Boston, on December 17, 1924. This address was one of a series sponsored by the National Civic Federation, Women's Department, Massachusetts Section, for the year 1924–25.

334. *Foreword:* Selected Essays on the Law of Torts
    Cambridge, Mass., Harvard Law Review Association, 1924.
    vii, 770 p. Foreword, p. iii–iv.

1925

335. [*Annual Report of the Dean of the Harvard Law School to the President of Harvard University*, 1923–24] [1]
    In: Report of the President and the Treasurer of Harvard College, 1923–24. Official Register of Harvard University, vol. 22, no. 5, February 24, 1925, p. 181–189.
    Reprint: Cambridge, Mass., 1925. 9 p.

[1] In this report Mr. Pound considers Endowment of Professorships [in the Harvard Law School], p. 185–187.

336. *Harvard Dean Warns of Hasty Action on Crime Problem* [1]
Boston Herald, August 29, 1925, p. 1:2, 3.
Reprinted in: New York Times, August 30, 1925, II, 1:6
and 3:3, 4.

[1] The article appeared in the New York Times under the title "Pound Deplores Crime Crusades; Harvard Law Dean Blames Judicial System, Not Officials for Present Situation."

337. *The Harvard Law School; Its History, Its Development, Its Needs* [1]
New York, 1925. 28 p. With 2 folding plates.

[1] A projet prepared by Mr. Pound and distributed by the Harvard Law School Endowment Fund Committee, New York City.

This pamphlet was reprinted in 31 pages without the plates but with two illustrations, one on the cover and one in the text. The sub-title "A Projet by Dean Roscoe Pound" was added.

338. *Introduction:* The Chief Sources of English Legal History. Percy H. Winfield.
Cambridge, Mass., Harvard University Press, 1925. xviii, 374 p. Introduction, p. xiii–xviii.

339. *Introduction:* The Supreme Court and Minimum Wage Legislation
New York,[1] National Consumers League, 1925. xxviii, 287 p. Introduction, p. xi–xxviii.

[1] Comments by various members of the legal profession compiled and published by the National Consumers League.

340. *It Isn't Done* [1]
Proceedings of the Eighteenth Annual Meeting of the Oklahoma State Bar Association, p. 68–74. 1925.

[1] These remarks are so inadequately reported that they do not represent with accuracy what Mr. Pound said.

1926

341. *The Prospect of Law and Order* [1]
Boston Herald, January 8, 1926, p. 1–2.
Boston Transcript, January 8, 1926, p. 11.

[1] Address delivered on January 7, 1926, at the Copley-Plaza Hotel, Boston, Mass., before the Massachusetts Bankers' Association at its annual banquet. It was reported in part in the Boston Herald under the title *Courts Blamed by Dean Pound*, and in the Boston Transcript under the title *Dean Pound Urges Care in Changing Criminal Law*.

342. [*Annual Report of the Dean of the Harvard Law School to the President of Harvard University*, 1924–25] [1]
> *In:* Report of the President and the Treasurer of Harvard College, 1924–25. Official Register of Harvard University, vol. 23, no. 2, January 20, 1926, p. 171–184.

[1] In this report Mr. Pound considers The Next Step in Legal Education, p. 177–180.

343. *Dean Pound, Harvard Law School, Discusses "Crime Wave"; Declares Silencing Trial Judges Crying Evil of Court System* [1]
> Boston Sunday Post, January 24, 1926, p. B 1.

[1] Mr. Pound's "views on the proposed reform to be initiated by Mr. Benton and in Massachusetts on the situation in general so far as the courts are concerned."

344. *Address at Dinner to Mr. Justice Stone*
> Year Book of the New York County Lawyers' Association, 1926 [vol. 18], p. 257–260. 1926.

345. *Dean Pound Tells Why Criminal Justice Fails*
> New York Times, April 18, 1926, IX, 17:1–8. [1]

[1] Portrait.

346. [*Address at Dinner of Associated Harvard Clubs*] [1]
> 29 Harvard Alumni Bulletin, Supplement to no. 1, p. 11–13. September 30, 1926.

[1] Address delivered June 3, 1926, at Chicago, Illinois, at the 28th meeting of the Associated Harvard Clubs.

347. [*Address Opening the Campaign to Raise Funds for the Harvard Law School*] [1]
> 29 Harvard Alumni Bulletin, Supplement to no. 9, p. 5–7. November 25, 1926.

[1] Address made at the Dinner at the Harvard Club of Boston, November 1, 1926. Mr. Pound also spoke at the Dinner at the Association of the Bar of the City of New York, November 9, 1926.

1927

348. Editorial: *Senator Walsh on Rule-Making Power on the Law Side of Federal Practice* [1]
> 13 American Bar Association Journal 84–86. February, 1927.

[1] The editorial is followed by Senator Walsh's address before the Oregon State Bar Association, October 2, 1926, p. 87 *et seq.*

349. [*Annual Report of the Dean of the Harvard Law School to the President of Harvard University*, 1925–26] [1]

> *In:* Report of the President and the Treasurer of Harvard College, 1925–26. Official Register of Harvard University, vol. 24, no. 8, March 9, 1927, p. 185–194.

[1] In this report Mr. Pound considers The Tasks of a National Law School, p. 185–191.

350. Letter: *Child Labor* [1]

> New York Times, November 29, 1927, 26:8.

[1] Letter read at Dinner of the National Consumers League, New York City, on November 28, 1927.

351. *Introduction:* A Selection of Cases on Criminal Law. Francis Bowes Sayre.

> Rochester, N. Y., Lawyers Cooperative Publishing Co., 1927. xxxix, 1135 p. Introduction, p. xxix-xxxix.
> *Reprint:* Rochester, N. Y., 1927. 11 p.

352. *Introduction:* A Working Bibliography of Greek Law.[1] George M. Calhoun and Catherine Delamere.

> Cambridge, Mass., Harvard University Press, 1927. xix, 144 p. Introduction, p. xiii–xiv.

[1] Harvard Series of Legal Bibliographies, I.

1928

353. [*Annual Report of the Dean of the Harvard Law School to the President of Harvard University*, 1926–27] [1]

> *In:* Report of the President and the Treasurer of Harvard College, 1926–27. Official Register of Harvard University, vol. 25, no. 8, March 9, 1928, p. 185–192.

[1] In this report Mr. Pound considers Graduate Instruction and Research [with Especial Reference to the Harvard Law School], p. 185–188.

354. *Review:* Handbook of the Law of Code Pleading. Charles E. Clark. 1928.

> 38 Yale Law Journal 127–130. November, 1928.

355. Letter: *Preventive Justice* [1]

> 7 Probation 3, 7.[2] December, 1928.

[1] Letter read at the Boston, Massachusetts, meeting of the National Probation Association, held to commemorate the passage of the first probation law.

"It is a brilliant statement of the genesis and growth of the ideals of preventive justice within the structure of the law. Dr. Pound is a member of the Advisory Committee of the National Probation Association and has long favored the extension of well organized probation work." — Editor's note. Portrait, p. 3.   [2] Official bulletin of the National Probation Association.

1929

356. *Foreword:* Predictability in the Administration of Criminal Justice. Sheldon Glueck and Eleanor T. Glueck.[1]

  42 Harvard Law Review 297–299. January, 1929.

[1] The article by Professor and Mrs. Glueck appears in 42 Harvard Law Review 300–329.

357. [*Annual Report of the Dean of the Harvard Law School to the President of Harvard University, 1927–28*] [1]

  In: Report of the President and the Treasurer of Harvard College, 1927–28. Official Register of Harvard University, vol. 26, no. 6, February 28, 1929, p. 197–207.

[1] In this report Mr. Pound considers both Administrative Reorganization [of the Harvard Law School], p. 197–199, and Aims in Legal Education, p. 199–204.

358. *"A Great Lawyer, a Great Statesman, a Strong Personality is Called to a Great Opportunity"* [1]

  15 American Bar Association Journal 263–264. May, 1929.

[1] This is a part of "A sheaf of expressions representative of the feeling of fellow lawyers toward distinguished member of profession" published under the title of *Mr. Hughes Goes to Permanent Court of International Justice.*

359. *Dean Pound Writes of Pioneer and Law*

  Sunday World-Herald, Omaha, Nebraska. October 27, 1929, p. 14–C:5–8.

360. *Fundamental Objectives of Business Management — Justice* [1]

  Publications, Bureau of Personnel Administration. 1929. 9 sheets, multigraphed.

[1] Bureau of Personnel Administration, New York City. Conference 17, April 3, 1929.

361. *Legal Education — The United States* [1]

  In: Encyclopaedia Britannica, 14th ed., vol. 13, p. 874–875. 1929.

[1] The phases treated: 1. Early history. . . . 2. Apprentice training. . . . 3. College teaching. . . . 4. Scientific study of jurisprudence.

1930

362. *Supreme Court or Supreme Congress?*

  Christian Science Monitor, vol. 22, no. 75, p. 14. February 24, 1930.

  6 State Bar Journal 203–204, 206.[1] August, 1931.

[1] Official organ of State Bar of California.

363. [*Annual Report of the Dean of the Harvard Law School to the President of Harvard University, 1928–29*] [1]
In: Report of the President and the Treasurer of Harvard College, 1928–29. Official Register of Harvard University, vol. 27, no. 8, March 3, 1930, p. 180–188.

[1] In this report Mr. Pound considers both Atmosphere of Study of Law, p. 180–183, and Institute of Criminal Law [of the Harvard Law School], p. 186.

364. *Washington's Birthday Memorial* [1]
72 Congressional Record,[2] p. 5534–5535. March 18, 1930.

[1] Address delivered at the tenth anniversary Dinner of the Federal Bar Association, Washington, D. C., held at the Mayflower Hotel, Washington, D. C., February 22, 1930.
[2] Proceedings and debates of the 2d Session, 71st Congress.

365. [*Address Upon the Occasion of the Acceptance of a Portrait of Mr. Justice Oliver Wendell Holmes by the President and Fellows of Harvard College*]
In: A Portrait of Mr. Justice Holmes,[1] 32 Harvard Alumni Bulletin, p. 741–748 at p. 745–747. March 27, 1930.

[1] Date of presentation, Thursday, March 20, 1930. "In the unavoidable absence of President Lowell, Rt. Rev. William Lawrence . . . one of the Fellows of Harvard College, presided." The portrait is now hanging in Langdell Hall, Harvard Law School.

366. *Address at Annual Dinner of the American Bar Association* [1]
Report of the 53rd Annual Meeting of the American Bar Association [vol. 55], p. 172–178. 1930.

[1] The meeting was held at Chicago, Illinois, August 20–22, 1930.

367. *Address on the Occasion of the Visit of the Bars from Across the Sea*
Bar Bulletin,[1] No. 39,[2] p. 25–29. December, 1930.

[1] Published by the Bar Association of the City of Boston.
[2] A "Special Number" of the Boston Bar publication — *The Addresses on the Occasion of the Visit of the Bars from Across the Sea*. Mr. Pound's address is part of V. At the Harvard Law School, p. 23 *et seq.* Reported in the New York Times, September 14, 1930, IX, 2:2.

368. *American Law Institute*
In: Encyclopaedia of the Social Sciences, vol. 2, p. 30–31. 1930.

369. *Foreword:* Law Dictionary with Pronunciations. James A. Ballentine.

Rochester, N. Y.,[1] Lawyers Cooperative Publishing Co., 1930. xi, 1494 p. Foreword, p. v.

[1] Portrait of Mr. Pound, with facsimile signature.

370. *William Reynell Anson, Bart. (1843–1914)*
In: Encyclopaedia of the Social Sciences, vol. 2, p. 71–72. 1930.

1931

371. [*Address of Acceptance of a Portrait of James Brown Scott*] [1]
In: Portrait of Dr. James Brown Scott, 33 Harvard Alumni Bulletin, p. 418–424 at 420–421. January 1, 1931.

[1] Date of acceptance of the portrait by Mr. Pound on behalf of the Faculty of the Harvard Law School, October 28, 1930. The portrait is now hanging in Langdell Hall, Harvard Law School.

372. [*Annual Report of the Dean of the Harvard Law School to the President of Harvard University,* 1929–30] [1]
In: Report of the President and the Treasurer of Harvard College, 1929–30. Official Register of Harvard University, vol. 28, no. 4, February 24, 1931. p. 198–203.

[1] In this report Mr. Pound considers both New Demands on Law Teachers, p. 198, and New Demands upon Law Schools, p. 199.

373. *Frank Irvine*
17 Cornell Law Quarterly 4–7.[1] December, 1931.

[1] A memorial address to Frank Irvine, 1858–1931, former Dean of Cornell Law School. The addresses of Hon. Cuthbert W. Pound and Hon. Riley H. Heath appear on pages 1–4 and 7–8, respectively.

374. *Introduction:* Cases on the Interpretation of Statutes. Frederick Joseph De Sloovere.

St. Paul, Minn., West Publishing Co.,[1] 1931. xxiii, 970 p. Introduction, p. v–viii.

[1] American Casebook Series.

375. *Preface:* The Inns of Court and Early English Drama. A. Wigfall Green.

New Haven, Conn., Yale University Press, 1931. xii, 199 p. Preface, p. vii–ix.

1932

376. [*Annual Report of the Dean of the Harvard Law School to the President of Harvard University*, 1930–31] [1]
    In: Report of the President and the Treasurer of Harvard College, 1930–31. Official Register of Harvard University, vol. 29, no. 2, January 29, 1932, p. 201–210.

    [1] In this report Mr. Pound considers Curriculum [and the Tasks of a Law School], p. 201–208.

377. [*The End of Individualism and Development of a "Relational" Society*] [1]
    New York Times, February 20, 1932, p. 17:7.

    [1] Address before the College of the City of New York Chapter of Phi Beta Kappa, at its annual meeting.

378. *Better Practitioners Needed*
    4 New York State Bar Association Bulletin 160. March, 1932.

379. *Introduction:* How to Find the Law, vol. 1. Adolphus Mosseau Ashcraft.
    Boston, Mass., Published by the Author, 1932. 807 p. Introduction, p. 63–67.

380. [*Speech*]
    Proceedings of the 38th Annual Session of the Iowa State Bar Association, p. 118–119. 1932.

1933

381. [*Annual Report of the Dean of the Harvard Law School to the President of Harvard University*, 1931–32] [1]
    In: Report of the President and the Treasurer of Harvard College, 1931–32. Official Register of Harvard University, vol. 30, no. 1, January 31, 1933, p. 202–211.

    [1] In this report Mr. Pound considers both The Curriculum [of the Harvard Law School], p. 202–205, and Progress of Research [in the Harvard Law School], p. 207–208.

382. *Driving the Country to Repeal*
    87 Review of Reviews *and* World's Work 33. February, 1933.

383. *Review:* American Interpretations of Natural Law. Benjamin Fletcher Wright, Jr. 1931.
    46 Harvard Law Review 864–869. March, 1933.

384. [*The Recurring Attacks upon the American Constitution*] [1]
New York Herald Tribune, October 14, 1933, p. 6.

[1] Delivered at the New York Herald Tribune's Conference on Current Problems. The general topic of the Conference was "This Crisis in History." Mr. Pound contributed to the specific topic of education and peace.

385. *Liability*
In: Encyclopaedia of the Social Sciences, vol. 9, p. 427–429.
1933.

1934

386. [*Annual Report of the Dean of the Harvard Law School to the President of Harvard University, 1932–33*] [1]
In: Report of the President and the Treasurer of Harvard College, 1932–33. Official Register of Harvard University, vol. 31, no. 3, February 5, 1934, p. 210–217.

[1] In this report Mr. Pound considers both Some Considerations as to Legal Education, p. 210–212, and Progress of Research [in the Harvard Law School], p. 215.

387. *Repeal of the Eighteenth Amendment*
1 The World To-Day [1] 19–20. [2] February, 1934.

[1] Published by the Encyclopaedia Britannica; containing new and supplementary articles by Britannica authors.

[2] Portrait, a group picture of former President Hoover and his Law Enforcement Commission at their first meeting in the White House, May 28, 1929, p. 20.

388. *Review:* The New Jurisprudence. Edward Jenks. 1933.
47 Harvard Law Review 890–897. March, 1934.

389. *Review:* For My Grandson; Remembrances of an Ancient Victorian. Sir Frederick Pollock. 1933.
47 Harvard Law Review 1075–1076. April, 1934.

390. *Introduction:* Five Hundred Delinquent Women. Sheldon and Eleanor T. Glueck.
New York, Alfred A. Knopf, 1934. xxiv, 539, x p. Introduction, p. vii–x.

391. *Joseph Story (1779–1845)*
In: Encyclopaedia of the Social Sciences, vol. 14, p. 413. 1934.

392. *500 Onondaga Lawyers Hear Dean Pound Talk* [1]
6 New York State Bar Association Bulletin 296–297. May, 1934.

[1] Summary of an address before the Research Bureau of the Onondaga County Bar Association.

1935

393. [*Annual Report of the Dean of the Harvard Law School to the President of Harvard University*, 1933–34] [1]
  In: Report of the President and the Treasurer of Harvard College, 1933–34. Official Register of Harvard University, vol. 32, no. 3, February 18, 1935, p. 236–243.

[1] In this report Mr. Pound considers [The] Curriculum [of the Harvard Law School], p. 241–242.

394. *Improvement of Criminal Justice in the United States; the Hindrances and the Possibilities of Betterment*
  2 The World To-Day 37–40.[1] February, 1935.

[1] Portrait, p. 38.

395. *Review:* Precedent in English and Continental Law. A. L. Goodhart. 1934.
  48 Harvard Law Review 863–867. March, 1935.

396. *Foreword:* Law and the Social Sciences. Huntington Cairns. New York, Harcourt, Brace and Co., 1935. xiv, 279 p. Foreword, p. xi–xiv.

397. *Foreword:* Mr. Justice Cardozo; A Liberal Mind in Action. Joseph P. Pollard.
  New York, Yorktown Press, 1935. 327 p. Foreword, p. 1–5.

1936

398. [*Annual Report of the Dean of the Harvard Law School to the President of Harvard University*, 1934–35] [1]
  In: Report of the President and the Treasurer of Harvard College, 1934–35. Official Register of Harvard University, vol. 33, no. 4, February 29, 1936, p. 193–198.

[1] In this report Mr. Pound considers The [Harvard] Legal Aid Bureau, p. 193–196.

399. *Address* [*of Welcome to the Members of the American Association of Law Libraries*] [1]
  29 Law Library Journal 99–101. October, 1936.

[1] Delivered at the 31st Annual Meeting which was held at Langdell Hall, Cambridge, Mass., August 26, 1936.

400. *Introduction:* Fundamental Principles of the Sociology of Law.[1] Eugen Ehrlich. English translation by Walter L. Moll.

[1] Harvard Studies in Jurisprudence, vol. 5.

Cambridge, Mass., Harvard University Press, 1936. xxxvi, 541 p. Introduction, p. xxix–xxxvi.

1937

401. *Review:* Art of Law and Other Essays, Juridical and Literary. John C. H. Wu. 1936.
   50 Harvard Law Review 847. March, 1937.

402. *Richard Burdon Haldane (1856–1928)*
   Proceedings of the American Academy of Arts and Sciences,[1] vol. 71, no. 10, p. 503–505. March, 1937.
   [1] Boston, Mass.

403. *Foreword:* Social Treatment in Probation and Delinquency. Pauline V. Young.
   New York, McGraw Hill, 1937. xxxvi, 646 p. Foreword, p. xxiii–xxxi.[1]
   [1] Introduction by Justin Miller, p. xxxiii–xxxvi.

404. [*Letter of Greeting to the 1937 Class, Philippine Law School*][1]
   In: The Advocate. 1937.
   [1] Letter addressed to M. G. Manzano, Philippine Law School, National University, Manila, P. I., November 9, 1936. The Advocate was edited and published by the class of 1937 of the Philippine Law School.

1938

405. *Statement by Dean Roscoe Pound*[1]
   In: United States Court of Appeals for Administration,[2] Part 4, p. 169–186. May 12, 14, 1938.
   [1] Saturday, May 14, 1938.
   [2] Hearings before a subcommittee of the Committee on the Judiciary, United States Senate, 75th Congress, 3rd Session, on S 3676 — A Bill to establish a United States Court of Appeals for Administration to Receive, Decide, and Expedite Appeals from Commissions, Administrative Authorities and Tribunals in which the United States is a Party or has an Interest for other purposes.

406. *The Need of Standards for Law Schools*
   Bar Bulletin,[1] no. 138, p. 4–6. July, 1938.
   [1] Publication of the Bar Association of the City of Boston.

407. *Every Man an Officer*
    3 The Key Reporter,[1] No. 3, p. 6. 1938.

[1] "The Phi Beta Kappa News Magazine."

408. *Introduction:* The Open Mind; Elmer Ernest Southard, 1876–1920. Frederick P. Gay.
    Chicago, Ill., Normandie House, 1938. xxiii, 324 p. Introduction, p. xix–xxiii.

1939

409. *The Fight for Intellectual Freedom; The Swing Away from the Humanities* [1]
    5 Vital Speeches of the Day 342. March 15, 1939.
    Under title: *The Humanities or Absolutism?* [2]
    4 The Key Reporter, No. 3, p. 1, 5. 1939.

[1] Remarks made before the Phi Beta Kappa at its symposium of February 20, 1939.
[2] Excerpts from the speech.

410. *The Revival of Absolutism* [1]
    Newark Evening News, April 6, 1939, p. 29:5.[2]

[1] An address delivered at the annual dinner of the Bond Club of New Jersey, April 5, 1939, at the Robert Treat Hotel.
[2] Under the title Bond Club Speaker Hits Absolutism. See item 411.

411. *Why Absolute Government Fails* [1]
    27 Nation's Business 11–13, 60, 61. July, 1939.

[1] A thorough revision of the text of the Bond Club address. See item *supra.*

412. *Training for the Bar in the United States* [1]
    15 New Zealand Law Journal 222–224. September 5, 1939.

[1] A historical review specially written for the New Zealand Law Journal.

413. *Frantz Dahl (1869–1937)*
    73 Proceedings of American Academy of Arts & Sciences, no. 6, p. 134–135. 1939.
    Reprint: n.p., n.d. 1 sheet.[1]

[1] Biographical note on one side of one unnumbered page.

414. *The Founding of the Harvard Law School*[1]
Harvard Law School Year Book,[2] vol. 3, 1939–1940, p. 17–24. 1939.[3]

[1] "In the past few years hitherto unpublished documents have been unearthed in the Harvard archives which reveal considerable information concerning details of the founding of the Law School and the appointment of Asahel Stearns as its first head, or University Professor, as the post was then called." In this article Mr. Pound again discusses the establishment of the Harvard Law School "in the light of the documentary evidence now available, and with respect to its importance and significance in the later development of the School." — Editor.

[2] "Published by the Law School Year Book Committee of the Phillips Brooks House Association, Harvard University, Cambridge, Massachusetts."

[3] Editorial note, p. 19; reproductions of documents, p. 18, 21, 23.

415. *General Introduction:* The National Law Library.[1] 1939.
In: The National Law Library, vol. 1, p. v–viii.

[1] New York, P. F. Collier and Son Corporation, 1939. 6 v.

416. *Introduction:* Criminal Appeals in America.[1] Lester Bernhardt Orfield.
Boston, Mass., Little, Brown and Company, 1939. 321 p. Introduction, p. 3–13.

[1] At head of title: The Judicial Administration Series, published under the auspices of The National Conference of Judicial Councils.
Roscoe Pound is Director of the National Conference of Judicial Councils.

1940

417. *Introduction:* Institutes of the Roman Law of Civil Procedure. Leopold Wenger. Revised edition.
English translation by Otis Harrison Fisk.
New York, N. Y., Veritas Press, 1940. xxix, 440 p. Introduction, p. ix–xii.

SECTION 3. ARTICLES AND REPORTS WRITTEN WITH OTHERS

1898

418. *Insurance*[1]
In: Encyclopaedia of Pleading and Practice, vol. 11, p. 375–434. 1898.[2]

[1] Roscoe Pound and Charles Sumner Lobingier.

[2] Northport, L. I., N. Y., Edward Thompson Co., 23 v., 1895–1902.

1909

419. *Report of the Special Committee to Suggest Remedies and Formulate Proposed Laws to Prevent Delay and Unnecessary Cost in Litigation* [1]
    Report of the 32nd Annual Meeting of the American Bar Association [vol. 34], p. 578–602. 1909.

[1] The Committee's Report, by Mr. Pound and fourteen others, presented at the meeting of the American Bar Association held at Detroit, Michigan, August 24–27, 1909.

1910

420. *Report of the Special Committee to Suggest Remedies and Formulate Proposed Laws to Prevent Delay and Unnecessary Cost in Litigation* [1]
    Report of the 33rd Annual Meeting of the American Bar Association [vol. 35], p. 614–619. 1910.

[1] The Committee's Report, by Mr. Pound and twelve others, presented at the meeting of the American Bar Association held at Chattanooga, Tennessee, August 30, 31 and September 1, 1910.

1911

421. *Report of the Special Committee to Suggest Remedies and Formulate Proposed Laws to Prevent Delay and Unnecessary Cost in Litigation* [1]
    Report of the 34th Annual Meeting of the American Bar Association [vol. 36], p. 448–483. 1911.

[1] The Committee's Report, by Mr. Pound and thirteen others, presented at the meeting of the American Bar Association held at Boston, Massachusetts, August 29–31, 1911.

1912

422. *Report of the Special Committee to Suggest Remedies and Formulate Proposed Laws to Prevent Delay and Unnecessary Cost in Litigation* [1]
    Report of the 35th Annual Meeting of the American Bar Association [vol. 37], p. 557–560. 1912.

[1] The Committee's Report, by Mr. Pound and thirteen others, presented at the meeting of the American Bar Association held at Milwaukee, Wisconsin, August 27–29, 1912.

1913

423. *Report of the Special Committee to Suggest Remedies and Formulate Proposed Laws to Prevent Delay and Unnecessary Cost in Litigation* [1]
    Report of the 36th Annual Meeting of the American Bar Association [vol. 38], p. 546–568. 1913.

[1] The Committee's Report, by Mr. Pound and twelve others, presented at the meeting of the American Bar Association held at Montreal, Canada, September 1–3, 1913.

1914

424. *Preliminary Report on Efficiency in the Administration of Justice* [1]
    Boston, Mass., Caustic-Claflin Company, 1914. 32 p.

[1] Prepared by several hands, Charles W. Eliot, Moorfield Storey, L. D. Brandeis, Adolph J. Rodenbeck, and Roscoe Pound, for the National Economic League of Boston.

1915

425. *Organization of the Courts* [1]
    3 New Republic 60–62.[2] May 22, 1915.

[1] In joint authorship with Felix Frankfurter and Austin W. Scott.
[2] Bibliography, p. 62, by R[oscoe] P[ound].

426. *Defective Judicial Procedure* [1]
    3 New Republic 252–255. July 10, 1915.

[1] Felix Frankfurter and Austin W. Scott, collaborators.

1920

427. *Report Upon the Illegal Practices of the United States Department of Justice* [1]
    Washington, D. C.,[2] The National Popular Government League, 1920. 67 p.

[1] At head of title: To the American People.
[2] Report of the Committee, Mr. Pound and eleven others, p. 3–9; a list of exhibits supplementing the report, p. 11–67.

1931

428. *Reports of the National Commission on Law Observance and Enforcement* [1]
    Report on the Enforcement of Prohibition Laws of the

[1] The Commission consisted of Geo. W. Wickersham, Chairman; Henry W. Anderson; Newton D. Baker; Ada L. Comstock; William I. Grubb; William S. Kenyon; Monte M. Lemann; Frank J. Loesch; Kenneth Mackintosh; Paul J. McCormick; Roscoe Pound.

United States, Dated January 7, 1931. (Confidential.) Washington, D. C., 1931. (4), 281 p. Commission Report, p. 1–148.[2]

Reprinted as: Enforcement of the Prohibition Laws of the United States: Message from the President of the United States Transmitting a Report of the National Commission on Law Observance and Enforcement Relative to the Facts as to the Enforcement, the Benefits, and the Abuses under the Prohibition Laws, both before and since the Adoption of the Eighteenth Amendment to the Constitution.[3] Washington, D. C., Government Printing Office, 1931. viii, 162 p. Commission Report, p. 1–84.[4] (House Document No. 722, 71st Congress, 3rd Session.)

Report on Criminal Statistics, April 1, 1931 [3] [Publication 3]. Washington, D. C., Government Printing Office, 1931. v, 205 p. Commission Report, p. 3–18.

Report on Prosecution, April 22, 1931 [3] [Publication 4]. Washington, D. C., Government Printing Office, 1931. v, 337 p. Commission Report, p. 3–38.

Report on the Enforcement of the Deportation Laws of the United States, May 27, 1931 [3] [Publication 5]. Washington, D. C., Government Printing Office, 1931. iii, 179 p. Commission Report, p. 1–8.

Report on the Child Offender in the Federal System of Justice, May 28, 1931 [3] [Publication 6]. Washington, D. C., Government Printing Office, 1931. iii, 175 p. Commission Report, p. 1–6.

Progress Report on the Study of the Federal Courts, June 30, 1931 [3] [Publication 7]. Washington, D. C., Government Printing Office, 1931. vii, 123 p.[5]

Report on Criminal Procedure, June 9, 1931 [3] [Publication 8]. Washington, D. C., Government Printing Office, 1931. v, 51 p. Commission Report, p. 1–48.

Report on Penal Institutions, Probation and Parole, June 23, 1931 [3] [Publication 9]. Washington, D. C., Government Printing Office, 1931. vi, 344 p. Commission Report, p. 1–174.

Report on Crime and the Foreign Born, June 24, 1931 [3] [Publication 10]. Washington, D. C., Government Printing Office, 1931. iii, 416 p. Commission Report, p. 1–5.

Report on Lawlessness in Law Enforcement, June 25, 1931 [3] [Publication 11]. Washington, D. C., Government Printing Office, 1931. v, 347 p. Commission Report, p. 1–10.

Report on the Cost of Crime, June 24, 1931 [3] [Publication 12]. Washington, D. C., Government Printing Office, 1931. v.p. Commission Report, p. 1–8.

Report on the Causes of Crime, June 26, 1931 [3] [Publication 13]. Washington, D. C., Government Printing Office, 1931. v. 1, lxxi, 390 p.; v. 2, xv, 401 p. Commission Report, vol. 1, p. vii–x.

Report on Police, June 26, 1931 [3] [Publication 14]. Washington, D. C., Government Printing Office, 1931. iii, 140 p. Commission Report, p. 1–10.

[2] Mr. Pound's statement, p. 279–281.
[3] These publications of the National Commission on Law Observance and Enforcement, with the President's Message, were bound in six volumes, issued by the Government Printing Office.
[4] Mr. Pound's statement, p. 159–160.
[5] Report of Advisory Committee.

1936

429. *Report* [1] *of the Special Committee to Consider and Report as to the Duplication of Law Books and Publications* [2]
Annual Report of the American Bar Association, vol. 61, p. 848–855.[3] 1936.

[1] Mr. Pound was chairman of the committee of five.
[2] 59th Annual Meeting held at Boston, Mass., Aug. 24–28, 1936.
[3] Bibliography, p. 853–855.

1938

430. *Report of the Special Committee on Administrative Law*
Annual Report of the American Bar Association,[1] vol. 63, p. 331–362. 1938.

[1] 61st Annual Meeting held at Cleveland, Ohio, July 25–29, 1938. Mr. Pound was Chairman of the Special Committee on Administrative Law.

The Report, p. 332–362, is divided into: I. Statement regarding recommendations, p. 332–333; II. Proposed legislation to provide for the more expeditious settlement of disputes with the United States, p. 333–338; III. General report, p. 338–362. With bibliographical notes. Appended to the Committee's Report is a "Proposed Act — A Bill to Provide for the More Expeditious Settlement of Disputes with the United States and for Other Purposes," p. 362–368.

PART II

JUDICIAL WRITINGS

Section 1. Nebraska Reports

"Dr. Roscoe Pound, whose studies on the phytogeography of Nebraska have made him well known as a botanist, has been appointed a member of the new Supreme Court Commission, which is to assist the Supreme Court of Nebraska to clear up its docket. The work of the Court is far in arrears, and the commissioners are *de facto* justices. Dr. Pound is winning laurels in his vocation as well as in his avocation." — 31 Botanical Gazette, no. 5, p. 367, May 1901.

Mr. Pound was appointed commissioner under the Act providing for Commissioners of the Supreme Court, Laws of Nebraska, 1901, chapter 25, page 331.

Abbreviations

Am. St. Rep.	— American State Reports
L. R. A.	— Lawyers Reports Annotated
L. R. A. (N.S.)	— Lawyers Reports Annotated (New Series)
Neb.	— Nebraska Reports
Neb. Unof.	— Nebraska Reports [Unofficial]
N. W.	— Northwestern Reporter

61 Nebraska Reports

Chief Justice: T. L. Norval; Judges: J. J. Sullivan, Silas A. Holcomb; Commissioners for Department No. 2: Samuel H. Sedgwick, Willis D. Oldham, and Roscoe Pound.

431. *George W. Ames v. Jerome B. Parrott*
61 Neb. 847 at 848–858; 86 N. W. 503 at 503–507; 87 Am. St. Rep. 536 at 537–546. May 22, 1901.

Attachment — Levy — Interested Witness — Pleading — New Trial.

62 Nebraska Reports

Chief Justice: T. L. Norval; Judges: J. J. Sullivan, Silas A. Holcomb; Commissioners for Department No. 2: Samuel H. Sedgwick, Willis D. Oldham, and Roscoe Pound.

432. *Martha E. Stuart, Appellee v. Henry Burcham et al., Impleaded with Jacob Rocke, Appellant*
62 Neb. 84 at 85–88; 86 N. W. 898 at 898–900; 89 Am. St. Rep. 739 at 739–742. June 5, 1901.

Creditor's Bill — Interest on Decree — Estoppel — Execution.

433. *Modern Woodmen of America v. Jennie Lane*
62 Neb. 89 at 92–98; 86 N. W. 943 at 943–946. June 5, 1901.

Benefit Insurance — Assignment of Error — Authority of Agent — Waiver of Forfeiture.

434. *C. A. Schrandt et al. v. W. E. Young*
62 Neb. 254 at 256–269; 86 N. W. 1085 at 1086–1091. June 19, 1901.

Replevin — Damages — Anticipated Profits — Transcript of Record — Agister's Lien — Tender — Contract Requiring Arbitration.

435. *Fred. A. Miller et al., Appellees v. FitzGerald Dry Goods Company et al., Appellants*
62 Neb. 270 at 271–273; 86 N. W. 1078 at 1079–1080. June 19, 1901.

Lease — Construction — Use of Stairway — Injunction — Signs.

436. *Robert H. Boggs et al. v. Ida M. Boggs*
62 Neb. 274 at 277–287; 87 N. W. 39 at 40–43. June 19, 1901.

Wills — Undue Influence — Confidential Relations.

437. *Philip H. Bender v. Kingman and Company*
62 Neb. 469 at 469–471; 87 N. W. 142 at 142–143. July 10, 1901.

Fraudulent Conveyance — Intent — Directing Verdict.

438. *Sturdevant Brothers and Company v. Farmers & Merchants Bank of Rushville*
62 Neb. 472 at 473–478; 87 N. W. 156 at 157–158. July 10, 1901.

Authority of Bank Cashier — Pledge of Credit — Estoppel — Replevin Bond.

439. *Leonard A. Davis v. Allen R. Kelly et al.*
62 Neb. 642 at 643–647; 87 N. W. 347 at 347–348. October 1, 1901.

Homestead — Constructive Occupancy — Intent — Impeachment of Acknowledgment.

440. *Charles Battelle, Appellant v. James H. McIntosh et al., Appellees*
62 Neb. 647 at 648–651; 87 N. W. 361 at 361–363. October 1, 1901.

Purchaser at Judicial Sale — Liens — Foreclosure of Tax Lien — Answer.

63 Nebraska Reports

Chief Justices: T. L. Norval (until January 9, 1902), J. J. Sullivan (after January 9, 1902); Judges: Silas A. Holcomb, Samuel H. Sedgwick (after January 9, 1902); Commissioners for Department No. 2: Samuel H. Sedgwick (until January 9, 1902), John Barnes (after January 9, 1902), Willis D. Oldham, and Roscoe Pound.

441. *Valentine Ulrich v. A. J. McConaughey*
63 Neb. 10 at 11–20; 88 N. W. 150 at 151–154. November 20, 1901.

Replevin — Answer — Judgment — Verdict — Partnership — Deposition.

442. *Ezekiel Johnston v. Phelps County Farmers' Mutual Insurance Company*
63 Neb. 21 at 22–26; 88 N. W. 142 at 142–143; 56 L. R. A. 127 at 128–129. November 20, 1901.

Mutual Insurance — Waiver — Payment of Assessment.

443. *Robert A. Batty et al., Appellees, v. City of Hastings et al., Appellants*
63 Neb. 26 at 27–34; 88 N. W. 139 at 139–141. November 20, 1901.

Quieting Title — Limitation — Special Assessments — Conveyance "Subject to Incumbrances" — Estoppel — Laches.

444. *Richard S. Horton, Trustee, v. State of Nebraska, ex rel. William Hayden et al.*
63 Neb. 34 at 36–43; 88 N. W. 146 at 147–149. November 20, 1901.

Mandate — Jurisdiction of Supreme Court — Dismissal — Restitution on Reversal.

445. *William C. Brown et al., Appellees, v. Hotel Association of Omaha et al., Appellants*
63 Neb. 181 at 181–184; 88 N. W. 175 at 175–176. December 4, 1901.

Assignment of Interest in Pledge — Transfer of Stock — Foreclosure.

446. *John Fox v. State of Nebraska, ex rel. Josie Powers*
63 Neb. 185 at 186–189; 88 N. W. 176 at 177–178. December 4, 1901.

Satisfaction of Judgment — Setting Aside — Contract Lawful on Face — Tender.

447. *Henry Gibson, Administrator, Appellant, v. Manetta Hammang et al., Appellees*
    63 Neb. 349 at 350–356; 88 N. W. 500 at 501–503. December 18, 1901.

Findings — Review — Gift — Parent and Child — Undue Influence.

448. *Alfred E. Hargreaves v. Orestes B. Tennis et al.*
    63 Neb. 356 at 357–363; 88 N. W. 486 at 486–488. December 18, 1901.

Fraudulent Conveyance — Creditor's Suit — Interest — Stolen Goods — Lien of Vendee — Defects in Cross-Petition.

449. *Richard O. Williams, Receiver, v. William J. Turner et al.*
    63 Neb. 575 at 575–578; 88 N. W. 668 at 668–669. January 8, 1902.

Insolvent Corporations — Preferring Creditors — Accounting — Powers of Receiver.

450. *Kingman & Company v. Newell A. Davis et al.*
    63 Neb. 578 at 579–580; 88 N. W. 777 at 778. January 8, 1902.

Error from County to Supreme Court — Offer in Writing — Parol Acceptance — Sale.

451. *Adam Kas, Sr., v. State of Nebraska, ex rel. School District No. 1, Sarpy County*
    63 Neb. 581 at 582–585; 88 N. W. 776 at 776–777. January 8, 1902.

Mandamus — Amendment — Performance of Official Duty after Expiration of Term — School District within Village — Distribution of License Money.

452. *Albert L. Steidl v. State of Nebraska, ex rel. School District of the City of Crete*
    63 Neb. 695 at 695–698; 88 N. W. 853 at 853–854. January 22, 1902.

Occupation Tax — License — Mandamus— Verification of Application — Amendment.

453. *J. K. Baker v. Union Stock Yards National Bank*
    63 Neb. 801 at 802–806; 89 N. W. 269 at 269–270; 93 Am. St. Rep. 484 at 484–488. February 6, 1902.

Jurisdiction — Special Appearance — Privilege — Accommodation Note — Consideration.

64 Nebraska Reports

Chief Justice: J. J. Sullivan; Judges: Silas A. Holcomb and Samuel H. Sedgwick; Commissioners for Department No. 2: John B. Barnes, Willis D. Oldham, and Roscoe Pound.

454. *Charles Weston, Auditor, v. Lee Herdman*
64 Neb. 24 at 30–31; [1] 89 N. W. 384 at 386.[1] February 19, 1902.

Specific Appropriations — Salary of Reporter of Supreme Court.
[1] Separate concurrence.

455. *George W. Leavitt, Appellee, v. S. D. Mercer Company et al., Appellants*
64 Neb. 31 at 32–35; 89 N. W. 426 at 426–427. February 19, 1902.

Appeal — Review of Ruling on Demurrer — Answer — Tax Sale Certificate as Evidence — Payment by Purchaser.

456. *County of Keith v. Ogalalla Power & Irrigation Company et al.*
64 Neb. 35 at 36–38; 89 N. W. 375 at 375–376. February 19, 1902.

Consideration of Bond — Internal Improvements — Contracts — Powers of County Commissioners.

457. *John A. Horbach, Revived in the Name of Mary A. Bourke, v. Matilda J. Boyd et al.*
64 Neb. 129 at 130–134; 89 N. W. 644 at 644–646. March 5, 1902.

Directing Verdict — Offer of Proof — Review — Conveyance — Possession — After-acquired title by Adverse Possession.

458. *Samuel Doane, Appellant, v. Ellen Dunham et al., Appellees*
64 Neb. 135 at 135–137; 89 N. W. 640 at 640–641. March 5, 1902.

Action to Establish Resulting Trust — Preponderance of Evidence — Conveyance to Wife — Presumption.

459. *Estate of John Fitzgerald, Deceased, v. First National Bank of Chariton, Iowa*
64 Neb. 260 at 269–274; [1] 89 N. W. 813 at 816–818.[1] March 19, 1902.

County Court — Jurisdiction — Administrator.
[1] Dissent.

460. *Jonathan Lydick, Appellant, v. Mary E. Chaney et al., Appellees*

64 Neb. 288 at 288–291; 89 N. W. 801 at 801–803. March 19, 1902.

Decree on Executor's Final Report — Personal Liability — Enforcement.

461. *Julius Poessnecker et al., Appellants, v. Fred Entenmann, Jr., Appellee*

64 Neb. 409 at 409–411; 89 N. W. 1033 at 1033. April 2, 1902.

Executor — Application to Sell Land — Review by Petition in Error.

462. *President and Directors of the Insurance Company of North America, Appellees, v. Emma A. Parker et al., Appellants*

64 Neb. 411 at 412–413; 89 N. W. 1040 at 1040–1041. April 2, 1902.

Errors at Trial — Review — Foreclosure of Mortgage — Counterclaim — Malicious Prosecution — Allegation of No Proceedings at Law — Evidence.

463. *Bernard Thurman, Appellee, v. City of Omaha et al., Appellants*

64 Neb. 490 at 491–496; 90 N. W. 253 at 253–255. April 17, 1902.

Contract of Sale — Approval of Purchaser — Legal Adviser — Opinion.

464. *State of Nebraska, ex rel. Grant S. Cobb, v. Jacob Fawcett, Judge*

64 Neb. 496 at 497–499; 90 N. W. 250 at 250. April 17, 1902.

Bill of Exceptions — Contents — Judicial Notice — Mandamus — Remedy at Law.

465. *Alvin L. Leigh, Appellee, v. Henry S. Green, Appellant* [1]

64 Neb. 533 at 534–546; 90 N. W. 255 at 255–260; 101 Am. St. Rep. 592 at 593–603. April 23, 1902.

Tax Foreclosure — Parties — Unknown Owner — Service by Publication — Notice — Description — Affidavit on Information and Belief — Proceedings in rem — Due Process of Law.

[1] Rehearing of 62 Neb. 344. Affirmed in 193 U. S. 79–93. February 23, 1904.

466. *John D. Knight, Executor, v. Amos H. Denman et al.* [1]

64 Neb. 814 at 815–821; 90 N. W. 863 at 864–866. May 21, 1902.

Pleading — Denial *ipsorum verborum* — Ejectment — Proof of Title — Adverse Possession.

[1] Affirmed on rehearing 68 Neb. 383, 94 N. W. 622.

467. *City of Lincoln v. William G. Morrison et al.*
64 Neb. 822 at 823–833; 90 N. W. 905 at 906–909; 57
L. R. A. 885 at 886–889. May 21, 1902.

Cestui que trust — Preferred Creditor — Trust Money — Stare Decisis.

468. *Mary A. Topping, Appellant, v. John Jeanette et al., Appellees*
64 Neb. 834 at 834–837; 90 N. W. 911 at 911–912. May 21, 1902.

Reformation of Mortgage — Evidence of Mistake.

469. *In Re William Rhea* [1]
64 Neb., Appendix A, 885 at 885–887; 97 N. W. 1119

Murder — Adoption of Statute of Other State — Construction

[1] Coram Sullivan, Chief Justice, at Chambers.

"Chief Justice Sullivan called to his assistance Ames and Pound, Commissioners, who sat with him." — p. 886. Mr. Justice Sedgwick dissented, p. 889–895.

The case of *Rhea* v. *State* is reported in 63 Neb. 461–496.

65 Nebraska Reports

Chief Justice: J. J. Sullivan; Judges: Silas A. Holcomb and Samuel H. Sedgwick; Commissioners for Department No. 2: John B. Barnes, Willis D. Oldham, Roscoe Pound (until November 4, 1903), and Charles B. Letton (after November 4, 1903).

470. *Philadelphia Mortgage & Trust Company, Appellant, v. City of Omaha et al., Appellees*
65 Neb. 93 at 94–97; 90 N. W. 1005 at 1005–1006; 57
L. R. A. 150 at 154–155. June 4, 1902.

Mortgage — Quia timet — Tax — Levy — Equitable Estoppel.

471. *Estate of John Fitzgerald et al. v. Union Savings Bank*
65 Neb. 97 at 99–104; 90 N. W. 994 at 995–997. June 4, 1902.

Stock Subscription — Decedent's Estate, Creditor's Claims — Stockholders — Claim against Estate — Supplemental Answer.

472. *County of Harlan, Appellee, v. Ezra S. Whitney et al., Appellants*
65 Neb. 105 at 106–109; 90 N. W. 993 at 993–994; 101
Am. St. Rep. 610 at 610–613. June 4, 1902.

Principal and Surety — Securities — Trust — Payment — Bond — Contingent Liability — Deed — Mortgage — Recital — County Treasurer — Indemnity — Limit of Liability.

473. *State of Nebraska v. William A. Paxton et al.*
    65 Neb. 110 at 113–136; 90 N. W. 983 at 984–992. June 4, 1902.

Law of the Case — Official Bond — Consideration — Delivery — Material Alteration — Waiver — Time of Defalcation.

474. *State of Nebraska, Appellee, v. German Savings Bank of Omaha et al., Impleaded with M. Wollstein & Co. et al., Appellants*
    65 Neb. 416 at 421–423; [1] 91 N. W. 414 at 416.[1] July 1, 1902.

Power of Receiver of Insolvent Bank to Compound Doubtful Debts.

[1] Separate concurrence.

475. *John Lind Carson et al., Appellants, v. May Jansen et al., Appellees*
    65 Neb. 423 at 424–426; 91 N. W. 398 at 398–399. July 1, 1902.

Independent Action for Injunction in Aid of Cause Pending.

476. *W. C. Murray v. John M. Burd, Receiver*
    65 Neb. 427 at 427–429; 91 N. W. 278 at 278–279. July 1, 1902.

Reference in Instructions to Pleadings — Burden of Proof — Preponderance of Evidence.

477. *Morris Ketelman v. Chicago Brush Company*
    65 Neb. 429 at 429–431; 91 N. W. 282 at 283. July 1, 1902.

Assignment of Error — Plea of Payment.

478. *Levi Bennett, Guardian, Appellee, v. Ezra Bennett, Appellant* [1]
    65 Neb. 432 at 434–441; 91 N. W. 409 at 409–412. July 1, 1902.

Descriptio Personae — Suit to Cancel Conveyance — Mental Weakness — Burden of Proof.

[1] Affirmed on rehearing 65 Neb. 441, 96 N. W. 994.

479. *Chicago, Burlington & Quincy Railroad Company v. E. H. Martelle*
    65 Neb. 540 at 549–550; [1] 91 N. W. 364 at 367. July 10, 1902.

Amended Pleadings — Right to File During Trial — Railroad Passenger Carried Beyond Destination.

[1] Separate concurrence.

480. *Marie Barge v. George Haslam*

    65 Neb. 656 at 656–661; 91 N. W. 528 at 529–530. July 22, 1902.

After Verdict Court May Order Case Reserved for Argument or Consideration of Some Point of Law.

481. *Cyrus S. Bowman et al. v. W. L. Wright*

    65 Neb. 661 at 662–666; 91 N. W. 580 at 581–582. July 22, 1902.

Written Executory Agreements — Subsequent Parol Agreement — Statute of Frauds — Lease — Deposition.

482. *William W. Carter et al., Appellees, v. E. O. Leonard, Trustee, et al., Impleaded with Alva L. Timblin, Appellant*

    65 Neb. 670 at 671–675; 91 N. W. 574 at 575–576. July 22, 1902.

Statute of Limitations — Reforming Conveyance — Discovery of Mistake — Recital of Mortgage in Deed.

483. *H. A. Merrill, Appellee, v. Joanna C. Wright, Appellee, Impleaded with George W. Scott, Appellant*

    65 Neb. 794 at 795–798; 91 N. W. 697 at 698–699; 101 Am. St. Rep. 645 at 645–649. September 18, 1902.

Writ of Assistance.

484. *William F. Bechel v. Pacific Express Company*

    65 Neb. 826 at 827–830; 91 N. W. 853 at 853–855. October 9, 1902.

Malicious Prosecution.

485. *Thomas Bonacum, Bishop, Appellant, v. Lewis J. Harrington, Appellee*

    65 Neb. 831 at 832–840; 91 N. W. 886 at 886–889. October 9, 1902.

Religious Organization — Ecclesiastical Law.

66 Nebraska Reports

Chief Justices: J. J. Sullivan (until January 4, 1904), Silas A. Holcomb (after January 4, 1904); Judges: Silas A. Holcomb (until January 4, 1904), Samuel H. Sedgwick, John B. Barnes (after January 4, 1904); Commissioners for Department No. 2: John B. Barnes (until January 4, 1904), Roscoe Pound (until November 4, 1903), Charles B. Letton (after November 4, 1903).

486. *Ruth Brown et al. v. Chicago, Rock Island & Pacific Railway Company*

66 Neb. 106 at 114–115; [1] 92 N. W. 128 at 129. October 22, 1902.

Eminent Domain — Compensation — Deposit with County Judge.

[1] Separate concurrence.

487. *Lola M. Hunt v. State Insurance Company of Des Moines, Iowa*
66 Neb. 121 at 126–129; [1] 92 N. W. 921 at 922–923. October 22, 1902.

Insurance Policy — Waiver of Provision by Agent.

[1] Pound, C., on rehearing.

488. *Coleridge Creamery Company, Appellee, v. George W. Jenkins, Appellant*
66 Neb. 129 at 130–132; 92 N. W. 123 at 123–124. October 22, 1902.

Interlocutory Orders — Appeal — Contract for Sale of Realty to Corporation — Erection of Improvements — Estoppel — Statute of Frauds — Specific Performance.

489. *J. C. Cleland et al. v. George F. Anderson et al.*
66 Neb. 252 at 256–272; 92 N. W. 306 at 307–313; 5 L. R. A. (N. S.) 136 at 139–146. November 6, 1902.
66 Neb. 252 at 273–276; [1] 96 N. W. 212 at 212–213; 5 L. R. A. (N. S.) 136 at 146–147. July 3, 1903.

Trusts — Special Legislation — Lumber Dealers' Association — Liability of Members — Evidence — Joint Wrong-Doers — Trustee in Bankruptcy — Interest in Pending Suit.

[1] Opinion on rehearing.

490. *Thomas Murray v. City of Omaha et al.*
66 Neb. 279 at 280–284; 92 N. W. 299 at 299–300; 103 Am. St. Rep. 702 at 703–706. November 6, 1902.

Municipal Corporation — Liability for Tort of Independent Board.

491. *Marie F. Nothdurft v. City of Lincoln*
66 Neb. 430 at 430–433; 92 N. W. 628 at 628–629. November 19, 1902.

Defective Sidewalk — Personal Injury — Notice of Defect — Directing Verdict — Appeal — Presumption.

492. *John Schumacher v. Crane-Churchill Company*
66 Neb. 440 at 441–445; 92 N. W. 609 at 610–611. November 19, 1902.

Ejectment.

493. *Willard E. Stewart v. Nels Rosengren, Administrator*
    66 Neb. 445 at 447–450; 92 N. W. 586 at 586–588. November 19, 1902.

Venue — Service of Process — Joinder of Defendants — *Bona-fide* Interest — Misjoinder of Causes of Action — Judicial Notice — Record on Appeal.

494. *Phoenix Insurance Company of Hartford, Connecticut, et al. v. Abram Zlotky et al.*
    66 Neb. 584 at 588–589; [1] 92 N. W. 736 at 737–738. December 3, 1902.

Insurance Policy — Provision for Arbitration — Validity.

[1] Separate concurrence.

495. *Swan W. Larson, Revived in the Name of Louisa Larson, Administratrix, v. First National Bank of Pender*
    66 Neb. 595 at 596–600; [1] 92 N. W. 729 at 729–731. December 3, 1902.

Pleading in Anticipation — Judicial Notice — Review — Errors Not Argued.

[1] Rehearing of 62 Neb. 303.

496. *Josephine Haslach v. Theodore Wolf et al.*
    66 Neb. 600 at 600–603; 92 N. W. 574 at 574–575; 60 L. R. A. 434 at 435–436; 103 Am. St. Rep. 736 at 736–738. December 3, 1902.

Negotiability of Note Payable with Exchange.

497. *Berteen D. Welch, Appellant, v. John W. Tippery et al., Appellees*
    66 Neb. 604 at 604–606; 92 N. W. 582 at 582. December 3, 1903 [*sic*].

Equity — Submission of Issues to Jury — County Road — Improvement in Lieu of Damages for Land Taken — Parol Evidence.

498. *City of South Omaha v. Vincent Wrzesinski*
    66 Neb. 790 at 801–803; [1] 92 N. W. 1045 at 1049–1050. December 17, 1902.

Defective Sidewalk — Claim for Personal Injury — Secondary Evidence of Filing — Instructions.

[1] Separate concurrence.

499. *George F. Gillian v. Thomas E. McDowall et al.*
    66 Neb. 814 at 815–822; 92 N. W. 991 at 991–994. December 17, 1902.

Mortgage — Assignment — Record — Foreclosure of Tax Lien — Designation of Parties — Service of Process — Foreclosure of Mortgage.

67 Nebraska Reports

Chief Justices: J. J. Sullivan (until January 4, 1904), Silas A. Holcomb (after January 4, 1904); Judges: Silas A. Holcomb (until January 4, 1904), Samuel H. Sedgwick, John B. Barnes (after January 4, 1904); Commissioners for Department No. 2: John B. Barnes (until January 4, 1904), Willis D. Oldham, Roscoe Pound, Charles B. Letton.

500. *Lusetta J. Solt et al., Appellees, v. Lewis C. Anderson, Appellant*

67 Neb. 103 at 105–111; 93 N. W. 205 at 205–207. January 8, 1903.

Judgment — Real Estate — Personal Representative — Homestead — Character of Purchase Money — Heirs at Law — Admission in Answer — Meaning of "Executed."

501. *Leonora S. Bronson v. Albion Telephone Company et al.*

67 Neb. 111 at 112–118; 93 N. W. 201 at 201–203; 60 L. R. A. 426 at 427–429. January 8, 1903.

Public Street — Damages — Corporation.

502. *Fremont, Elkhorn & Missouri Valley Railroad Company v. George Gayton et al.*

67 Neb. 263 at 264–268; 93 N. W. 163 at 163–165. January 21, 1903.

Owner of Land — Easements — Nuisance — Surface Water — Railroad Company.

503. *William Dougherty et al., Appellants, v. Emma Kubat et al., Appellees*

67 Neb. 269 at 270–275; 93 N. W. 317 at 318–319. January 21, 1903.

Stare Decisis — Title to Act — Redemption from Foreclosure Sale — Tenant in Common — Mortgage Debt.

504. *Allen E. Goble et al. v. Edward W. Simeral et al.*

67 Neb. 276 at 276–281; 93 N. W. 235 at 236–237. January 21, 1903.

Statute Adopted from Another State — Construction of Statute — Guardian and Ward — Statute of Limitations.

505. *Northern Assurance Company of England v. August D. Borgelt*

67 Neb. 282 at 284–289; 93 N. W. 226 at 226–228. January 21, 1903.

Foreign Corporation — Bond — Principal and Agent — Insurance Agents.

506. *Jens C. Meng, Appellant, v. Charles F. Coffee et al., Appellees*

> 67 Neb. 500 at 502–522; 93 N. W. 713 at 713–721; 60 L. R. A. 910 at 911–918; 108 Am. St. Rep. 697 at 698–715. February 4, 1903.

Common Law — Riparian Owners — Rights Defined — Irrigation — Squatter's Right — Appropriation of Waters.

507. *Clayton F. Tidball, Appellant, v. Chalburg Brothers, Appellees*

> 67 Neb. 524 at 525–526; 93 N. W. 679 at 679. February 4, 1903.

Written Agreement — Withdrawal of Offer.

508. *Edgar C. Smith v. John A. Thompson*

> 67 Neb. 527 at 527–529; 93 N. W. 678 at 678–679. February 4, 1903.

Negotiable Instruments — Indorsee.

509. *Home Fire Insurance Company, Appellant and Appellee, v. Charles J. Barber, Appellee and Appellant*

> 67 Neb. 644 at 645–678; 93 N. W. 1024 at 1025–1036; 60 L. R. A. 927 at 930–941; 108 Am. St. Rep. 716 at 717–744. February 17, 1903.

Corporation — Prior Management — Subsequent Stockholders — Stockholders' Right to Sue — Acquiring of Stock — Title to Corporate Property — Contract of Employment.

68 Nebraska Reports

Chief Justice: J. J. Sullivan; Judges: Silas A. Holcomb, Samuel H. Sedgwick; Commissioners for Department No. 2: John B. Barnes, Willis D. Oldham, Roscoe Pound.

510. *German Insurance Company of Freeport, Illinois, v. Arthur L. Shader*

> 68 Neb. 1 at 2–14; 93 N. W. 972 at 973–977; 60 L. R. A. 918 at 919–923. February 17, 1903.

Pleading — Policy of Insurance — Provisions of Policy — Receiving Premium after Total Destruction — Misconduct of Counsel — Instruction to Jury.

511. *Riley E. Haskell, Appellee, v. Henry B. Read et al., Appellants*

> 68 Neb. 107 at 109–115; 93 N. W. 997 at 997–999. March 4, 1903.

68 Neb. 107 at 115–117; 96 N. W. 1007 at 1007. October 7, 1903.

Written Contract — Right to Vote Pledged Shares of Stock — Corporation — Excessive Issue of Stock — Estoppel — Private Corporation — Validity of Election — Voting Shares.

512. *Henry H. Genau v. Raymond J. Abbott, Executor of the Last Will and Testament of Joseph Genau, Deceased*
68 Neb. 117 at 118–120; 93 N. W. 942 at 942. March 4, 1903.

Equitable Relief — Probate Court — Rules of Pleading — Petition — Striking from Files.

513. *Aetna Life Insurance Company v. Jennie M. Rehlaender*
68 Neb. 284 at 295; [1] 94 N. W. 129 at 133. March 18, 1903.

Revival of Policy — Statement by the Assured — Warranty — False Representation — Proof — Verdict — Theory of the Case — Instruction.

[1] Separate concurrence.

514. *Francis C. Faulkner et al., Appellants, v. Benjamin M. Simms et al., Appellees*
68 Neb. 295 at 300–307; [1] 94 N. W. 113 at 113–116. March 18, 1903.

Appeal — Conflicting Evidence — Review of Findings Based on Oral Evidence, on Written Testimony — Rule in Case of Written Evidence — Remanding Cause.

[1] Opinion on rehearing.

515. *Frank Fiala et al. v. John V. Ainsworth, Receiver of the State Bank of Milligan, Nebraska*
68 Neb. 308 at 308–314; 94 N. W. 153 at 154–156. March 18, 1903.

Bond — Negligence — Liability of Sureties — Verdict.

516. *Amanda M. Williams et al. v. Ed Fuller*
68 Neb. 354 at 362–363; [1] 97 N. W. 246 at 246. October 21, 1903.

Assignment of Error Too General — Pleading — Inconsistency — Exclusion of Evidence.

[1] Opinion on rehearing.

517. *Joseph Williams et al., Appellants, v. Joseph H. Miles et al., Appellees*
68 Neb. 463 at 465–479; 94 N. W. 705 at 706–711; 62

L. R. A. 383 at 384–389; 110 Am. St. Rep. 431 at 433–445. April 9, 1903.

68 Neb. 479 at 479–481; [1] 96 N. W. 151 at 151–152. July 3, 1903.

Will in Custody of Testator — Destruction of Subsequent Will Revoking Former by Implication — Intention of Testator — Term "Common Law of England" in Statute — Lost Will — Heirs — Evidence as to Declarations of Testator — Execution of Will — Subscribing Witnesses — Commissioner's Opinions; Matters Not Essential.

[1] Opinion on motion to modify the former judgment.

518. *First National Bank of Columbus, Nebraska, v. State of Nebraska ex rel. William O'Brien et al.*

68 Neb. 482 at 482–483; 94 N. W. 633 at 633. April 9, 1903.

Assignment of Salary of Public Officer.

519. *Thomas Sorenson et al. v. Alfred Hans Sorenson*

68 Neb. 483 at 484–490; 94 N. W. 540 at 540–542. April 9, 1903.

Petition — Sufficiency after Trial — Right to Open and Close — Denial — Burden of Proof — Heirs — Pleading and Proof — Admission and Denial — Burden of Proof.

520. *Walter W. Hackney, Trustee, v. Raymond Brothers Clarke Company*

68 Neb. 624 at 626–633; 94 N. W. 822 at 822–825. April 22, 1903.

Bankruptcy Act — Preferred Creditor — Sufficiency of Notice — Preference — Transfer of Account — Remedy — Good Faith — Cross-examination of Hostile Witness — Questions Not Raised in Brief.

521. *First National Bank of Holdrege, Nebraska, v. John A. Johnson, Trustee in Bankruptcy of the Estate of Nels Anderson et al.*

68 Neb. 641 at 642–647; 94 N. W. 837 at 837–839. April 22, 1903.

Chattel Mortgage — Recording — Lien — Bankruptcy — Preference.

522. *Bee Publishing Company et al. v. George W. Shields*

68 Neb. 750 at 759–763; [1] 99 N. W. 822 at 822–824. May 18, 1904.

Libel — Liberty of Press — Privilege — Limitation — Evidence — Malice — Damage — Exclusion of Evidence — Construction of Language in Article, Question for Jury — Instruction — Damages.

[1] Opinion on motion for rehearing.

523. *Chicago, Rock Island & Pacific Railway Company v. George Holmes, Jr., Administrator of the Estate of John E. Oakleaf, Deceased*
68 Neb. 826 at 827–832; 94 N. W. 1007 at 1007–1009. April 30, 1903.

Action under Lord Campbell's Act — Evidence — Expert Witness — Conclusion.

524. *George Gatzemeyer v. Dovey Peterson*
68 Neb. 832 at 833–836; 94 N. W. 974 at 974–975. April 30, 1903.

Continuance — Cross-examination — Discretion of Court — Bastardy — Admission — Instruction — Verdict — Testimony of Prosecutrix — Amount of Award in Bastardy Proceedings — Bastardy Statute Held Constitutional.

69 Nebraska Reports

Chief Justice: J. J. Sullivan; Associate Justices: Silas A. Holcomb, Samuel H. Sedgwick; Commissioners for Department No. 3: Edward R. Duffie, John S. Kirkpatrick, Roscoe Pound.

525. *Curtis W. Ribble, Administrator of the Estate of James M. Bullion, Deceased, v. Nettie Furmin*
69 Neb. 38 at 39–43; 94 N. W. 967 at 968–969. May 6, 1903.

Appeal and Error — Final Order — Section 582, Code.

526. *Bryon E. Inglehart v. Lyman C. Lull et al.*
69 Neb. 173 at 174–180; [1] 95 N. W. 25 at 25–28. May 20, 1903.

Justice of the Peace — Appeal — Issue — Extrinsic Evidence.
[1] Rehearing of 64 Neb. 758.

527. *L. O. Roblee et al. v. Union Stock Yards National Bank*
69 Neb. 180 at 181–187; 95 N. W. 61 at 61–63. May 20, 1903.

Negotiable Instrument — Promissory Note — Negotiability — Collateral Security — Notice.

528. *Alvin H. Armstrong et al. v. Simon D. Mayer et al.*
69 Neb. 187 at 189–202; 95 N. W. 51 at 52–57. May 20, 1903.

Cross-petition, Scope — Cross-suit, Basis of Right, When Maintainable — Cross-bill, Chancery Practice — Chancery Enlarged by Code — Supersedas Bond.

529. *George N. Youngson, Administrator of the Estate of Warren Bond, Deceased, Appellee, v. Harriet M. Bond et al., Appellants*
> 69 Neb. 356 at 357–361; [1] 95 N. W. 700 at 700–702. June 3, 1903.

County Court: Jurisdiction — Suit by Administrator with Will Annexed for Construction of Will — Distinction between Suit by Administrator and by Trustee under a Will — Construction of Will by Probate Court — Constitutional Provision, s. 16, art. 6.

[1] Rehearing of 64 Nebraska 615.

530. *Dodge County, Nebraska, v. Herman Diers*
> 69 Neb. 361 at 362–364; 95 N. W. 602 at 602–603. June 3, 1903.

Counties — Non-liability for Necessaries Furnished Quarantined Persons.

531. *George H. Downing, Appellee, v. Charles D. Hartshorn et al., Appellants*
> 69 Neb. 364 at 365–371; 95 N. W. 801 at 801–803; 111 Am. St. Rep. 550 at 551–555. June 3, 1903.

Homestead in Life Estate — Right of Tenant for Life Who Has Paid Mortgage — Reimbursement and Contribution — Mortgage Kept Alive by Assignment — Where Preservation of Lien Operates Fraudulently — Assignment of Mortgage by Life Tenant — Foreclosure.

532. *Allen C. Abbott v. P. N. Campbell*
> 69 Neb. 371 at 371–372; 95 N. W. 591 at 592. June 3, 1903.

Verification of Pleading — The Word "Instrument."

533. *Knights of the Maccabees of the World v. Louise Nitsch*
> 69 Neb. 372 at 373–375; 95 N. W. 626 at 626–627. June 3, 1903.

Fraternal Beneficiary Associations — Statute re Obligations of Contracts.

534. *Almira C. Van Every v. Abisha Sanders*
> 69 Neb. 509 at 510–511; 95 N. W. 870 at 870. June 18, 1903.

Judgment — Vacation — Equity — Petition — Statute Declaratory of Power of Court of Equity.

535. *Robert A. Batty et al., Appellees, v. City of Hastings, et al., Appellants*
  69 Neb. 511 at 512–514; [1] 95 N. W. 866 at 866–867. June 18, 1903.

Appeal — Questions Not Considered Below — Questions Not Raised in Briefs.

[1] Former opinion in 63 Neb. 26.

536. *Henry Bolton v. Nebraska Chicory Company*
  69 Neb. 681 at 681–683; 96 N. W. 148 at 148. July 3, 1903.

Manufacturing Corporation — Construction of Statute, s. 37, c. 16, Compiled Statutes.

537. *Joseph F. Dunn et al., Appellants, v. Samuel M. Thomas, Appellee*
  69 Neb. 683 at 683–684; 96 N. W. 142 at 142–143. July 3, 1903.

Riparian Owner — Prescription — Easement.

538. *Nathan Hart, Appellee, v. G. H. Dietrich, Appellant*
  69 Neb. 685 at 685–686; 96 N. W. 144 at 145. July 3, 1903.

Partnership — Equity — Accounting.

539. *In Re Anderson et al.*
  69 Neb. 686 at 687–690; 96 N. W. 149 at 149–150. July 3, 1903.

Police Power — Constitutionality of Ordinance re Circulating and Distributing Printed or Written Dodgers, Handbills or Circulars on Public Streets, etc., s. 5, art. 1, State Constitution.

540. *George Mitchell et al. v. County of Clay*
  69 Neb. 779 at 780–795; 96 N. W. 673 at 673–679. September 17, 1903.

County Commissioners — Powers — Judicial Functions — Ministerial Acts — Quasi-judicial Act — Passing upon Claims against County.

541. *Michael Cizek v. Anna Cizek*
  69 Neb. 797 at 798–800; 96 N. W. 657 at 657–658. September 17, 1903.

Decree — Collateral Attack — Findings — Homestead — Powers of Court to Quiet Title — Divorce — Possession.

542. *Charles Best, Appellee, v. Helen Gralapp et al., Appellants*
69 Neb. 811 at 812–815; 96 N. W. 641 at 641–642. September 17, 1903.

Specific Performance — Agreement to Devise Land — Trust — Part Performance — Statute of Frauds.

543. *Dupont M. Newbro et al., Appellees, v. Andrew L. Undeland, Appellant*
69 Neb. 821 at 821–826; 96 N. W. 635 at 635–636. September 17, 1903.

Trade-mark — Injunction — Deceit — False Representation.

70 Nebraska Reports

Chief Justice: J. J. Sullivan; Associate Justices: Silas A. Holcomb, Samuel H. Sedgwick.

544. *McCook Irrigation & Water Power Company, Appellee, v. Charles G. Crews et al., Appellants*
70 Neb. 109 at 110–114; 96 N. W. 996 at 996–998. October 7, 1903.

Riparian Owner — Use of Water — Injury to Rights — Remedy — Equitable Relief — Damages — Prescription — Amendment — Demand — New Parties.

545. *Henry R. Penney et al. v. Thomas Bryant et al.*
70 Neb. 127 at 128–132; 96 N. W. 1033 at 1033–1035. October 7, 1903.

Corporation — Liability of Agent — Action for Joint and Several Liability.

546. *In the Matter of the Estate of Robert N. James, Deceased, et al., Appellees, v. Lillie O'Neill, Appellant*
70 Neb. 132 at 133–134; 97 N. W. 22 at 23. October 7, 1903.

Probate Proceedings — Equity — Fraud — Final Judgment — Allowance to Widow — Proceeding in Error.

547. *Keeley Institute of Kansas v. James E. Riggs et al.*
70 Neb. 134 at 135–136; 96 N. W. 1010 at 1010. October 7, 1903.

Transcript of Record — Diminution of the Record — When Stricken — Correctness — Affidavit.

548. *John Barton et al. v. Henry B. Shull et al.*
70 Neb. 324 at 325–331; 97 N. W. 292 at 293–295. November 5, 1903.

Replevin Undertaking — Exceptions to Sureties — Waiver of Objections — Witness — Impeachment — Trial — Statement of Testimony — Exceptions.

71 Nebraska Reports

Chief Justice: Silas A. Holcomb; Associate Justices: Samuel H. Sedgwick, John B. Barnes.

549. *Union Pacific Railroad Company v. Sarah N. Stanwood*
71 Neb. 150 at 158–159; [1] 98 N. W. 656 at 657; February 17, 1904.

Evidence as to Value — Offer Motion to Strike — Instructions — Waiver — Trial — Evidence — Error.

[1] Opinion on Rehearing.

SECTION 2. NEBRASKA UNOFFICIAL REPORTS

1 Nebraska Reports (Unofficial)

Department No. 2

Commissioners: Hon. Samuel H. Sedgwick, Hon. Willis D. Oldham, Hon. Roscoe Pound.

550. *Caroline Sanely, Administratrix of the Estate of Benedict Sanely, Deceased, v. Chris Crapenhoft et al., Impleaded with Daniel Sanely, Appellee, W. H. Greenslit, Appellant, et al.*
1 Neb. Unof. 8 at 9–14; 95 N. W. 352 at 352–354. May 22, 1901.

Pleadings — Mortgages — Appeal and Error.

551. *The Northwestern Mutual Life Insurance Company, Appellee, v. Whitney J. Marshall et al., Appellants, Impleaded with Phoenix Mutual Life Insurance Company*
1 Neb. Unof. 36 at 36–38; 95 N. W. 357 at 357–358. May 22, 1901.

Certificate of Liens by Officer without Seal in Mortgage Foreclosure — Mortgages.

552. *Charles P. Lundgren v. John Kerkow et al.*
1 Neb. Unof. 66 at 67–68; 95 N. W. 501 at 501–502. May 22, 1901.

Ejectment.

553. *United States National Bank, Appellee, v. Gustave A. Hanson et al., Appellants*

    1 Neb. Unof. 87 at 87–88; 95 N. W. 364 at 364. May 22, 1901.

Judicial Sales — Appeal and Error.

554. *Herman Oldig v. Caroline H. Fisk, Administratrix of the Estate of John L. Fisk, Deceased*

    1 Neb. Unof. 124 at 124–127; 95 N. W. 492 at 492–494. May 22, 1901.

Appeal and Error — Vendor and Purchaser.

555. *Henry L. Pratt, Appellee, v. William C. Galloway et al., Appellants, Impleaded with Rochester Loan & Banking Company, Appellee*

    1 Neb. Unof. 172 at 174–175; [1] 95 N. W. 329 at 331–332. February 6, 1902.

Mortgages.

[1] Separate concurrence. Rehearing of 1 Neb. Unof. 168.

556. *Sarah Biddle v. Spatz & Miner*

    1 Neb. Unof. 175 at 175–177; 95 N. W. 354 at 354–355. June 5, 1901.

Pleading — Process.

557. *The Farmers Mutual Insurance Company of Nebraska v. The Phoenix Insurance Company of Brooklyn, New York*

    1 Neb. Unof. 239 at 239; 95 N. W. 482 at 482. June 19, 1901.

Insurance.

558. *Henry Herpolsheimer et al. v. Carl Funke et al.*

    1 Neb. Unof. 304 at 306–308; 95 N. W. 687 at 687–688. June 19, 1901.

Contracts in Restraint of Trade.

559. *Curtis Cohee et al. v. The First National Bank of West Point*

    1 Neb. Unof. 321 at 321–322; 95 N. W. 610 at 610. June 19, 1901.

Chattel Mortgages.

560. *Charles Edward Wiley, Appellee, v. Gertrude M. Wiley et al., Appellants*

    1 Neb. Unof. 350 at 351–352; 95 N. W. 702 at 702. June 19, 1901.

Wills.

561. *William Stull, Contestant of the Will of Lefler Stull, Deceased, v. John S. Stull, Proponent*

1 Neb. Unof. 389 at 399–403; [1] 96 N. W. 196 at 203–204. February 6, 1902.

Appeal and Error — Wills — Depositions — Trial.

[1] Separate concurrence. Rehearing of 1 Neb. Unof. 380.

562. *William R. Winterringer v. The Warder, Bushnell & Glessner Company*

1 Neb. Unof. 414 at 414–415; [1] 95 N. W. 619 at 619–620. February 6, 1902.

Evidence — Trial.

[1] Rehearing of 1 Neb. Unof. 413.

563. *Southard A. Henton et al. v. Farmers & Merchants Insurance Company*

1 Neb. Unof. 425 at 425–429; 95 N. W. 670 at 670–671. June 19, 1901.

Insurance.

564. *Martha W. Warren et al. v. Harry Wales*

1 Neb. Unof. 446 at 447–448; 95 N. W. 610 at 610–611. June 19, 1901.

Mortgage — Pleadings — Bill of Exceptions.

565. *Commercial State Bank of Crawfordsville, Appellee, v. William H. Ketchum et al., Appellants*

1 Neb. Unof. 454 at 455–457; 96 N. W. 614 at 614–615. June 19, 1901.

Injunction against Judgment — Injunction — Appeal and Error.

566. *Henry Herpolsheimer et al. v. Carl Funke et al.*

1 Neb. Unof. 471 at 472–477; 95 N. W. 688 at 689–690. July 10, 1901.

Landlord and Tenant — Evidence — Appeal and Error.

567. *Adolph Steinkamp v. Henry Gaebel*

1 Neb. Unof. 480 at 480–482; 95 N. W. 684 at 684–685. July 10, 1901.

Attorney and Client.

568. *Frank Murphy v. The City of Omaha*

1 Neb. Unof. 488 at 489–490; 95 N. W. 680 at 681. July 10, 1901.

Action for Money Had and Received — Municipal Corporations.

569. *Z. Boughn v. Security State Bank of Randolph*
    1 Neb. Unof. 490 at 491; 95 N. W. 680 at 680. July 10,
    1901.
Appeal and Error — Evidence.

570. *L. Letitia Cochran, Appellee, v. Warren Cochran et al.,
    Impleaded with Elmer G. Cochran, Appellant*
    1 Neb. Unof. 508 at 509–510; 95 N. W. 778 at 779. July
    10, 1901.
Creditor's Suit — Appeal and Error.

571. *State of Nebraska v. the Bloomfield State Bank, George M.
    Reed, Receiver, et al., Appellants, Impleaded with Mrs. J. H.
    Walker, Appellee*
    1 Neb. Unof. 526 at 528; [1] 95 N. W. 791. February 6, 1902.
Appeal and Error.
[1] Opinion on rehearing of 1 Neb. Unof. 524. Separate concurrence.

572. *Frank W. Bissell et al. v. Harris & Company*
    1 Neb. Unof. 535 at 537–540; 95 N. W. 779 at 779–780.
    July 10, 1901.
Bailment without Reward — Bailment.

573. *Melvin L. Rawlings v. Anheuser-Busch Brewing Association*
    1 Neb. Unof. 555 at 556–557; 95 N. W. 792 at 792–793.
    July 10, 1901.
Appeal and Error — Trial.

574. *Margaret M. Milner, Appellant, v. Albertina Harris et al.
    Appellees*
    1 Neb. Unof. 584 at 584–585; 95 N. W. 682 at 683.
    July 10, 1901.
Pleading — Agreement.

575. *William H. Crary et al. v. Truman Buck*
    1 Neb. Unof. 596 at 596–598; 95 N. W. 839 at 839–840.
    July 10, 1901.
Mortgages.

576. *Voorheis, Miller & Co. v. T. A. Leisure et al.*
    1 Neb. Unof. 601 at 602; 95 N. W. 676 at 676. July 10,
    1901.
Replevin — Appeal and Error.

577. *Parsons Band Cutter & Self-Feeder Company v. O. A. Gadeke et al.*

 1 Neb. Unof. 605 at 606–608; 95 N. W. 850 at 850–851. July 10, 1901.

Trial — Vendor and Purchaser — Oral Notice Acted upon Waives Written Notice — Appeal and Error.

578. *Western Mattress Company v. Burton W. Potter*

 1 Neb. Unof. 631 at 631–632; 95 N. W. 841 at 842.[1] February 6, 1902.

Bills and Notes.

[1] Opinion on rehearing of 1 Neb. Unof. 627. Joint concurrence.

579. *Catherine A. Walsh, Appellant, Impleaded with William Walsh, v. Michael Walsh, Sr., Appellee*

 1 Neb. Unof. 719 at 720–723; 95 N. W. 1024 at 1024–1025. October 1, 1901.

Appeal and Error — Homestead.

580. *In the Matter of the Application of Hans Thomsen for a Writ of Habeas Corpus*

 1 Neb. Unof. 751 at 751–753; 95 N. W. 805 at 806. October 1, 1901.

Parent and child.

581. *Anna P. Hillebrand v. Lind Nelson et al.*

 1 Neb. Unof. 783 at 785–789; 95 N. W. 1068 at 1069–1070. October 16, 1901.

Chattel Mortgage — Mortgage of Realty and Personalty — Pleading — Fixtures — Personal Property — Trial.

582. *Robert L. Payne v. Pettibone & Nixon*

 1 Neb. Unof. 789 at 790; 96 N. W. 117 at 117. October 16, 1901.

Appeal and Error.

583. *Herman C. Brinker et al. v. John W. Ashenfelter et al.*

 1 Neb. Unof. 793 at 794–795; 95 N. W. 1124 at 1124–1125. October 16, 1901.

Chattel Mortgage with Power of Sale in Mortgagor — Chattel Mortgage — Appeal and Error.

584. *Union State Bank v. Margaret Hutton et al.*

 1 Neb. Unof. 795 at 796–797; 95 N. W. 1061 at 1061–1062. October 16, 1901.

Estoppel — Evidence — Trial.

585. *Thomas Langan et al., Appellants, v. David W. Parkhurst et al., Appellees*

1 Neb. Unof. 804 at 808; [1] 96 N. W. 63 at 65. November 7, 1901.

New Trial — Judgment.

[1] Separate concurrence.

586. *Morris Adkins et al. v. H. B. Andrews*

1 Neb. Unof. 810 at 810–812; 96 N. W. 228 at 228. November 7, 1901.

Forcible Entry and Detainer.

2 Nebraska Reports (Unofficial)

Department No. 2

Commissioners: Hon. Samuel H. Sedgwick (until January 7, 1902), Hon. John B. Barnes (after January 9, 1902), Hon. Willis D. Oldham, Hon. Roscoe Pound.

587. *Nathan Campbell et al. v. D. Laue*

2 Neb. Unof. 63 at 64; 95 N. W. 1043 at 1044. November 20, 1901.

Statutes — Replevin Bond — Effect of Appeal Bond on Replevin Undertaking.

588. *John Schmuck v. Cora Bell Hill*

2 Neb. Unof. 79 at 80–84; 96 N. W. 158 at 158–159. November 20, 1901.

Libel — Witnesses — Evidence of Handwriting — Expert Witnesses — Appeal and Error — Several Causes of Action — Preponderance of Evidence.

589. *The First National Bank of Hastings, Nebraska, v. The Farmers & Merchants Bank of Platte Center, Nebraska, et al.*

2 Neb. Unof. 104 at 116;[1] 95 N. W. 1062 at 1064. November 20, 1901.

Election to Plead Over — Rule When Amended Petitions Filed — Bills and Notes — "The Law of the Case."

[1] Separate concurrence.

590. *Robert B. Morton et al. v. The Western Seed & Irrigation Company*

2 Neb. Unof. 131 at 131–133; 96 N. W. 183 at 183–184. December 4, 1901.

Judgment.

591. *Joseph Johns v. Louis Kamarad et al.*
2 Neb. Unof. 157 at 157–158; 96 N. W. 118 at 118. December 4, 1901.

Unfiled Chattel Mortgage — Growing Crops.

592. *Lavina A. Boales et al., Appellants, v. E. I. Ferguson, Administrator of the Estate of Emily A. Praul, Deceased, Appellee*
2 Neb. Unof. 172 at 173; 96 N. W. 337 at 337. December 4, 1901.

Appeal and Error.

593. *Isham B. Pope v. Kingman & Company*
2 Neb. Unof. 184 at 184–188; 96 N. W. 519 at 519–520. December 18, 1901.

Garnishment — Fraudulent Conveyances — Appeal and Error.

594. *David S. Gray et al., Appellees, v. Wilhelmina Eurich, Appellant, Impleaded with Henry Eurich et al.*
2 Neb. Unof. 194 at 194–195; 96 N. W. 343 at 343. December 18, 1901.

Judicial Sales — Appeal and Error.

595. *Mary B. Shelby v. John A. Creighton*
2 Neb. Unof. 264 at 265–266; 96 N. W. 382 at 383. January 8, 1902.

Appeal and Error — Judgments — Contracts.

596. *The Omaha Brewing Association v. Herman Tillenburg*
2 Neb. Unof. 277 at 277–280; 96 N. W. 107 at 107–108. January 8, 1902.

Appeal and Error.

597. *Laura J. McKee, Appellee, v. John McKee, Appellant*
2 Neb. Unof. 322 at 322–325; 96 N. W. 489 at 489–490. January 8, 1902.

Divorce.

598. *Farmers Loan & Trust Company, Appellant, v. Byron R. Hastings et al., Appellees*
2 Neb. Unof. 337 at 337–340; 96 N. W. 104 at 105. January 8, 1902.

Taxation — Appeal and Error.

599. *The Kitchen Brothers Hotel Company v. Philip H. Philbin*
2 Neb. Unof. 340 at 341–343; 96 N. W. 487 at 488–489. January 8, 1902.

Landlord and Tenant.

600. *B. M. Webster v. Citizens Bank of Omaha*
   2 Neb. Unof. 353 at 354–361; 96 N. W. 118 at 119–121.
   January 8, 1902.

Limitation of Actions.

601. *William H. Carnahan, Appellant, v. Charles M. Brewster et al., Impleaded with John L. Means, Appellee*
   2 Neb. Unof. 366 at 371; [1] 96 N. W. 590 at 591. January 8, 1902.

Estoppel — Appeal and Error — Default — Mortgages.

[1] Separate concurrence.

602. *George W. Marsh et al. v. State of Nebraska, ex rel. Hannah North, et al.*
   2 Neb. Unof. 372 at 376; [1] 96 N. W. 520 at 522. January 8, 1902.

Appeal and Error — Pleading — Mandamus.

[1] Separate concurrence.

603. *Eunice Baldwin, Appellant, v. Wellington R. Burt et al., Impleaded with Marion G. Rohrbough, Appellees*
   2 Neb. Unof. 377 at 377–382; 96 N. W. 401 at 401–403.
   January 8, 1902.

Judgment — Process — Vacation of Judgments — Enforcing Void Judgment — Appeal and Error.

604. *Eunice Baldwin, Appellant, v. Wellington R. Burt et al., Impleaded with Marion G. Rohrbough, Appellees*
   2 Neb. Unof. 383 [1] at 385; [2] 96 N. W. 401 at 403–404.[3]
   October 22, 1902.

Judgment.

[1] Rehearing of case reported 2 Neb. Unof. 377.
[2] Separate concurrence.
[3] Separate concurrence on rehearing.

605. *The Fidelity & Casualty Company of New York v. Field & Brown*
   2 Neb. Unof. 442 at 442–443; 89 N. W. 249 at 249. February 6, 1902.

Principal and Agent.

606. *People's Building, Loan & Savings Association of Geneva, New York, Appellant, v. Marion S. Palmer et al., Appellees*
   2 Neb. Unof. 460 at 461–462; 89 N. W. 316 at 317. February 6, 1902.

Building and Loan Associations — Usury.

607. *People's Building, Loan & Savings Association of Geneva,
New York, Appellant, v. Angeline M. Welton et al., Appellees*
    2 Neb. Unof. 462 at 462–463; 89 N. W. 317 at 317. February 6, 1902.
Building and Loan Associations.

608. *People's Building, Loan & Savings Association of Geneva,
New York, Appellant, v. Lewis S. Backus et al., Appellees*
    2 Neb. Unof. 463 at 463–465; 89 N. W. 315 at 315–316.
    February 6, 1902.
Evidence — Usury.

609. *People's Building, Loan & Savings Association of Geneva,
New York, Appellant, v. William L. Carricker et al., Appellees*
    2 Neb. Unof. 465 at 465; 89 N. W. 316 at 317. February 6, 1902.
Building and Loan Associations.

610. *Edward A. Livingston et al. v. George W. Moore et al.*
    2 Neb. Unof. 498 at 498–500; 89 N. W. 289 at 290. February 6, 1902.
Appeal and Error — Replevin.

611. *William P. Chambers, Executor of the Estate of Nathan P.
Rice, Deceased, Appellee, v. George E. Barker, Appellant, et al.*
    2 Neb. Unof. 523 at 524–525; 89 N. W. 388 at 389. February 19, 1902.
Appeal and Error — Vendor and Purchaser — Receiver.

612. *O. C. Randall v. The Phelps County Mutual Hail Insurance
Association*
    2 Neb. Unof. 530 at 530–532; 89 N. W. 398 at 398–399.
    February 19, 1902.
Mutual Insurance.

613. *Charles S. Taylor, Appellee, v. Urban Reis et al., Impleaded
with Bessie Kavan et al., Appellants*
    2 Neb. Unof. 533 at 533–534; 89 N. W. 374 at 375. February 19, 1902.
Mortgage Foreclosure.

614. *School District No. 80 of Nemaha County v. J. M. Burress
et al.*
    2 Neb. Unof. 554 at 555–560; 89 N. W. 609 at 610–611.
    March 5, 1902.
Officers — Appeal and Error.

615. *Joseph Storey v. William Kerr*
> 2 Neb. Unof. 568 at 568–573; 89 N. W. 601 at 601–603. March 5, 1902.

Action upon Lost Instrument — Pleading — Partial Payment — Trial.

616. *The City of Lincoln v. William D. Sager*
> 2 Neb. Unof. 598 at 598–600; 89 N. W. 617 at 617–618. March 5, 1902.

Trial — Appeal and Error.

617. *Charles H. Hannah et al. v. James H. Perkins*
> 2 Neb. Unof. 614 at 614; 89 N. W. 599 at 599. March 5, 1902.

Judgment.

618. *D. Murray Cheston, Executor of the Last Will and Testament of Ellen R. Cheston, Deceased, Appellee, v. Sarah A. Wilson, Appellant, et al.*
> 2 Neb. Unof. 674 at 675–676; 89 N. W. 764 at 764. March 19, 1902.

Appeal and Error — Evidence.

619. *Joseph B. Carter et al., Appellants, v. Asher D. Warner, Appellee*
> 2 Neb. Unof. 688 at 694; [1] 89 N. W. 747 at 749. March 19, 1902.

Equity — Tortious Trespass.
[1] Separate concurrence.

620. *Annie D. Wright, Appellee, v. Frank G. Patrick et al., Appellants*
> 2 Neb. Unof. 695 at 695–696; 89 N. W. 746 at 746–747. March 19, 1902.

Mortgage Foreclosure.

621. *Mercantile Co-operative Bank, Appellant, v. Conrad A. Schaaf, Appellee*
> 2 Neb. Unof. 703 at 703–704; 89 N. W. 990 at 990–991. March 19, 1902.

Building and Loan Associations.

622. *William Bokhoof v. John M. Stewart, Sheriff of Holt County*
> 2 Neb. Unof. 714 at 715–716; 89 N. W. 759 at 759–760. March 19, 1902.

Judgment — Vendor and Purchaser.

623. *The State of Nebraska, ex rel. The Chadron Loan & Building Association, Relator, v. Wm. H. Westover, Judge of the District Court of Dawes County, Respondent*
    2 Neb. Unof. 768 at 769–770; 89 N. W. 1002 at 1002. April 2, 1902.

Mandamus.

624. *P. H. Peterson et al. v. James E. Mannix*
    2 Neb. Unof. 795 at 795–797; 90 N. W. 210 at 210–211. April 17, 1902.

Interest.

625. *Omaha Loan & Trust Company, Appellee, v. Mary Walenz et al., Appellants*
    2 Neb. Unof. 806 at 806–807; 90 N. W. 222 at 222. April 17, 1902.

Judicial Sale.

626. *Union Stock Yards National Bank, Appellant, v. Riley E. Haskell et al., Appellees*
    2 Neb. Unof. 839 at 846; [1] 90 N. W. 233 at 235–236. April 17, 1902.

Appeal and Error — Mortgage Foreclosure — Pleading — Principal and Agent — Trusts.

[1] Separate concurrence.

627. *Michigan Mutual Life Insurance Company, Appellee, v. Fritz Klatt et al., Impleaded with James E. Ebersole, Administrator of the Estate of Fred Klatt, Deceased, Appellants*
    2 Neb. Unof. 872 at 874–875; [1] 92 N. W. 325 at 326. November 6, 1902.

Bills and Notes — Case Distinguished.

[1] Separate concurrence. Rehearing of 2 Neb. Unof. 870.

3 Nebraska Reports (Unofficial)

Department No. 2

Commissioners: Hon. John B. Barnes, Hon. Willis D. Oldham, Hon. Roscoe Pound (until November 4, 1903), Hon. Charles B. Letton (after November 4, 1903).

628. *Morris Levy, Appellee, v. Charles Hinz et al., Appellants*
    3 Neb. Unof. 11 at 11–12; 90 N. W. 640 at 640. May 8, 1902.

Mortgage Foreclosure.

629. *Mary E. Gandy v. The Estate of William C. Bissell, Deceased*
> 3 Neb. Unof. 47 at 48–51; 90 N. W. 883 at 883–884. May 21, 1902.

Evidence.

630. *William G. Ure, Appellee, v. Conrad Bunn et al., Appellants, Impleaded with Union Life Insurance Company, Appellee, et al.*
> 3 Neb. Unof. 61 at 61–64; 90 N. W. 904 at 904–905. May 21, 1902.

Mortgage Foreclosure — Taxation.

631. *Frank J. Sharp v. Delmar W. Call et al.*
> 3 Neb. Unof. 64 at 64–65; 90 N. W. 765 at 765. May 21, 1902.

Appeal and Error.

632. *John T. Jones v. The First National Bank of Lincoln, Nebraska*
> 3 Neb. Unof. 73 at 75–79; 90 N. W. 912 at 912–914. May 21, 1902.

Banks and Banking — Evidence.

633. *Union Pacific Railroad Company v. Sarah N. Stanwood*
> 3 Neb. Unof. 123 at 123.[1] June 4, 1902.

[1] Opinion reported in 71 Neb. 150 at 158–159, February 17, 1904. See title no. 549 *supra.*

634. *Estate of John Fitzgerald, Deceased, and Mary Fitzgerald, Administratrix of Said v. Union Savings Bank of Lincoln, Nebraska*
> 3 Neb. Unof. 123 at 124. June 4, 1902.

Corporations.

635. *Herman G. Weilage v. Lysle I. Abbott et al.*
> 3 Neb. Unof. 157 at 157–158; 90 N. W. 1128 at 1128–1129. June 4, 1902.

Costs and Attorneys' Fees — Statute of Frauds.

636. *State of Nebraska, ex rel. Christopher G. Reiss, v. Edward P. Holmes, Judge of the Third Judicial District of Nebraska*
> 3 Neb. Unof. 183 at 183–186; 91 N. W. 175 at 175–176. June 4, 1902.

Mandamus — Mandamus to Settle Bill of Exceptions.

637. *Charles S. Joslin et al., Appellees, v. Dora E. Williams, Appellant, et al.*
   3 Neb. Unof. 192 at 192–193; 90 N. W. 1124 at 1124–1125. June 18, 1902.
   Receiver for Mortgaged Property.

638. *Charles S. Joslin et al., Appellees, v. Dora E. Williams, Appellant, et al.*
   3 Neb. Unof. 194 at 194–196; [1] 93 N. W. 701 at 701–702. February 4, 1903.
   Receiver of Mortgaged Premises.
   [1] Rehearing of 1 Neb. Unof. 192.

639. *Sarah A. Allyn v. Mary Cole*
   3 Neb. Unof. 235 at 235–237; 91 N. W. 505 at 505. July 1, 1902.
   Attachment.

640. *Orville G. Ellsworth et al. v. Mary F. Newby et al.*
   3 Neb. Unof. 285 at 285–286; 91 N. W. 517 at 517–518. July 1, 1902.
   Trial — Appeal and Error.

641. *Patrick Murray v. Samuel W. Allerton*
   3 Neb. Unof. 291 at 291–292; 91 N. W. 518 at 518–519. July 1, 1902.
   Trial — Appeal and Error.

642. *Samuel H. Reed, Appellee, v. John T. Hopkins et al., Appellants, Impleaded with Sarah G. Foote et al.*
   3 Neb. Unof. 308 at 308–309; 91 N. W. 1126 at 1126. July 1, 1902.
   Mortgage Foreclosure.

643. *Chicago, Burlington & Quincy Railroad Company, Appellant, v. Dundy County, Nebraska, et al., Appellees*
   3 Neb. Unof. 391 at 391–393; 91 N. W. 554 at 554–555. July 22, 1902.
   Waters and Water Courses — Bonds — Municipal Bonds.

644. *Charles A. Stitzer, Appellant, v. John B. Whittaker, Trustee for Minor Heirs, et al., Appellees*
   3 Neb. Unof. 414 at 415–423; 91 N. W. 713 at 713–716. September 18, 1902.
   Trusts — Mortgage Foreclosure.

645. *Charles Broadway Rouss v. Jacob Goldgraber*
   3 Neb. Unof. 424 at 424–425; 91 N. W. 712 at 712. September 18, 1902.
Evidence.

646. *The Chicago, Burlington & Quincy Railroad Company v. Moses Roberts*
   3 Neb. Unof. 425 at 426–431; 91 N. W. 707 at 707–709. September 18, 1902.
Railroads.

647. *Patrick J. Creedon v. Eliza W. Patrick et al.*
   3 Neb. Unof. 459 at 460–463; 91 N. W. 872 at 872–873. October 9, 1902.
Reference — Contracts — Appeal and Error.

648. *Hannah R. Dillon, Appellee, v. John C. Watson et al., Appellants*
   3 Neb. Unof. 530 at 531–534; 92 N. W. 156 at 157–158. October 22, 1902.
Contracts — Attorney and Client — Statute of Frauds.

649. *Lydia E. Shuster, Appellant, v. James E. Shuster, Appellee*
   3 Neb. Unof. 610 at 610–613; 92 N. W. 203 at 203–204. November 6, 1902.
Divorce.

650. *Ida M. Jones, Appellee, v. Thomas I. Dutch, Appellant, et al.*
   3 Neb. Unof. 673 at 674–676; 92 N. W. 735 at 735–736. November 19, 1902.
Mortgages.

651. *John N. Ritter et al. v. Fanny Piatt Myers*
   3 Neb. Unof. 684 at 684–686; 92 N. W. 638 at 639. November 19, 1902.
Adverse Possession.

652. *The German Mutual Fire Insurance Company v. William E. Palmer*
   3 Neb. Unof. 688 at 688–689; 92 N. W. 624 at 624–625. November 19, 1902.
Appeal and Error.

653. *Charles F. Iddings, Appellant, v. Citizens' State Bank of Council Bluffs, Iowa, Appellee, et al.*
   3 Neb. Unof. 750 at 750–752; 92 N. W. 578 at 578–579. December 3, 1902.
Judgment.

654. *Christopher G. Reiss v. George W. Argubright*
   3 Neb. Unof. 756 at 756–757; 92 N. W. 988 at 988–989.
   December 17, 1902.
   Pleading — Chattel Mortgages.

655. *H. M. Brabham et al., Remonstrators, v. The County of Custer et al., Petitioners*
   3 Neb. Unof. 801 at 802–803; 92 N. W. 989 at 989–990.
   December 17, 1902.
   Highways — Appeal and Error — Parties.

656. *Christopher G. Reiss, Appellant, v. George W. Argubright, Appellee*
   3 Neb. Unof. 816 at 816; 92 N. W. 985 at 985–986. December 17, 1902.
   Trial.

657. *Nebraska Shirt Company v. Richard S. Horton, Trustee of the Greater American Exposition*
   3 Neb. Unof. 888 at 889–890; 93 N. W. 225 at 225–226.
   January 8, 1903.
   Corporations.

4 Nebraska Reports (Unofficial)

Department No. 3

Commissioners: Hon. Edward R. Duffie, Hon. John S. Kirkpatrick, Hon. Roscoe Pound (1904 and 1905).

658. *The Village of Atkinson v. Edward F. Fisher*
   4 Neb. Unof. 21 at 21–23; 93 N. W. 211 at 212. January 8, 1903.
   Municipal Corporations.

659. *The Village of Holstein et al. v. Katie Klein*
   4 Neb. Unof. 33 at 33–34; 93 N. W. 214 at 214. January 8, 1903.
   Appeal and Error.

660. *Alexander N. Baker v. The Grand Island Banking Company et al.*
   4 Neb. Unof. 100 at 101–103; 93 N. W. 428 at 429. January 21, 1903.
   Taxation — Homestead Claimant.

661. *Hector McLean v. Charlotte L. McCormick et al.*
    4 Neb. Unof. 187 at 187–189; 93 N. W. 697 at 697–698.
    February 4, 1903.
Mortgages.

662. *Joseph Lee Chamberlain v. Chamberlain Banking House*
    4 Neb. Unof. 278 at 279–281; 93 N. W. 1021 at 1021–1022.
    February 17, 1903.
Trial — Trusts.

663. *The Chicago, Burlington & Quincy Railroad Company et al.*
    v. Eliza A. Lilley, Administratrix of the Estate of Michael W.
    Lilley, Deceased
    4 Neb. Unof. 300 at 301–302.[1] November 18, 1903.
Negligence.
[1] Rehearing of 4 Neb. Unof. 286.

664. *Frank J. Black v. Cloud H. Fuller, Sheriff of Pawnee*
    County, et al.
    4 Neb. Unof. 303 at 303–304; 93 N. W. 1010 at 1010.
    February 17, 1903.
Chattel Mortgages.

665. *Frank E. Moores v. Medora Allayne Jones*
    4 Neb. Unof. 319 at 319–320; 93 N. W. 1016 at 1016–1017.
    March 4, 1903.
Appeal and Error.

666. *The Nebraska Loan & Trust Company, Appellant, v. Orson*
    S. Haskell et al., Appellees
    4 Neb. Unof. 330 at 331–334; 93 N. W. 1045 at 1045–
    1046. March 4, 1903.
Mortgages.

667. *Rudolph B. Kummer v. The Dubuque Turbine and Roller*
    Mills Company
    4 Neb. Unof. 347 at 347–348; 93 N. W. 938 at 938.
    March 4, 1903.
Appeal and Error — Contracts.

668. *Charles Spence v. C. D. Apley*
    4 Neb. Unof. 358 at 358–359; 94 N. W. 109 at 109.
    March 18, 1903.
Appeal and Error — Statute of Frauds.

669. *Nebraska Loan & Trust Company, Appellee, v. Ernest B. Corning et al., Appellants*
 4 Neb. Unof. 364 at 364; 94 N. W. 1135 at 1135. March 18, 1903.
Mortgages.

670. *Alexander Buchanan, Appellant, v. Saunders County National Bank et al., Appellees*
 4 Neb. Unof. 410 at 410; 94 N. W. 631 at 631. April 9, 1903.
Banks and Banking.

671. *The City of South Omaha v. Grace Fennell*
 4 Neb. Unof. 427 at 427–429; 94 N. W. 632 at 632–633. April 9, 1903.
Negligence — Trial.

672. *Mary Genau et al., Appellants, v. Lena K. Roderick et al., Appellees*
 4 Neb. Unof. 436 at 437–439; 94 N. W. 523 at 524. April 9, 1903.
Courts.

673. *Alexander Strowbridge, Appellant, v. Jacob Miller, Sheriff of Lincoln County, et al., Appellees*
 4 Neb. Unof. 449 at 460–461; [1] 94 N. W. 825 at 829. April 22, 1903.
Process — Limitation of Actions — Justices of the Peace.
[1] Separate concurrence.

674. *Henry D. Rhea et al. v. Clark K. Brown et al.*
 4 Neb. Unof. 461 at 462–464; 94 N. W. 716 at 716–717. April 22, 1903.
Courts.

675. *A. P. Bovier v. Michael McCarthy*
 4 Neb. Unof. 490 at 490–491; 94 N. W. 965 at 965. April 30, 1903.
Usury — Pleading.

676. *Irwin H. Emery v. David Hanna et al.*
 4 Neb. Unof. 491 at 492–493; 94 N. W. 973 at 973. April 30, 1903.
Trial — Appeal and Error — Mortgages.

677. *The McCormick Harvesting Machine Company v. D. J. Hiatt*
    4 Neb. Unof. 587 at 587–591; 95 N. W. 627 at 628–629.
    June 3, 1903.

Pleading — Evidence — Contracts — Trial.

678. *Catherine A. Walsh, Appellee, v. William Walsh et al.,*
    Appellees, Impleaded with Michael Walsh, Sr., Appellant
    4 Neb. Unof. 683 at 684–685; 95 N. W. 1025 at 1025–
    1026. June 18, 1903.

Res Judicata — Trusts.

679. *Charles H. Chase v. The Nebraska Chicory Company of*
    Schuyler, Nebraska
    4 Neb. Unof. 755 at 756; 96 N. W. 1134 at 1134. July 3,
    1903.

Manufacturing Corporations.

680. *Sarah C. Figg v. John P. Hanger et al.*
    4 Neb. Unof. 792 at 792–794; 96 N. W. 658 at 658–659.
    September 17, 1903.

Malicious Prosecution.

681. *Ray C. Merrill v. F. R. Garver*
    4 Neb. Unof. 830 at 831–832; 96 N. W. 619 at 619–620.
    September 17, 1903.

Gaming — Appeal and Error.

682. *John B. Staunchfield et al., Executors of the Estate of*
    H. C. Spaulding, Deceased, v. Karl Jeutter
    4 Neb. Unof. 847 at 847–850; 96 N. W. 642 at 643–644.
    September 17, 1903.

Mortgages — Trust Deeds — Evidence.

683. *The State of Nebraska, ex rel. Joseph L. Baker, Relator,*
    v. Irving F. Baxter, Judge of the District Court of the Fourth
    Judicial District of Nebraska, Respondent
    4 Neb. Unof. 869 at 869–871; 96 N. W. 647 at 647–648.
    September 17, 1903.

Pledges.

684. *William B. Smith et al. v. The County of Clay in the State*
    of Nebraska
    4 Neb. Unof. 872 at 872; 96 N. W. 1002 at 1002. Octo-
    ber 7, 1903.

Counties.

685. *John E. Hanson, Appellant, v. Hans E. Hanson, Appellee*
    4 Neb. Unof. 880 at 886–889; [1] 97 N. W. 23 at 25–26.
    October 7, 1903.
Partition.
[1] Separate concurrence.

SECTION 3. AMERICAN AND BRITISH CLAIMS ARBITRATION

Mr. Pound was a member of the Arbitral Tribunal appointed under the Special Agreement concluded between the United States and Great Britain on August 18, 1910. He acted as American Arbitrator during the third session which met at Washington, D. C. beginning October 26, 1925, under the presidency of Alfred Nerincx. The reports of the awards in this arbitration were published in AMERICAN AND BRITISH CLAIMS ARBITRATION, Report of Fred K. Nielsen, Agent and Counsel for the United States. Washington, D. C., Government Printing Office, 1926. The references are to pages in that volume.

The manuscripts of the awards, in Mr. Pound's handwriting, are in the Harvard Law School Library.

Arbitrators: Alfred Nerincx, Sir Charles Fitzpatrick, Roscoe Pound.

686. *Fishing Claims — Group I*, p. 554.
    Award, p. 565–567. November 6, November 9, December 22, 1925.

Refund of Duties, Light Duties, and Other Charges Imposed on American Fishing Vessels in Newfoundland — Interpretation of the Treaty of October 20, 1818, between the United States and Great Britain — Award of the Permanent Court of Arbitration at The Hague in 1910, under the Special Agreement of January 27, 1909, between the United States and Great Britain.

687. *The Sarah B. Putnam*, p. 568.
    Award, p. 568–569. November 6, 1925.

Breach of the *Modus Vivendi* of February 15, 1888, between the United States and Great Britain with Respect to the Issuance of Fishing Licenses.

688. *The Horace B. Parker*, p. 570.
    Award, p. 570–572. November 6, 1925.

Damages on Account of Refusal of Newfoundland Authorities to Allow an American Fishing Vessel to Make Repairs in Newfoundland Waters — Treaty of October 20, 1818, between the United States and Great Britain — Award of the Permanent Court of Arbitration at The Hague in 1910, under the Special Agreement of January 27, 1909, between the United States and Great Britain.

689. *The Thomas F. Bayard*, p. 573.

Award, p. 573–574. November 6, 1925.

Damages on Account of Refusal of Newfoundland Authorities to Permit Fishing in Newfoundland Water — Treaty of October 20, 1818, between the United States and Great Britain — Award of the Permanent Court of Arbitration at The Hague in 1910, under the Special Agreement of January 27, 1909, between the United States and Great Britain.

690. *Hawaiian Claims*, p. 85.

Award, p. 160–161. November 10, 1925.

Succession of States; Annexation by Conquest and Annexation by Peaceful Methods — International Law; Nature and Sources, Evidence Required to Establish the Existence of a Rule — General Principles in Relation to the Treatment of Aliens; Expulsion, Arrests in Time of Peace, War, or Martial Law — Nationality of Claimants; Evidence of Birth, Collective Naturalization of Hawaiian Citizens, Naturalization by Marriage, Effect of Annexation on Political Status of Inhabitants, Dual Nationality, Registration Certificates as Evidence of Nationality, Domicile, Political Activities of Aliens — Right of Interposition in Behalf of Aliens — Denial of Justice.

691. *Iloilo Claims*, p. 382.

Award, p. 403–405. November 19, 1925.

Date of the Acquisition of Sovereignty by the United States over the Philippine Islands — Date of the Coming into Force of the Treaty of Peace, Concluded between the United States and Spain, December 10, 1898 — Effect of the Signing of a Treaty — Protection of Aliens against Acts of Insurrectionists or Brigands — War Losses — Criticism of Military Operations — Nationality.

692. *The Zafiro*, p. 578.

Award, p. 579–585. November 30, 1925.

Looting by the Crew of a Vessel — Status of a Vessel Engaged in Carrying Supplies to a Fleet of War Vessels — Character of Evidence — Burden of Proof — Responsibility of a Government for Damages Not Proved to Have Been Committed by Persons in Its Service.

693. *Luzon Sugar Refining Company, Limited*, p. 586.

Award, p. 586. November 30, 1925.

Destruction of Property during Military Operations — War Losses.

694. *J. Parsons*, p. 587.

Award, p. 587. November 30, 1925.

Destruction of Poisonous Liquors by Military Authorities — Police Powers.

695. *William Webster*, p. 537.

Award, p. 540–546. December 12, 1925.

Preservation of Private Rights following Changes of Sovereignty — Article V of the Claims Convention of February 8, 1853.

696. *Cayuga Indians*, p. 203.
Award, p. 307–331. January 22, 1926.
Violation of Article IX of the Treaty of Ghent Concluded December 24, 1814 — Liability of the United States on Agreements Concluded by the State of New York with the Cayuga Nation of Indians — Legal Status of Indian Tribes — Interpretation of Article V of the Claims Convention of February 8, 1853, between Great Britain and the United States — Interpretation of Treaties — Denial of Justice — The Meaning of "Equity" in the Terms of Submission — Nationality — Matters Relating to Procedure.

SECTION 4. REPORT AS SPECIAL EXAMINER IN ADMINISTRATIVE HEARING

697. *United Air Lines Transport Corporation, application for approval of a proposed acquisition of control of, and merger with or purchase of all of the assets of Western Air Express Corporation, under section 408(b) of the Civil Aeronautics Act of 1938.* Civil Aeronautics Authority, Docket No. 270. [1940.] Report of Roscoe Pound, Examiner. 41 p. multigraphed.

PART III

NON-LEGAL BOOKS AND PAPERS

1889

698. *Herbarium Notes — An Alphabetical Arrangement*
   American Naturalist, vol. 23, no. 266, p. 177–178. February, 1889.

699. *The Algae Fungi and Lichens*
   American Naturalist, vol. 23, no. 266, p. 178. February, 1889.

700. *As to the Citation of Authorities*
   American Naturalist, vol. 23, no. 267, p. 161–163. March, 1889.

701. *A Question Regarding the Application of the Law of Priority*
   American Naturalist, vol. 23, no. 267, p. 163. March, 1889.

702. *Of Generic and Specific Names Too Nearly Alike* [1]
   American Naturalist, vol. 23, no. 267, p. 163–164. March, 1889.

[1] *The Royal Society Catalogue of Scientific Papers* (Fourth Series, 1884–1900), vol. 17, p. 991 [Cambridge, The University Press, 1921], lists this title nos. 704, 708, 711, 720, 722, and 723, *infra.*

703. *The Treatment of Exsiccati in the Herbarium*
   American Naturalist, vol. 23, no. 268, p. 263–264. April, 1889.

704. *As Regards Some Botanical Latin*
   American Naturalist, vol. 23, no. 269, p. 444–445. May, 1889.

1892

705. *Review: Revisio Generum Plantarum Vascularium omnium et Cellularium multarum secundum Leges Nomenclaturae Internationales cum Enumeratione Plantarum in Itinere Mundi Collectarum — Mit Erlaeuterungen.* Dr. Otto Kuntze. 1891.
   American Naturalist, vol. 26, no. 302, p. 147–155; *ibid.* no.

303, p. 226–231; [1] vol. 27, no. 323, p. 1010–1013. February, March, 1892; November, 1893.

[1] The review of Dr. Kuntze's work was originally intended to be published in two parts — signed and dated, "Roscoe Pound, Lincoln, Nebraska, February 8, 1892." A supplementary installment followed in November, 1893.

706. *Botanical Survey of Nebraska. I* [1]
Lincoln, Neb., University of Nebraska: Botanical Seminar, 1892. 5–8 p.

[1] This is the initial Report of the Botanical Survey. Preliminary: The Plan and Scope of the Survey.

1893

707. *Flora of the Sand Hill Region of Sheridan and Cherry Counties, and List of Plants Collected on a Journey through the Sand Hills in July and August, 1892* [1]
Botanical Survey of Nebraska, Part 2, p. 5–30. April, 1893.

[1] By Jared G. Smith and Roscoe Pound.

708. *Symbiosis and Mutualism* [1]
American Naturalist, vol. 27, no. 318, p. 509–520. June, 1893.

[1] Paper read before the Botanical Seminar of the University of Nebraska on December 17, 1892.

1894

709. *Translation:* The Number of Plants.[1] P. A. Saccardo.
American Naturalist, vol. 28, no. 326, p. 173–180. February, 1894.

[1] Published in *Atti Cong. Bot. Int.* 1892.

710. *Bibliography of the Flora of Nebraska*
Botanical Survey of Nebraska. Part 3,[1] p. 43–48. June, 1894.

[1] Report for 1893.

711. *A Revision of the Mucoraceae with Especial Reference to Species Reported from North America*
Minnesota Botanical Studies,[1] vol. 1, p. 87–104. June, 1894. Minnesota Geological and Natural History Survey, Bulletin No. 9, Part 3.[2]

[1] Geological and Natural History Survey of Minnesota, Paper No. 13.
[2] Botanical Series 2 (1894–1898).

712. *Thaxter's Studies of the Laboulbeniaceae*
American Naturalist, vol. 28, no. 331, p. 605–607. July, 1894.

713. *The Synchytria, Mucoraceae and Entomophthoraceae of Nebraska*
In: Flora of Nebraska,[1] Part 1, p. 35, 48–53. August, 1894.
[1] Published by the University of Nebraska Botanical Seminar.

714. *Comment on "The Meaning of Tree Life"*
Botanical Gazette, vol. 19, no. 10, p. 422. October, 1894.

715. *Dr. Kuntze's "Nomenclatur-Studien"* [1]
American Naturalist, vol. 28, no. 336, p. 1030–1034. December, 1894.
[1] Paper read before the Botanical Seminar of the University of Nebraska, September 22, 1894.

1895

716. *The Vienna Propositions* [1]
American Naturalist, vol. 29, no. 348, p. 1093–1100; vol. 30, no. 349, p. 55–58. December, 1895; January, 1896.
Les Propositions Viennoises de Nomenclature [2]
Journal de Botanique, vol. 10, no. 6, p. 108–112. March, 1896.
Die Wiener Nomenclatur-Vorschläge [2]
Allgemeine Botanische Zeitschrift, 2 Jahrgang, no. 6, p. 101–103. June, 1896.
[1] In this paper, Mr. Pound translated and commented (with special reference to Dr. Otto Kuntze) upon the Report of Ascherson and Engler concerning the work of the Geneva Congress Committee. The transactions of the said Committee appear in the January, 1894, number of the *Oesterreichische Botanische Zeitschrift.*
[2] Translated by Otto Kuntze.

1896

717. *[The Fungi of Nebraska]* [1]
Botanical Survey of Nebraska. Part 4,[2] *passim.* January, 1896.
[1] It is stated on page 3 of the Report that the list of *Anthophyta* was prepared by P. A. Rydberg, the algae, except *Bacillariaceae* by D. A. Saunders, the *Bacillariaceae* by C. J. Elmore, the fungi by Roscoe Pound and Frederic E. Clements.
[2] Report on Collections made in 1894–1895.

718. *The Plant-Geography of Germany*
American Naturalist, vol. 30, no. 354, p. 465–468. June, 1896.

719. *Some Recent Papers on Nomenclature*
Botanical Gazette, vol. 22, no. 4, p. 338–339. October, 1896.

720. *A Re-Arrangement of the North American Hyphomycetes* [1]
Minnesota Botanical Studies, vol. 1, p. 644–673; 726–738. November, 1896; May, 1897.
Minnesota Geological and Natural History Survey,[2] Bulletin No. 9, Part 9, Parts 10–11.

[1] In joint authorship with Frederic E. Clements. Published in two parts. Part 2 published in advance, April 21, 1897.
[2] Geological and Natural History Survey of Minnesota, Papers Nos. 39, 44.

1897

721. *Review:* Observations on the Distribution of Plants Along Shore at Lake of the Woods.[1] Conway MacMillan.[2]
American Naturalist, vol. 31, no. 371, p. 980–984. November, 1897.

[1] Philadelphia, The Edwards and Docker Co., 1897.
[2] Reviewed jointly with Frederic E. Clements.

1898

722. *A Method of Determining the Abundance of Secondary Species* [1]
Minnesota Botanical Studies, vol. 2, p. 19–24.[2] June, 1898.
Minnesota Geological and Natural History Survey,[3] Reports Second Series, Part 1. June 15, 1898.

[1] With Frederic E. Clements.
[2] Geological and Natural History Survey of Minnesota, Paper No. 2.
[3] Botanical Series 4 (1898–1902).

723. *The Vegetation Regions of the Prairie Province* [1]
Botanical Gazette, vol. 25, no. 6, p. 381–394.[2] June, 1898.

[1] This paper was prepared in joint authorship with Frederic E. Clements and was presented at the 1897 meeting of the British Association for the Advancement of Science, held August 20th, at Toronto, Canada, and is noted in the Report of the 67th Meeting of the British Association for the Advancement of Science, p. 863, August, 1897.
[2] With 1 plate, map no. 21, facing p. 394. See title no. 724 *infra*.

724. *Confused Species of Agropyron* [1]
Botanical Gazette, vol. 26, no. 5, p. 355. November, 1898.

[1] Published to correct some errors made in the paper, title no. 723 *supra*, *The Vegetation Regions of the Prairie Province*.

725. THE PHYTOGEOGRAPHY OF NEBRASKA. I. GENERAL SURVEY [1]
Lincoln, Neb., Jacob North & Co., 1898. xxi, 329 p. 4 maps.
Bibliography, p. xiv–xxi.
2d ed. Lincoln, Neb., University of Nebraska: Botanical
Seminar,[2] 1900. 442 p. 4 maps. Bibliography, p. 22–30.

[1] In collaboration with Frederic E. Clements. This work is based on the doctoral dissertation submitted by Mr. Pound at the University of Nebraska in 1897. No further parts were published.

[2] Revised and brought up to date. The need for a second edition was brought about by a "fire which destroyed the entire stock of Jacob North & Sons, in Lincoln, Nebraska, [and] all the unsold copies of Pound & Clements' 'Phytogeography of Nebraska' were burned." — Botanical Gazette, vol. 28, no. 4, p. 285, October, 1899.

See Botanical Gazette, vol. 28, no. 4, p. 286, October, 1899, where the following item appears: "The international scientific medal of the *Academie Internationale de Geographie Botanique* has been conferred upon Dr. Roscoe Pound of Lincoln, Nebraska, for his phytogeographical researches."

1900

726. *Progress of the Botanical Survey of Nebraska* [1]
Nebraska Academy of Sciences. Publications, vol. 7,[2] p. 138–
139.[3] December, 1900.

[1] Paper read at the eleventh annual meeting, November 30, December 1, 1900, of the Nebraska Academy of Sciences, held at the University of Nebraska.

[2] Jacob North & Co., Lincoln, Nebraska, November, 1901. This volume contains the proceedings for 1897–1900.

[3] An abstract of the paper presented.

1901

727. *Additions to the Reported Flora* [1]
Botanical Survey of Nebraska, Part 5, p. 12–27.[2] March 30,
1901.

[1] See note on page 4 of the Report: "In the list of the additions to the reported flora, Messrs. Pound and Clements have identified the fungi. . . ."

[2] In Report on Recent Collections — Studies in the Vegetation of the State, 1.

728. *New Species of Fungi* [1]
   Botanical Survey of Nebraska, Part 5, p. 5–11.[2] March 30,
   1901.

[1] By Roscoe Pound and Frederic E. Clements.
[2] In Report on Recent Collections — Studies in the Vegetation of the
State, 1.

729. *An Addition to the Parasites of the Human Ear* [1]
   Transactions of the American Microscopical Society, vol. 22,
   p. 81–88, 1 plate. May, 1901.

[1] Paper presented at the twenty-third annual meeting of the American
Microscopical Society, held at Schemerhorn Hall, Columbia University,
New York City, June 28, 29, and 30, 1900.
At the fifth session, Saturday, June 30th, "a paper on 'A New Ear Fungus
of Man' by Dr. Roscoe Pound was read by title in the absence of the author."
The parasite discussed by Mr. Pound was Sterigmatocystis candida.

1909

730. A BRIEF OUTLINE OF THE HISTORY OF BOTANY [1]
   Lincoln, Neb., University of Nebraska: Botanical Seminar,
   1909. 12 p. Bibliography, p. 9–12.

[1] "For the Use of Candidates Preparing for Examinations for Admission
to the Botanical Seminar of the University of Nebraska."

SECTION 2. FREEMASONRY

Evaluations of Mr. Pound's Contributions to Masonic Literature:

The Builder, vol. 1, p. 14–15, 131; vol. 2, p. 25, 90, 105, 157, 186;
vol. 9, p. 55–58. *In* Nocalore (Proceedings of the North Carolina Lodge of
Research), vol. 1 (pt. 1), p. 4–16. Shepardson, *A Modern Masonic Philosopher*, The Builder, vol. 2, p. 83–84 (March, 1916). Haywood, *The Great
Teachings of Masonry* (ch. xviii, "Typical Schools of Masonic Philosophy"),
p. 155–163; contains a discussion of Pound's philosophy of Masonry 1921–
1923.

1902

731. *Transplantation of Freemasonry to the United States*
   The Acacia, vol. 4, p. 30–36. July, 1902.

1903

732. *Oration* [*Karl Christian Friedrich Krause*] [1]
   Proceedings of the Grand Lodge Ancient Free and Accepted
   Masons, of the State of Nebraska, 1903, p. 533–542. 1903.

[1] Oration delivered on June 3, 1903.

Under title: *Krause*

The Acacia, vol. 5, p. 316–323. June, 1903.

Proceedings of the Most Worshipful Grand Lodge of Ancient Free and Accepted Masons of the Commonwealth of Massachusetts, for the Year 1914, p. 490–509. 1914.

The Builder, vol. 1, no. 2, p. 31–36. February, 1915.

Under title: *Krause: [Masonry in Its Relation to Morals and Law]*

In: Lectures on the Philosophy of Freemasonry,[2] p. 23–39. 1915.

[2] See title no. 739 *infra*.

1908

733. *Oration [A Twentieth-Century Masonic Philosophy]* [1]

Proceedings [2] of the Grand Lodge Ancient Free and Accepted Masons of the State of Nebraska, 1908, p. 754–762. 1908.

Under title: *A Twentieth-Century Masonic Philosophy*

The Builder, vol. 1, no. 5, p. 106–110.[3] May, 1915.

Proceedings of the Most Worshipful Grand Lodge of Ancient Free and Accepted Masons of the Commonwealth of Massachusetts for the Year 1914, p. 545–562. 1915.

Under title: *A Twentieth-Century Masonic Philosophy: The Relation of Masonry to Civilization*

In: Lectures on the Philosophy of Freemasonry, p. 73–88.[4] 1915.

[1] The first draft of Mr. Pound's fifth and concluding part of LECTURES ON THE PHILOSOPHY OF FREEMASONRY (title no. 739 *infra*).

[2] Fifty-First Annual Communication, held in Omaha, June 9, 10, and 11, 1908. The oration delivered on June 9th.

[3] Portrait, p. 106.

[4] See title no. 739 *infra*.

1914

734. *Address [On the Feast of Saint John the Evangelist]* [1]

Proceedings of the Most Worshipful Grand Lodge of Ancient Free and Accepted Masons of the Commonwealth of Massachusetts, for the Year 1913, p. 371–378. 1914.

[1] Boston, Massachusetts, December 30, 1913.

1915

735. *William Preston*
The Builder, vol. 1, no. 1, p. 7–13.[1] January, 1915.
Proceedings [2] of the Most Worshipful Grand Lodge of Ancient Free and Accepted Masons of the Commonwealth of Massachusetts, for the Year 1914, p. 467–489. 1915.
Under title: *Preston: [Masonry in Its Relation to Education]*
In: Lectures on the Philosophy of Freemasonry,[3] p. 3–21. 1915.

[1] At head of title: The Philosophy of Masonry; Five Lectures Delivered under the Auspices of the Grand Master of Massachusetts, Masonic Temple, Boston.
[2] At head of title: Lectures on the Philosophy of Masonry.
[3] See title no. 739 *infra*.

736. *Oliver*
The Builder, vol. 1, no. 3, p. 54–58. March, 1915.
Proceedings of the Most Worshipful Grand Lodge of Ancient Free and Accepted Masons of the Commonwealth of Massachusetts, for the Year 1914, p. 510–526. 1915.
Under title: *Oliver: Masonry in Its Relation to Religion*
In: Lectures on the Philosophy of Freemasonry,[1] p. 41–55. 1915.

[1] See title no. 739 *infra*.

737. *Pike*
The Builder, vol. 1, no. 4, p. 78–82. April, 1915.
Proceedings of the Most Worshipful Grand Lodge of Ancient Free and Accepted Masons of the Commonwealth of Massachusetts, for the Year 1914, p. 527–544. 1915.
Under title: *Pike: Masonry in Its Relation to Metaphysics and the Problem of Reality*
In: Lectures on the Philosophy of Freemasonry,[1] p. 57–71. 1915.

[1] See title no. 739 *infra*.

738. *Our Thucydides* [1]
The Builder, vol. 1, no. 6, p. 125–126. June, 1915.

[1] An appreciation of Robert Freke Gould, English Masonic historian.

739. LECTURES ON THE PHILOSOPHY OF FREEMASONRY [1]
Anamosa, Iowa. National Masonic Research Society, 1915.
96 p. Bibliography, p. 89–92.

[1] "By Roscoe Pound, Carter Professor of Jurisprudence in Harvard University, Deputy Grand Master of Masons in Massachusetts."
The preface states that these lectures were first delivered before the Harvard Chapter of the Acacia Fraternity in 1911–1912, except the lecture on Krause, which was first delivered before the Grand Lodge of Nebraska in 1903 and was originally printed in the proceedings of that body for that year. Afterwards all five lectures, revised and corrected, were delivered before the Grand Lodge of Massachusetts in 1914 and appear in its proceedings for that year. In the latter form they were published in successive numbers of The Builder, from January to May, 1915, from which they are now reprinted.

1916

740. *The Causes of Divergence in Ritual*
Proceedings of the Most Worshipful Grand Lodge of Ancient Free and Accepted Masons of the Commonwealth of Massachusetts for the Year 1915, p. 143–166. 1916.
Under title: *Address Before the Grand Lodge of Massachusetts [June 9th] 1915*
Correspondence Circle Bulletin,[1] No. 11, p. four–ten. November, 1917.

[1] Published separately with The Builder, vol. 3, no. 11, November, 1917.

741. *Non-Christian Candidates* [1]
Proceedings of the Most Worshipful Grand Lodge of Ancient Free and Accepted Masons of the Commonwealth of Massachusetts for the Year 1915, p. 379–388. 1916.
The Builder, vol. 2, no. 10, p. 302–304. October, 1916.

[1] By a "Special Committee on Dispensation" (Roscoe Pound and four others).

1917

742. *The Data of Masonic Jurisprudence*
Proceedings of the Most Worshipful Grand Lodge of Ancient Free and Accepted Masons of the Commonwealth of Massachusetts for the Year 1916, p. 783–804. 1917.
The Builder, vol. 3, no. 4, p. 105–110. April, 1917.
In: Lectures on Masonic Jurisprudence, 1st ed., 1920, p. 1–20; 2d ed., 1924, p. 1–25.

743. *The Landmarks*
Proceedings of the Most Worshipful Grand Lodge of Ancient Free and Accepted Masons of the Commonwealth of Massachusetts for the Year 1916, p. 805–825. 1917.
The Builder, vol. 3, no. 7, p. 211–216. July, 1917.
In: Lectures on Masonic Jurisprudence, 1st ed., 1920, p. 21–40; 2d ed., 1924, p. 26–49.

744. *Masonic Common Law — Part 1*
Proceedings of the Most Worshipful Grand Lodge of Ancient Free and Accepted Masons of the Commonwealth of Massachusetts for the Year 1916, p. 826–849. 1917.
The Builder, vol. 4, no. 4, p. 117–123. April, 1918.
In: Lectures on Masonic Jurisprudence, 1st ed., 1920, p. 41–62; 2d ed., 1924, p. 50–75.

745. *Masonic Common Law — Part 2*
Proceedings of the Most Worshipful Grand Lodge of Ancient Free and Accepted Masons of the Commonwealth of Massachusetts for the Year 1916, p. 850–872. 1917.
The Builder, vol. 4, no. 5, p. 136–141. May, 1918.
In: Lectures on Masonic Jurisprudence, 1st ed., 1920, p. 63–82; 2d ed., 1924, p. 76–99.

746. *Masonic Law Making*
Proceedings of the Most Worshipful Grand Lodge of Ancient Free and Accepted Masons of the Commonwealth of Massachusetts for the Year 1916, p. 872a–872s. 1917.
The Builder, vol. 4, no. 11, p. 317–321. November, 1918.
In: Lectures on Masonic Jurisprudence, 1st ed., 1920, p. 83–99; 2d ed., 1924, p. 100–120.

1918

747. *A Preface to Masonic Symbolism* [1]
Proceedings of the Most Worshipful Grand Lodge of Ancient Free and Accepted Masons of the Commonwealth of Massachusetts for the Year 1917, p. 93–109. 1918.

[1] Delivered March 14, 1917.

1920

748. LECTURES ON MASONIC JURISPRUDENCE [1]
Anamosa, Iowa, National Masonic Research Society, 1920.
112 p.[2]
2nd ed. Washington, D. C., Masonic Service Association of
the United States, 1924. 120 p.[3]

[1] "By Roscoe Pound, 33°, Past Master Lancaster Lodge No. 54, A. F. &
A. M., Lincoln, Nebraska; Past Deputy Grand Master, Massachusetts; Carter
Professor of Jurisprudence in Harvard University."
The prefatory part of the volume states that these lectures were delivered originally before the Harvard Chapter of the Acacia Fraternity in
the school-year 1911–1912 (see titles no. 742–746), that afterwards "they
were delivered under the auspices of the Grand Lodge of Massachusetts and
printed in its proceedings for 1916. They were also printed in The Builder
from which they are now reprinted . . . some notes and bibliographies
[have been added]."
[2] Bibliography: *passim*.   [3] Bibliography: *passim*.

1930

749. *What Came We Here to Know?*
New York Masonic Outlook, vol. 6, no. 5, p. 131–132, 149.
January, 1930.

1938

750. *A Balanced Government* [1]
Grand Lodge Bulletin,[2] vol. 39, no. 5, p. 557–558. May,
1938.
New Age Magazine,[3] vol. 46, no. 10, p. 601–602. October,
1938.
Reprint: n.p., n.d. 2 p.

[1] "Prepared at the request of the Iowa Masonic Service Committee for
the Simultaneous Meetings [held by all the Lodges of Iowa in observance of
the 150th Anniversary of the Constitution of the United States] of April 12,
1938."
[2] Of the Grand Lodge of Iowa, A. F. & A. M.
[3] The official organ of the Supreme Council 33rd Degree, Ancient and
Accepted Scottish Rite of Freemasonry, S. J., U. S. A. (Washington, D. C.).

1939

751. *Address: [Remarks on Receiving Distinguished Achievement
Medal]* [1]
Proceedings of the Grand Lodge of Free and Accepted
Masons of the State of New York, 1939, p. 87–92.[2] 1939.

[1] Address delivered on May 3, 1939.
[2] Portrait, "eminent citizen, lawyer, educator, scientist and philosopher;
Belmont Lodge, Belmont, Mass.," facing p. 312.

Section 3. Miscellaneous

1896

752. *The Price of Wheat* [1]
Nebraska State Journal. 1896.

[1] "I remember now that in the summer of 1896 when the free silver agitation was on I published an article 'The Price of Wheat' in the Nebraska State Journal which was widely commented on and used in that campaign. . . . I remember that it involved an immense amount of work going over the consular statistics and reports of the Department of Agriculture and such documents. . . ."

1919

753. *Society and the Individual*
Proceedings of the National Conference of Social Work at the 46th Annual Session,[1] p. 103–107. 1919.

[1] Held at Atlantic City, New Jersey, June 1–8, 1919.

1920

754. *The Place of the University in Training for Citizenship* [1]
12 School and Society 505–513. November 27, 1920.
Reprint: n.p., n.d. 9 p.
23 Harvard Alumni Bulletin 217–222. December 2, 1920.

[1] Address made on the occasion of the inauguration of Marion LeRoy Burton as President of the University of Michigan, October 14, 1920.

1921

755. *The University and Civilization* [1]
7 St. Louis Law Review 1–15. December, 1921.

[1] Address to graduating class of Washington University, June 9, 1921.

1925

756. *The Prospects of the American University* [1]
12 Indiana University Alumni Quarterly 265–282.[2] July, 1925.
Reprint: n.p., n.d. 20 p.
22 School and Society 217–229. August 22, 1925.
Reprint: n.p., n.d. 13 p.

[1] Commencement address, Indiana University, June 9, 1925.
[2] Portrait facing p. 265. A group picture, Mr. Pound in academic gown.

1926

757. *Must Again Exert Political Genius* [1]
Boston Herald, March 18, 1926, p. 13.

[1] Address at Mechanics Building, Boston, Mass., March 17, 1926, to commemorate the 150th Anniversary of the Evacuation of Boston by the British troops.

758. *The State Library in Modern Society* [1]
17 Special Libraries 127–131. April, 1926.

[1] Address delivered on the occasion of the One-Hundredth Anniversary of the Massachusetts State Library, March 3, 1926.

759. *Culture and Population* [1]
University of Pittsburgh Bulletin (unnumbered issue). 30 p. June, 1926.

[1] Address delivered at the Commencement Day exercises, University of Pittsburgh, Wednesday, June 9, 1926.

760. *The Task of Organized Education* [1]
Wheaton Alumnae Quarterly, vol. 6, no. 5, p. 1–3.[2] November, 1927.

[1] This address was delivered on Founder's Day, October 15, 1927.
[2] An abstract of the address. This address was also reported in the Boston Sunday Herald, October 23, 1927, p. 13, 16, under the title *Organized Education Ousts Organized Religion*.

761. *The Abdication of Reason* [1]
26 School and Society 471–481. October, 1927.
Reprint: n.p., n.d. 11 p.
Oberlin Alumni Magazine, p. 22.[2] July, 1927.

[1] Commencement address delivered June 21, 1927, at Oberlin College. Reported in the New York Times, June 22, 1927, 8:2.
[2] Several extracts from the Commencement address.

1928

762. *The Social Order and Modern Life*
In: The Creative Intelligence and Modern Life,[1] University of Colorado Semicentennial Series, vol. 5, p. 71–103. 1928.

[1] Boulder, Colo., University of Colorado Semicentennial Publications, 1928. xiii, 213 p.

1929

763. *The Problem of an Ordered Society* [1]
Portland Evening News, May 8 or 9, 1929.
[1] Address delivered before the Institute of Social Science of Bowdoin College, May 8, 1929.

764. *The Cult of the Irrational* [1]
Wellesley Alumnae Magazine, vol. 13, no. 6, p. 367–370.[2]
August, 1929.
[1] Commencement address delivered June 18, 1929, at Wellesley College.
[2] A condensation of the address.

765. *What We Can Do Through Education* [1]
Publications, Northwestern University. 1929. 14 p.
Under title: *What Can We Do Through Education?* [2]
Bulletin of Emory University, vol. 15, no. 9. September, 1929. 19 p.
[1] Address made at the first annual Honors Convocation at Northwestern University, Evanston, Illinois, January 15, 1929. The caption title on page 2 reads: *What Can We Do Through Education?*
[2] The "Baccalaureate Address" for the eighty-ninth Commencement of Emory University, Atlanta, Georgia, June 4, 1929. This is identical with the address at Northwestern University.

766. *The Rejection of Liberalism* [1]
31 University of California Chronicle 229–247. July, 1929.
Reprint: n.p., n.d. 229–247 p.
2 The Summons 11, 13, 15, 18.[2] Spring, 1929.[3]
[1] An address made at the sixty-first Charter Day Exercises, University of California, held at Berkeley, California, March 22, 1929.
[2] Excerpts from the above address.
[3] Issued at intervals by the Bancroft-Whitney Co.

1930

767. *Information and Learning* [1]
10 Bryn Mawr Alumnae Bulletin, no. 7, p. 2–7. July, 1930.
[1] Delivered at the Commencement Exercises of Bryn Mawr College, June 4, 1930.

1932

768. *Some Analogies from History* [1]
19 Rice Institute Pamphlet 352–367. October, 1932.
[1] Address at the seventeenth Commencement Convocation of the Rice Institute, Houston, Texas, held on June 6, 1932.

1933

769. *Our Times before the Tribunal of History*[1]
6 Bostonia,[2] no. 10, p. 9–12. June, 1933.
112 Christian Register[3] 679–681. October 19, 1933.

[1] Commencement address at Boston University, June 12, 1933. Reported in the New York Times, June 13, 1933, 14:3.
[2] The Boston University alumni magazine. There is a group portrait of the recipients of honorary degrees including Mr. Pound, p. 3; a separate portrait of Mr. Pound, p. 10.
[3] Republished by "the courtesy of Bostonia and with the consent of Dean Pound."

1934

770. *The Task of Education*[1]
29 University Record, University of Florida, Series 1, no. 9, p. 323–331. September, 1934.

[1] Commencement address delivered at Gainesville, Florida, June 4, 1934.

1936

771. *Stresses Need of High Level of Education*[1]
Chattanooga News, April 25, 1936, p. 18: 5, 6.
Under title: *Pound Scores Teacher Oath*
Chattanooga Times, April 26, 1936, p. 1:2, p. 16:7.

[1] Address delivered at the Semi-Centennial Celebration of the University of Chattanooga, held at Chattanooga, Tennessee, April 25, 1936.

772. *The Place of Higher Learning in American Life*[1]
44 School and Society 161–168. August 8, 1936.
Brown University Papers 13.[2] 1936. 10 p.
2 Education Digest 18–21. September, 1936.

[1] Address before the Graduate Convocation, Brown University, on June 13, 1936. Reported in the New York Times, June 14, 1936, II, 6:5.
[2] Reprinted from School and Society, vol. 44, no. 1128, August 8, 1936.

1939

773. *Fashions in Thinking*[1]
17 The Barnwell Bulletin,[2] no. 68, p. 5–21. 1939.

[1] An address delivered on April 14, 1939.
[2] Printed for Students and Alumni of the Central High School of Philadelphia by the Mary Gaston Barnwell Foundation, The Fidelity-Philadelphia Trust Company, Trustee.

APPENDICES

APPENDIX A

WRITINGS ABOUT ROSCOE POUND

1. Principal Papers

1914

A1. *American Contributions to Jurisprudence.*[1]
28 Harvard Law Review 337–339. January, 1915.

[1] A review and translation by Felix Frankfurter of parts of Dr. Rudolf Leonhard's paper Zwei Amerikanische Beiträge zur Weltrechtswissenschaft in 8 Archiv für Rechts- und Wirtschaftsphilosophie 144–147, October 1914. See items A46 and A47.

1923

A2. *A Plea for Historical Interpretation.*[1] Sir Frederick Pollock.
39 Law Quarterly Review 163–169. April, 1923.

[1] Though essentially a review of the volume INTERPRETATIONS OF LEGAL HISTORY (see title no. 118), in it the late Sir Frederick Pollock gives an admirable critique of Mr. Pound's philosophy touching historico-legal interpretations.

1924

A3. *The Juristic Philosophy of Roscoe Pound.* John C. H. Wu.
18 Illinois Law Review 285–304. January, 1924.
Also in: Juridical Essays and Studies. 1st ed. Commercial Press, Shanghai, 1928. p. 120 *et seq.* 2d ed. Commercial Press, Shanghai, 1933. p. 120 *et seq.*

1925

A4. *Pragmatism As a Philosophy of Law.* Walter B. Kennedy.
9 Marquette Law Review 63–77. February, 1925.

1927

A5. プラグマテイズムの法律理論 Puragumateizumu no hôritsu riron [1]
In: 現代法律思想の研究 Gendai hôritsu-shisô no kenkyû. Kenzo Takayanagi. p. 43–175.[2] Tokyo, 1927.

[1] This may be translated as Pragmatic Legal Thought, an article by Professor Takayanagi; it forms a chapter in the Professor's book, the translated title of which is *Studies in Modern Legal Thought.*
[2] Bibliography: p. 166–175.

A6. [*Roscoe Pound*]. Dr. Joseph Schutzner.
Introduction: *Právní Věda Našeho Času Ve Svých Význačných Rysech A Problémech.* Bratislava, Czechoslovakia, 1927.

1930

A7. *Dean Pound: The Scope of His Life and Work.* Lewis C. Cassidy.
7 New York University Law Quarterly Review 897–940. June, 1930.

A8. *Roscoe Pound and Sociological Jurisprudence.*[1] Walter Pollak.
47 South African Law Journal 247–258; 374–384. August, November, 1930.

[1] Lecture delivered by Walter Pollak, member of the Faculty of Law of the University of the Witwatersrand, before the Law Students' Society of that University.

A9. *Dean Roscoe Pound and the Search for Legal Certainty*
In: Law and the Modern Mind.[1] Jerome Frank. p. 207–216. 1930.

[1] New York, Brentano's. xvii, 362 p.

A10. *Notes on Pound's Views*
In: Law and the Modern Mind.[1] Jerome Frank. p. 289–301. 1930.

[1] See item above.

1931

A11. *Some Realism about Realism — Responding to Dean Pound.* Karl N. Llewellyn.
44 Harvard Law Review 1222–1264. June, 1931.

1933

A12. *Roscoe Pound.* Sir Maurice Sheldon Amos, K.C.
In: Modern Theories of Law,[1] p. 86–104. 1933.

[1] The text of ten public lectures delivered at the London School of Economics and Political Science, University of London, during the Lent and Summer Terms of 1932. London, Oxford University Press, 1933. vi, 229 p.

A13. *Roscoe Pound*
In: Law and the Social Order.[1] Morris Raphael Cohen.
p. 327–351. 1933.

[1] Essays in legal philosophy. New York, Harcourt Brace & Co. xii, 403 p. Notes: p. 371–390.

1934

A14. *Dean Roscoe Pound — His Significance in American Legal Thought.* George R. Farnum.
    14 Boston University Law Review 715–727.[1] November, 1934.
    [1] Portrait.

A15. *Juristic Thought in the United States, with Special Reference to Roscoe Pound.* Harold G. Reuschlein.
    Cornell University Doctoral Dissertation, 1934.

1935

A16. *The Legal Philosophy of Roscoe Pound.* William L. Grossman.
    44 Yale Law Journal 605–618. February, 1935.

A17. *A Critique of Pound's Theory of Justice.* Julius Stone.
    20 Iowa Law Review 531–550. March, 1935.

1936

A18. *The Thought and Work of Roscoe Pound.*[1] Henry T. Lummus.
    11 Tulane Law Review 4–17. December, 1936.
    42 Case and Comment 3–5.[2] Winter, 1936–1937.

[1] A tribute, by an Associate Justice of the Supreme Judicial Court of Massachusetts, read at a dinner in honor of Mr. Pound at New Orleans, Louisiana, on October 31, 1936.
[2] Portrait. Condensed from the above.

1937

A19. *The Roscoe Pound Fund*
    Cambridge, Mass.[1] 19 p.[2] February, 1937.

[1] Published by the Harvard Law School Association for the purpose of creating a Roscoe Pound University Professorship in Harvard University.
[2] Cover title; front.; [p. 1] *Roscoe Pound* by A. Lawrence Lowell (reprinted from 50 Harvard Law Review 169–170, December, 1936, *q.v.* title no. A 39); [p. 3] *The Plan for the Roscoe Pound Fund* by Reginald Heber Smith, Treasurer, Harvard Law School Association; [p. 7] *Letters Concerning the Plan* by James B. Conant; [p. 9] Joseph H. Beale, [p. 11] Samuel Williston, [p. 15] E. M. Morgan, [p. 17] James M. Landis; [p. 19] *Letter [of appreciation]* by Roscoe Pound.

A20. *The Sociologic Jurisprudence of Roscoe Pound.* Morris Raphael Cohen.
   In: Law — A Century of Progress, 1835–1935, vol. 2, p. 296–300.[1] 1937.

[1] New York, New York University Press, Washington Square, 1937.

1940

A21. *Dean Pound and the End of Law.* Karl Kreilkamp.
   9 Fordham Law Review, p. 196–232. May, 1940.

2. BRIEF ARTICLES AND NOTICES

1899

A22. *[Roscoe Pound]*
   Botanical Gazette, vol. 28, no. 4, p. 285–286.[1] October, 1899.[2]

[1] The fire at Jacob North & Sons and the Phytogeography of Nebraska. See note 2, item 760 *supra.*

[2] The award to Mr. Pound of the international scientific medal of the Academie Internationale de Geographie Botanique. See note 2, item 760 *supra.*

1901

A23. *[Roscoe Pound]*
   Botanical Gazette, vol. 31, no. 5, p. 367.[1] May, 1901.

[1] Mr. Pound's botanical studies and his appointment as Commissioner of Appeals of the Supreme Court of Nebraska. See Prefatory note to "Judicial Writings," *supra.*

1909

A24. *[Roscoe Pound]*
   21 Green Bag 369.[1] July, 1909.

[1] Concerning the appointment of Mr. Pound to the faculty of the University of Chicago Law School; his work at Northwestern; organizing the National Conference on Criminal Law and Criminology; the Illinois Law Review.

1916

A25. *The New Dean of the Law School*
   18 Harvard Alumni Bulletin 397–398. March 1, 1916.

A26. *Roscoe Pound, Dean of the Law School*
   18 Harvard Alumni Bulletin 400–402.[1] March 1, 1916.

[1] With an appended bibliography at pages 401–402. Portrait, p. 400.

A27. *New Leadership in the Law.*[1] Morris Raphael Cohen.
6 New Republic 148–150. March 11, 1916.
Also in: Law and the Social Order,[2] p. 32–37. 1933.

[1] On the election of Roscoe Pound as Dean of the Harvard Law School.
[2] Reprinted with some slight changes from the original text (New Republic, 1916) and an addition of bibliographical footnotes.

A28. *Dean Pound*
14 Michigan Law Review 479–480. April, 1916.

A29. *The Appointment of Dean Pound.* O[rrin] K[ip] M[cMurray].
4 California Law Review 319–320. May, 1916.

A30. *The New Dean of a Great Law School*
1 Massachusetts Law Quarterly 154–155.[1] May, 1916.

[1] *A List of [Pound's] Legal Writings* is appended to the article at pages 155–158.

A31. *Dean Pound of the Law School*[1]
24 Harvard Graduates' Magazine 659. June, 1916.

[1] A brief notice signed "The University Editor" (William Bennett Munro).

A32. *Roscoe Pound, Dean of the Harvard Law School*
53 American Review of Reviews 734–735.[1] June, 1916.

[1] Portrait, p. 734.

A33. *Roscoe Pound, Dean of the Harvard Law School.* Lawrence B. Evans.
23 Case and Comment 167–169.[1] July, 1916.

[1] Portrait, p. 168.

A34. *Thayer's Successor as Dean*
In: Ezra Ripley Thayer; An Estimate of His Work as Dean of the Harvard Law School, a Sketch of His Life and Reprints of Certain of His Writings, p. 102–103.[1] 1916.

[1] See title no. 300 *supra.*

1923

A35. *[Dean Pound].* Frederick Pollock.
39 Law Quarterly Review 285. July, 1923.

1925

A36. *A Letter from Dean Pound*
3 New York Law Review 303–305. August, 1925.

1926

A37. *Your Memory Is as Good as You Care to Make It.* Charles Lane Callen.

> 102 American Magazine 34–35, 108, 110, 112, 114.[1] December, 1926.

[1] Portrait, full page photogravure, p. 35.

1934

A38. *Dean Roscoe Pound in München* [1]

> 4 Deutsches Recht 337. July 25, 1934.

[1] An account of a lecture delivered before the Law Faculty of the University of Munich, July 13, 1934.

1936

A39. *Roscoe Pound.* A. Lawrence Lowell.[1]

> 50 Harvard Law Review 169–170.[2] December, 1936.

[1] Remarks by Harvard's President Emeritus, A. Lawrence Lowell, upon Mr. Pound's retirement from the deanship of the Law School. Reprinted in *The Roscoe Pound Fund, q.v.* title no. A 19 *supra.*
[2] Portrait.

1937

A40. *Roscoe Pound — An Appreciation and a Tribute.* Anna Ginsbourg.[1]

> 80 China Weekly Review 292.[2] April 24, 1937.

[1] Written upon the occasion of Mr. Pound's arrival in the City of Shanghai, in February, 1937, to lecture before various educational institutions and learned societies of China.
[2] Shanghai, China.

A41. *Roscoe Pound's Notable Address* [1]

> 6 South Dakota Bar Journal 81–83. July, 1937.

[1] With reference to *What Is the Common Law,* address delivered at the Conference on the Future of the Common Law, at the Harvard Law School, August 19–21, as part of the Harvard Tercentenary Celebration. See item no. 223 *supra.*

1938

A42. *The Cover: Dean Roscoe Pound.*[1] Sisenando Villaluz.

> 6 Lawyers' Journal 665–667.[2] July 31, 1938.

[1] Portrait on cover.
[2] Manila, P. I.

1939

A43. *Dean Pound Returns to Texas* [1]
2 Texas Bar Journal 197–198. July, 1939.

[1] Portrait on cover with title "Harvard's Dean Pound Returns after Twenty-One Years."

APPENDIX B

REVIEWS OF BOOKS AND PAPERS OF ROSCOE POUND

1898

A44. THE PHYTOGEOGRAPHY OF NEBRASKA. 1st ed.
Henry C. Cowles. Botanical Gazette, vol. 25, no. 5, p. 370–372. May, 1898.

1901

A45. THE PHYTOGEOGRAPHY OF NEBRASKA. 2d ed.
Henry C. Cowles. Botanical Gazette, vol. 32, no. 5, p. 374. November, 1901.
Colton Russell. American Naturalist, vol. 35, no. 415, p. 600–602. July, 1901.

1913

A46. *Justice According to Law*
R. Leonhard.[1] 8 Archiv für Rechts und Wirtschaftsphilosophie, Heft 1. Translated by Felix Frankfurter.[1] 28 Harvard Law Review 337–339. January, 1915.

[1] Reviewed jointly with item no. A47 *infra*.

1914

A47. *Law as Developed in Legal Rules and Doctrines*
R. Leonhard.[1] 8 Archiv für Rechts und Wirtschaftsphilosophie, Heft 1. Translated by Felix Frankfurter.[1] 28 Harvard Law Review 337–339. January, 1915.

[1] Reviewed jointly with item no. A46 *supra*.

1915

A48. *Report upon Uniformity of Laws Governing the Establishment of Regulations of Corporations and Joint Stock Companies
in the American Republics*
  E. H. Warren. 29 Harvard Law Review 113–114. November, 1915.

1919

A49. *Outline of a Course on the History and System of the Common Law*
  H. J. Laski. 33 Harvard Law Review 491. January, 1920.

A50. OUTLINE OF LECTURES ON JURISPRUDENCE. 3d ed.
  C. A. Huston. 34 Harvard Law Review 800–802. May,
  1921.

1921

A51. THE SPIRIT OF THE COMMON LAW
  S. E. Baldwin. 31 Yale Law Journal 788–790. May, 1922.
  Phillips Bradley. Springfield Republican, p. 9a. Febru-
  ary 26, 1922.
  E. M. Borchard. 12 Yale Review (N.S.) 415. January,
  1923.
  Zechariah Chafee, Jr. 73 Dial 222. August, 1922.
  M. R. Cohen. 33 New Republic, sup. 5. November 29, 1922.
  W. W. Cook. 7 Cornell Law Quarterly 284–286. April,
  1922.
  A. L. Corbin. Literary Review, p. 466. March 4, 1922.
  T. P. Hardman. 28 West Virginia Law Quarterly 325–327.
  June, 1922.
  C. M. Hough. 22 Columbia Law Review 385–387. April,
  1922.
  E. W. Patterson. 7 Iowa Law Bulletin 271–272. May, 1922.
  E. W. Patterson. 20 Michigan Law Review 809. May,
  1922.
  T. R. Powell. 16 American Political Science Review 326–
  327. May, 1922.
  Max Radin. 11 California Law Review 455–461. Sep-
  tember, 1923.

T. W. Swan. 35 Harvard Law Review 481–482. February, 1922.

L. P. Wilson. 8 Virginia Law Review 474–476. April, 1922.
18 Booklist 176. March, 1922.
115 Catholic World 258. May, 1922.
65 Review of Reviews 222. February, 1922.
133 Saturday Review 67. January 21, 1922.

1922

A52. INTRODUCTION TO THE PHILOSOPHY OF LAW
M. R. Cohen. 22 Columbia Law Review 774–781. December, 1922.
A. L. Corbin. 32 Yale Law Journal 515–517. March, 1923.
T. P. Hardman. 29 West Virginia Law Quarterly 285–288. June, 1923.
James Hart. 9 Virginia Law Review 246–247. January, 1923.
Nathan Isaacs. 21 Michigan Law Review 615–617. March, 1923.
F. R. Mechem. 17 American Political Science Review 114–117. February, 1923.
W. H. Page. 36 Harvard Law Review 115–117. November, 1922.
Max Radin. 11 California Law Review 455–461. September, 1923.
86 Justice of the Peace 371–372. August 5, 1922.
38 Law Quarterly Review 509–510. October, 1922.
67 Solicitors' Journal 30–31. October 21, 1922.

1923

A53. INTERPRETATIONS OF LEGAL HISTORY
S. E. Baldwin. 29 American Historical Review 322. January, 1924.
W. H. Buck. 9 Virginia Law Review 666–668. June, 1923.
B. N. Cardozo. 27 Harvard Law Review 279–283. December, 1923.
C. T. Carr. 5 Journal of Comparative Legislation (3rd Series) 144–146. February, 1923.
W. F. Dodd. 17 American Political Science Review 656–658. November, 1923.

C. G. Haines. 2 Texas Law Review 131–134. December, 1923.

Nathan Isaacs. 22 Michigan Law Review 394–397. February, 1924.

C. Kenny. 1 Cambridge Law Journal 378–381. 1923.

A. M. Kidd. 12 California Law Review 152–154. January, 1924.

W. H. Lloyd. 71 University of Pennsylvania Law Review 424–426. May, 1923.

G. H. Montague. Literary Review, p. 235. November 10, 1923.

F. Pollock. 39 Law Quarterly Review 163–169. April, 1923.

F. Thilly. 9 Cornell Law Quarterly 226–229. February, 1924.

J. H. Tufts. 10 American Bar Association Journal 328–330. May, 1924.

Paul Vinogradoff. 38 English Historical Review 298. April, 1923.

H. E. Yntema. 24 Columbia Law Review 107–108. January, 1924.

34 International Journal of Ethics 91. October, 1923.

87 Justice of the Peace. 67–68. January 27, 1923.

135 Saturday Review 539. April, 1923.

130 Spectator 632. April 14, 1923.

The Times [London] Literary Supplement, p. 85. February 8, 1923.

1924

A54. LAW AND MORALS

M. R. Cohen. 38 Harvard Law Review 1123–1126. June, 1925.

J. Corbin. New York Times, p. 6:1, October 19, 1924.

F. J. De Sloovere. 13 Georgetown Law Journal 164–172. January, 1925.

John Dewey. 25 Columbia Law Review 245–246. February, 1925.

A. M. Dobie. 11 Virginia Law Review 84. November, 1924.

A. L. Goodhart. 2 Cambridge Law Journal 275–278. February, 1925.

I. Husik. 73 University of Pennsylvania Law Review 218–220. January, 1925.

A. M. Kidd. 13 California Law Review 185–186. January, 1925.

K. N. Llewellyn. 34 Yale Law Journal 113–114. November, 1924.

H. B. MacMahon, S. J. 9 Marquette Law Review 212. November, 1925.

C. Morse. 6 Canadian Bar Review 375–382. May, 1928.[1]

F. Pollock. 41 Law Quarterly Review 108. January, 1925.

Max Radin. 23 Michigan Law Review 553–558. March, 1925.

C. J. Ritchey. Springfield Republican, p. 7a. January 25, 1925.

W. L. Roberts. 13 Kentucky Law Journal 324–325. May, 1925.

Salander. 6 Zeitschrift für Völkerpsychologie und Soziologie 472.

Norman Wilde. 36 International Journal of Ethics 97. October, 1925.

91 Justice of the Peace 83. January 29, 1927.[1]

[1] Review of 2d edition, 1926.

1927

A55. READINGS ON THE HISTORY AND SYSTEM OF THE COMMON LAW (3d ed. with Theodore F. T. Plucknett)

W. F. Dodd. 37 Yale Law Journal 1177. June, 1928.

P. L. Sayre. 3 Indiana Law Journal 490–492. March, 1928.

33 Case and Comment 121. September–October, 1927.

13 Minnesota Law Review 168. January, 1929.

1930

A56. CRIMINAL JUSTICE IN AMERICA

Nels Anderson. 156 Outlook 551. December 3, 1930.

Nels Anderson. 35 Pittsburgh Monthly Bulletin 80. November, 1930.

Nels Anderson. 28 St. Louis Magazine 290. December, 1930.

F. R. Black. 26 Illinois Law Review 478–480. December, 1931.

F. R. Black. 19 Kentucky Law Journal 346–348. May, 1931.

R. L. Duffus. New York Times, IV, p. 1. August 24, 1930.

J. Hall. 3 Dakota Law Review 329–330. April, 1931.

W. H. Holly. 14 World Tomorrow 25. January, 1931.

V. J. Keane. 5 St. John's Law Review 165–167. December, 1930.

Hastings Lyon. 65 Survey 170. November, 1930.

H. L. McBain. Books, p. 4. August 17, 1930.

W. H. McMasters. Boston Transcript, p. 2. August 23, 1930.

R. Moley. 25 American Political Science Review 1087–1089. November, 1931.

W. L. Morse. 11 Oregon Law Review 306–310. April, 1932.

J. J. Parker. 17 Virginia Law Review 619–621. April, 1931.

R. M. Perkins. 16 Iowa Law Review 602–605. June, 1930.

J. J. Robinson. 6 Indiana Law Journal 530–534. May, 1931.

P. L. Sayre. 16 Iowa Law Review 462. April, 1931.

J. B. Waite. 44 Harvard Law Review 870–873. March, 1931.

27 Booklist 94. November, 1930.

65 New Republic 120. December 10, 1930.

A57. Cases on Equitable Relief against Defamation and Injuries to Personality. Supplementary to Chafee, Cases on Equitable Relief against Torts, and Ames, Cases on Equity Jurisdiction, 2d ed. Vol. 1

M. L. Ernst. 30 Columbia Law Review 1079. November, 1930.

J. R. Long. 44 Harvard Law Review 142–143. November, 1930.

S. Smith. 8 Canadian Bar Review 551–552. September, 1930.

C. M. Updegraff. 16 Iowa Law Review 612. June, 1931.

14 Minnesota Law Review 586. April, 1930.

1934

A58. Harvard Legal Essays

F. C. Auld. 13 Canadian Bar Review 50–53. January, 1935.

H. D. Hazeltine. 30 Illinois Law Review 120–128. May, 1935.

W. S. Holdsworth. 21 American Bar Association Journal 235–236. April, 1935.

J. G. Rogers. 48 Harvard Law Review 1455–1459. June, 1935.

1938

A59. FORMATIVE ERA OF AMERICAN LAW

J. C. Bassett. Boston Transcript, p. 1. June 17, 1939.

W. R. Blackard. 16 Tennessee Law Review 253–254. February, 1940.

H. M. Bowman. 24 Iowa Law Review 812–814. May, 1939.

Joseph Calderon. 29 Commonweal 725. April 21, 1939.

L. L. Fuller. 34 Illinois Law Review 372–374. November, 1939.

A. L. Goodhart. 13 Tulane Law Review 482–485. April, 1939.

J. Hall. 52 Harvard Law Review 1191–1194. May, 1939.

C. J. Hilkey. 25 Cornell Law Quarterly 156–159. December, 1939.

W. S. Holdsworth. 3 University of Toronto Law Journal 432–434. Lent Term, 1940.

M. De W. Howe. Books, p. 10. January 29, 1939.

W. P. Keeton. 18 Texas Law Review 245. February, 1940.

M. R. Konvitz. 16 New York University Law Quarterly Review 513–514. March, 1939.

H. T. Lummis. 2 Louisiana Law Review 206–207. November, 1939.

J. D. O'Reilly, Jr. 19 Boston University Law Review 344–347. April, 1939.

K. B. Umbreit. 25 American Bar Association Journal 339–340. April, 1939.

T. Williams. 24 Washington University Law Quarterly 297–299. February, 1939.

25 Virginia Law Review 1002. June, 1939.

1939

A60. NATIONAL LAW LIBRARY

Chester Rohrlich. New York Times, VI, p. 8. October 15, 1939.

1940

A61. JUBILEE LAW LECTURES

James T. Connor. 14 Tulane Law Review 477–480. April, 1940.

J. J. Kearney. 2 Louisiana Law Review 568–572. March, 1940.

Franz L. Neumann. 40 Columbia Law Review 951–953. May, 1940.

D. C. O'Grady. 15 Notre Dame Lawyer 262–265. March, 1940.

John D. O'Reilly, Jr. 20 Boston University Law Review 415–417. April, 1940.

TABLE OF CASES

TABLE OF CASES

ITEM
NO.

Abbott *v.* Campbell, 69 Neb. 371; 95 N. W. 591 532
Adkins *v.* Andrews, 1 Neb. Unof. 810; 96 N. W. 228 586
Aetna Life Ins. Co. *v.* Rehlaender, 68 Neb. 284; 94 N. W. 129 513
Allyn *v.* Cole, 3 Neb. Unof. 235; 91 N. W. 505 639
Ames *v.* Parrott, 61 Neb. 847; 86 N. W. 503; 87 Am. St. Rep. 536 431
Anderson *in re*, 69 Neb. 686; 96 N. W. 149 539
Armstrong *v.* Mayer, 69 Neb. 187; 95 N. W. 51 528

Baker *v.* Grand Island Banking Co., 4 Neb. Unof. 100; 93 N. W. 428 .. 660
Baker *v.* Union Stock Yards National Bank, 63 Neb. 801; 89 N. W. 269;
    93 Am. St. Rep. 484 453
Baldwin *v.* Burt, 2 Neb. Unof. 377; 96 N. W. 401 603
Baldwin *v.* Burt, 2 Neb. Unof. 383; 96 N. W. 401 604
Barge *v.* Haslam, 65 Neb. 656; 91 N. W. 528 480
Barton *v.* Shull, 70 Neb. 324; 97 N. W. 292 548
Battelle *v.* McIntosh, 62 Neb. 647; 87 N. W. 361 440
Batty *v.* City of Hastings, 63 Neb. 26; 88 N. W. 139 443
Batty *v.* City of Hastings, 69 Neb. 511; 95 N. W. 866 535
Bechel *v.* Pacific Express Co., 65 Neb. 826; 91 N. W. 853 484
Bee Publishing Co. *v.* Shields, 68 Neb. 750; 99 N. W. 822. 522
Bender *v.* Kingman and Co., 62 Neb. 469; 87 N. W. 142 437
Bennett *v.* Bennett, 65 Neb. 432; 91 N. W. 409 478
Best *v.* Gralapp, 69 Neb. 811; 96 N. W. 641 542
Biddle *v.* Spatz & Miner, 1 Neb. Unof. 175; 95 N. W. 354 556
Bissell *v.* Harris & Co., 1 Neb. Unof. 535; 95 N. W. 779 572
Black *v.* Fuller, 4 Neb. Unof. 303; 93 N. W. 1010 664
Boales *v.* Ferguson, 2 Neb. Unof. 172; 96 N. W. 337 592
Boggs *v.* Boggs, 62 Neb. 274; 87 N. W. 39 438
Bokhoof *v.* Stewart, 2 Neb. Unof. 714; 89 N. W. 759 622
Bolton *v.* Nebraska Chicory Co., 69 Neb. 681; 96 N. W. 148 536
Bonacum *v.* Harrington, 65 Neb. 831; 91 N. W. 886 485
Boughn *v.* Security State Bank of Randolph, 1 Neb. Unof. 490; 95
    N. W. 680 569
Bovier *v.* McCarthy, 4 Neb. Unof. 490; 94 N. W. 965 675
Bowman *v.* Wright, 65 Neb. 661; 91 N. W. 580 481
Brabham *v.* County of Custer, 3 Neb. Unof. 801; 92 N. W. 989 655
Brinker *v.* Ashenfelter, 1 Neb. Unof. 793; 95 N. W. 1124 583
Bronson *v.* Albion Telephone Co., 67 Neb. 111; 93 N. W. 201; 60
    L. R. A. 426 501
Brown *v.* Chicago, R. I. & P. Co., 66 Neb. 106; 92 N. W. 128 486
Brown *v.* Hotel Association of Omaha, 63 Neb. 181; 88 N. W. 175 445
Buchanan *v.* Saunders County National Bank, 4 Neb. Unof. 410; 94
    N. W. 631 670

ITEM
NO.

Campbell *v.* Laue, 2 Neb. Unof. 63; 95 N. W. 1043 587
Carnahan *v.* Brewster, 2 Neb. Unof. 366; 96 N. W. 590 601
Carson *v.* Jansen, 65 Neb. 423; 91 N. W. 398 475
Carter *v.* Leonard, 65 Neb. 670; 91 N. W. 574 482
Carter *v.* Warner, 2 Neb. Unof. 688; 89 N. W. 747 619
Cayuga Indians, American and British Claims Arbitration, Report of
    F. K. Nielson, p. 203 696
Chamberlain *v.* Chamberlain Banking House, 4 Neb. Unof. 278; 93
    N. W. 1021 662
Chambers *v.* Barker, 2 Neb. Unof. 523; 89 N. W. 388 611
Chase *v.* Nebraska Chicory Co. of Schuyler, 4 Neb. Unof. 755; 96
    N. W. 1134 679
Cheston *v.* Wilson, 2 Neb. Unof. 674; 89 N. W. 764 618
Chicago, B. & Q. R.R. Co. *v.* Lilley, 4 Neb. Unof. 300 663
Chicago, B. & Q. R.R. Co. *v.* Martelle, 65 Neb. 540; 91 N. W. 364 .. 479
Chicago, B. & O. R.R. Co. *v.* Roberts, 3 Neb. Unof. 425; 91 N. W. 707 646
Chicago, R. I. P. Ry. Co. *v.* Holmes, 68 Neb. 826; 94 N. W. 1007 523
Cizek *v.* Cizek, 69 Neb. 797; 96 N. W. 657 541
Cleland *v.* Anderson, 66 Neb. 252; 92 N. W. 306; 5 L. R. A. (N.S.) 136;
    96 N. W. 212 489
Cochran *v.* Cochran, 1 Neb. Unof. 508; 95 N. W. 778 570
Cohee *v.* First National Bank of West Point, 1 Neb. Unof. 321; 95
    N. W. 610 559
Coleridge Creamery Co. *v.* Jenkins, 66 Neb. 129; 92 N. W. 123 488
Commercial State Bank of Crawfordsville *v.* Ketchum, 1 Neb. Unof.
    454; 96 N. W. 614 565
Crary *v.* Buck, 1 Neb. Unof. 596; 95 N. W. 839 575
Creedon *v.* Patrick, 3 Neb. Unof. 459; 91 N. W. 872 647

Davis *v.* Kelly, 62 Neb. 642; 87 N. W. 347 439
Dillon *v.* Watson, 3 Neb. Unof. 530; 92 N. W. 156 648
Doane *v.* Dunham, 64 Neb. 135; 89 N. W. 640 458
Dodge County *v.* Diers, 69 Neb. 361; 95 N. W. 602 530
Dougherty *v.* Kubat, 67 Neb. 269; 93 N. W. 317 503
Downing *v.* Hartshorn, 69 Neb. 364; 95 N. W. 801; 111 Am. St. Rep. 550 531
Dunn *v.* Thomas, 69 Neb. 683; 96 N. W. 142 537

Ellsworth *v.* Newby, 3 Neb. Unof. 285; 91 N. W. 517 640
Emery *v.* Hanna, 4 Neb. Unof. 491; 94 N. W. 973 676
Estate of Fitzgerald *v.* First National Bank of Chariton, 64 Neb. 260;
    89 N. W. 813 459
Estate of Fitzgerald *v.* Union Savings Bank of Lincoln, 3 Neb. Unof. 123 634
Estate of Fitzgerald *v.* Union Savings Bank, 65 Neb. 97; 90 N. W. 994 471

Farmers Loan & Trust Co. *v.* Hastings, 2 Neb. Unof. 337; 96 N. W. 104 598
Farmers Mutual Ins. Co. *v.* Phoenix Ins. Co. of Brooklyn, N. Y., 1 Neb.
    Unof. 239; 95 N. W. 482 557
Faulkner *v.* Simms, 68 Neb. 295; 94 N. W. 113 514

ITEM
NO.

Fiala *v.* Ainsworth, 68 Neb. 308; 94 N. W. 153 515
Fidelity & Casualty Co. of N. Y. *v.* Field & Brown, 2 Neb. Unof. 442;
    89 N. W. 249 605
Figg *v.* Hanger, 4 Neb. Unof. 792; 96 N. W. 658 680
First National Bank of Columbus *v.* State ex rel. O'Brien, 68 Neb.
    482; 94 N. W. 633 518
First National Bank of Hastings *v.* Farmers & Merchants Bank of Platte
    Center, 2 Neb. Unof. 104; 95 N. W. 1062 589
First National Bank of Holdrege *v.* Johnson, 68 Neb. 641; 94 N. W.
    837 521
Fishing Claims — Group I, American and British Claims Arbitration,
    Report of F. K. Nielson, p. 554 686
Fitzgerald, Estate of, *v.* First National Bank of Chariton, 64 Neb. 260;
    89 N. W. 813 459
Fitzgerald, Estate of, *v.* Union Savings Bank of Lincoln, 3 Neb. Unof.
    123 634
Fitzgerald, Estate of, *v.* Union Savings Bank, 65 Neb. 97; 90 N. W. 994 471
Fox *v.* State, 63 Neb. 185; 88 N. W. 176 446
Fremont, E. & M. V. R.R. Co. *v.* Gayton, 67 Neb. 263; 93 N. W. 163 502

Gandy *v.* Bissell, 3 Neb. Unof. 47; 90 N. W. 883 629
Gatzemeyer *v.* Peterson, 68 Neb. 832; 94 N. W. 974 524
Genau *v.* Abbott, 68 Neb. 117; 93 N. W. 942 512
Genau *v.* Roderick, 4 Neb. Unof. 436; 94 N. W. 523 672
German Ins. Co. of Freeport, Illinois, *v.* Shader, 68 Neb. 1; 93 N. W.
    972; 60 L. R. A. 918 510
German Mutual Fire Ins. Co. *v.* Palmer, 3 Neb. Unof. 688; 92 N. W.
    624 652
Gibson *v.* Hammang, 63 Neb. 349; 88 N. W. 500 447
Gillian *v.* McDowall, 66 Neb. 814; 92 N. W. 991 499
Goble *v.* Simeral, 67 Neb. 276; 93 N. W. 235 504
Gray *v.* Eurich, 2 Neb. Unof. 194; 96 N. W. 343 594

Hackney *v.* Raymond Bros. Clarke Co., 68 Neb. 624; 94 N. W. 822 .. 520
Hannah *v.* Perkins, 2 Neb. Unof. 614; 89 N. W. 599 617
Hanson *v.* Hanson, 4 Neb. Unof. 880; 97 N. W. 23 685
Hargreaves *v.* Tennis, 63 Neb. 356; 88 N. W. 486 448
Harlan County *v.* Whitney, 65 Neb. 105; 90 N. W. 993; 101 Am. St.
    Rep. 610 472
Hart *v.* Dietrich, 69 Neb. 685; 96 N. W. 144 538
Haskell *v.* Read, 68 Neb. 107; 93 N. W. 997; 96 N. W. 1007 511
Haslach *v.* Wolf, 66 Neb. 600; 92 N. W. 574; 60 L. R. A. 434; 103
    Am. St. Rep. 736 496
Hawaiian Claims, American and British Claims Arbitration, Report of
    F. K. Nielson, p. 85 690
Henton *v.* Farmers & Merchants Ins. Co., 1 Neb. Unof. 425; 95 N. W.
    670 563
Herpolsheimer *v.* Funke, 1 Neb. Unof. 304; 95 N. W. 687 558

ITEM
NO.

Herpolsheimer v. Funke, 1 Neb. Unof. 471; 95 N. W. 688 566
Hillebrand v. Nelson, 1 Neb. Unof. 783; 95 N. W. 1069 581
Home Fire Ins. Co. v. Barber, 67 Neb. 644; 93 N. W. 1024; 60 L. R. A.
    927; 108 Am. St. Rep. 716 509
The Horace B. Parker, American and British Claims Arbitration, Re-
    port of F. K. Nielson, p. 570 688
Horbach v. Boyd, 64 Neb. 129; 89 N. W. 644 457
Horton v. State, 63 Neb. 34; 88 N. W. 146 444
Hunt v. State Ins. Co. of Des Moines, 66 Neb. 121; 92 N. W. 921 487

Iddings v. Citizens' State Bank of Council Bluffs, 3 Neb. Unof. 750;
    92 N. W. 578 653
Iloilo Claims, American and British Claims Arbitration, Report of
    F. K. Nielson, p. 382 691
Inglehart v. Lull, 69 Neb. 173; 95 N. W. 25 526

James, in the Matter of, v. O'Neill, 70 Neb. 132; 97 N. W. 22 546
Johns v. Kamarad, 2 Neb. Unof. 157; 96 N. W. 118 591
Johnston v. Phelps County Farmers' Mutual Ins. Co., 63 Neb. 21;
    88 N. W. 142; 56 L. R. A. 127 442
Jones v. Dutch, 3 Neb. Unof. 673; 92 N. W. 735 650
Jones v. First National Bank of Lincoln, 3 Neb. Unof. 73; 90 N. W. 912 632
Joslin v. Williams, 3 Neb. Unof. 192; 90 N. W. 1124 637
Joslin v. Williams, 3 Neb. Unof. 194; 93 N. W. 701 638

Kas v. State, 63 Neb. 581; 88 N. W. 776 451
Keeley Institute of Kansas v. Riggs, 70 Neb. 134; 96 N. W. 1010 547
Keith County v. Ogalalla Power & Irrigation Co., 64 Neb. 35; 89 N. W.
    375 456
Ketelman v. Chicago Brush Co., 65 Neb. 429; 91 N. W. 282 477
Kingman & Co. v. Davis, 63 Neb. 578; 88 N. W. 777 450
Kitchen Bros. Hotel Co. v. Philbin, 2 Neb. Unof. 340; 96 N. W. 487 .. 599
Knight v. Denman, 64 Neb. 814; 90 N. W. 863 466
Knights of the Maccabees of the World v. Nitsch, 69 Neb. 372; 95 N. W.
    626 533
Kummer v. Dubuque Turbine and Roller Mills Co., 4 Neb. Unof. 347;
    93 N. W. 938 667

Langan v. Parkhurst, 1 Neb. Unof. 804; 96 N. W. 63 585
Larson v. First National Bank of Pender, 66 Neb. 595; 92 N. W. 729 495
Leavitt v. S. D. Mercer Co., 64 Neb. 31; 89 N. W. 426 455
Leigh v. Green, 64 Neb. 533; 90 N. W. 255; 101 Am. St. Rep. 592 465
Levy v. Hinz, 3 Neb. Unof. 11; 90 N. W. 640 628
Lincoln, City of, v. Morrison, 64 Neb. 822; 90 N. W. 905, 57 L. R. A.
    885 467
Lincoln, City of, v. Sager, 2 Neb. Unof. 598; 89 N. W. 617 616
Livingston v. Moore, 2 Neb. Unof. 498; 89 N. W. 289 610

ITEM
NO.

Lundgren *v.* Kerkow, 1 Neb. Unof. 66; 95 N. W. 501 552
Luzon Sugar Refining Co. Lt., American and British Claims Arbitration,
Report of F. K. Nielson, p. 586 693
Lydick *v.* Chaney, 64 Neb. 288; 89 N. W. 801 460

McCook Irrigation & Water Power Co. *v.* Crews, 70 Neb. 109; 96 N. W.
996 544
McCormick Harvesting Machine Co. *v.* Hiatt, 4 Neb. Unof. 587; 95
N. W. 627 677
McKee *v.* McKee, 2 Neb. Unof. 322; 96 N. W. 489 597
McLean *v.* McCormick, 4 Neb. Unof. 187; 93 N. W. 697 661
Marsh *v.* State, 2 Neb. Unof. 372; 96 N. W. 520 602
Meng *v.* Coffee, 67 Neb. 500; 93 N. W. 713; 60 L. R. A. 910; 108 Am.
St. Rep. 697 506
Mercantile Co-operative Bank *v.* Schaaf, 2 Neb. Unof. 703; 89 N. W.
990 621
Merrill *v.* Garver, 4 Neb. Unof. 830; 96 N. W. 619 681
Merrill *v.* Wright, 65 Neb. 794; 91 N. W. 697; 101 Am. St. Rep. 645 483
Michigan Mutual Life Ins. Co. *v.* Klatt, 2 Neb. Unof. 872; 92 N. W. 325 627
Miller *v.* Fitzgerald Dry Goods Co., 62 Neb. 270; 86 N. W. 1078 435
Milner *v.* Harris, 1 Neb. Unof. 584; 95 N. W. 682 574
Mitchell *v.* County of Clay, 69 Neb. 779; 96 N. W. 673 540
Modern Woodmen of America *v.* Lane, 62 Neb. 89; 86 N. W. 943 .. 433
Moores *v.* Jones, 4 Neb. Unof. 319; 93 N. W. 1016 665
Morton *v.* Western Seed & Irrigation Co., 2 Neb. Unof. 131; 96 N. W.
183 590
Murphy *v.* City of Omaha, 1 Neb. Unof. 488; 95 N. W. 680 568
Murray *v.* Allerton, 3 Neb. Unof. 291; 91 N. W. 518 641
Murray *v.* Burd, 65 Neb. 427; 91 N. W. 278 476
Murray *v.* City of Omaha, 66 Neb. 279; 92 N. W. 299; 103 Am. St.
Rep. 702 490

Nebraska Loan & Trust Co. *v.* Corning, 4 Neb. Unof. 364; 94 N. W.
1135 669
Nebraska Loan & Trust Co. *v.* Haskell, 4 Neb. Unof. 330; 93 N. W.
1045 666
Nebraska Shirt Co. *v.* Horton, 3 Neb. Unof. 888; 93 N. W. 225 657
Newbro *v.* Undeland, 69 Neb. 821; 96 N. W. 635 543
Northern Assurance Co. of England *v.* Borgelt, 67 Neb. 282; 93 N. W.
226 505
Northwestern Mutual Life Ins. Co. *v.* Marshall, 1 Neb. Unof. 36; 95
N. W. 357 551
Nothdurft *v.* City of Lincoln, 66 Neb. 430; 92 N. W. 628 491

Oldig *v.* Fisk, 1 Neb. Unof. 124; 95 N. W. 492 554
Omaha Brewing Association *v.* Tillenburg, 2 Neb. Unof. 277; 96 N. W.
107 596
Omaha Loan & Trust Co. *v.* Walenz, 2 Neb. Unof. 806; 90 N. W. 222 625

ITEM
NO.

J. Parsons, American and British Claims Arbitration, Report of F. K.
Nielson, p. 587 694
Parsons Band Cutter & Self-Feeder Co. *v.* Gadeke, 1 Neb. Unof. 605;
95 N. W. 850 577
Payne *v.* Pettibone & Nixon, 1 Neb. Unof. 789; 96 N. W. 117 582
Penney *v.* Bryant, 70 Neb. 127; 96 N. W. 1033 545
People's Building, Loan & Savings Association of Geneva, N. Y., *v.*
Backus, 2 Neb. Unof. 463; 89 N. W. 315 608
People's Building, Loan & Savings Association of Geneva, N. Y., *v.*
Carricker, 2 Neb. Unof. 465; 89 N. W. 316 609
People's Building, Loan & Savings Association of Geneva, N. Y., *v.*
Palmer, 2 Neb. Unof. 460; 89 N. W. 316 606
People's Building, Loan & Savings Association of Geneva, N. Y., *v.*
Welton, 2 Neb. Unof. 462; 89 N. W. 317 607
Peterson *v.* Mannix, 2 Neb. Unof. 795; 90 N. W. 210 624
Philadelphia Mortgage & Trust Co. *v.* City of Omaha, 65 Neb. 93;
90 N. W. 1005; 57 L. R. A. 150 470
Phoenix Ins. Co. of Hartford, Conn., *v.* Zlotky, 66 Neb. 584; 92 N. W.
736 494
Poessnecker *v.* Entenmann, 64 Neb. 409; 89 N. W. 1033 461
Pope *v.* Kingman & Co., 2 Neb. Unof. 184; 96 N. W. 519 593
Pratt *v.* Galloway, 1 Neb. Unof. 172; 95 N. W. 329 555
President and Directors of the Ins. Co. of North America *v.* Parker,
64 Neb. 411; 89 N. W. 1040 462

Randall *v.* Phelps County Mutual Hail Ins. Association, 2 Neb. Unof.
530; 89 N. W. 398 612
Rawlings *v.* Anheuser-Busch Brewing Association, 1 Neb. Unof. 555;
95 N. W. 792 573
Reed *v.* Hopkins, 3 Neb. Unof. 308; 91 N. W. 1126 642
Reiss *v.* Argubright, 3 Neb. Unof. 756; 92 N. W. 988 654
Reiss *v.* Argubright, 3 Neb. Unof. 816; 92 N. W. 985 656
William Rhea, *in re*, 64 Neb. Appendix A 885; 97 N. W. 1119 469
Rhea *v.* Brown, 4 Neb. Unof. 461; 94 N. W. 716 674
Ribble *v.* Furmin, 69 Neb. 38; 94 N. W. 967 525
Ritter *v.* Myers, 3 Neb. Unof. 684; 92 N. W. 638 651
Roblee *v.* Union Stock Yards National Bank, 69 Neb. 180; 95 N. W. 61 527
Rouss *v.* Goldgraber, 3 Neb. Unof. 424; 91 N. W. 712 645

Sanely *v.* Crapenhoft, 1 Neb. Unof. 8; 95 N. W. 352 550
The Sarah B. Putnam, American and British Claims Arbitration, Re-
port of F. K. Nielson, p. 568 687
Schmuck *v.* Hill, 2 Neb. Unof. 79; 96 N. W. 158 588
School District No. 80 of Nemaha County *v.* Burress, 2 Neb. Unof.
554; 89 N. W. 609 614
Schumacher *v.* Crane-Churchill Co., 66 Neb. 440; 92 N. W. 609 492
Schrandt *v.* Young, 62 Neb. 254; 86 N. W. 1085 434
Sharp *v.* Call, 3 Neb. Unof. 64; 90 N. W. 765 631

ITEM
NO.

Shelby v. Creighton, 2 Neb. Unof. 264; 96 N. W. 382 595
Shuster v. Shuster, 3 Neb. Unof. 610; 92 N. W. 203 649
Smith v. County of Clay, 4 Neb. Unof. 872; 96 N. W. 1002 684
Smith v. Thompson, 67 Neb. 527; 93 N. W. 678 508
Solt v. Anderson, 67 Neb. 103; 93 N. W. 205 500
Sorenson v. Sorenson, 68 Neb. 483; 94 N. W. 540 519
South Omaha, City of, v. Fennell, 4 Neb. Unof. 427; 94 N. W. 632 .. 671
South Omaha, City of, v. Wrzesinski, 66 Neb. 790; 92 N. W. 1045 .. 488
Spence v. Apley, 4 Neb. Unof. 358; 94 N. W. 109 668
State v. Bloomfield State Bank, 1 Neb. Unof. 526; 95 N. W. 791 571
State v. German Savings Bank of Omaha, 65 Neb. 416; 91 N. W. 414 474
State v. Paxton, 65 Neb. 110; 90 N. W. 983 473
State ex rel. Baker v. Baxter, 4 Neb. Unof. 869; 96 N. W. 647 683
State ex rel. the Chadron Loan & Building Association v. Westover, 2
    Neb. Unof. 768; 89 N. W. 1002 623
State ex rel. Cobb v. Fawcett, 64 Neb. 496; 90 N. W. 250 464
State ex rel. Reiss v. Holmes, 3 Neb. Unof. 183; 91 N. W. 175 636
Staunchfield v. Jeutter, 4 Neb. Unof. 847; 96 N. W. 642 682
Steidl v. State, 63 Neb. 695; 88 N. W. 853 452
Steinkamp v. Gaebel, 1 Neb. Unof. 480; 95 N. W. 684 567
Stewart v. Rosengren, 66 Neb. 445; 92 N. W. 586 493
Stitzer v. Whittaker, 3 Neb. Unof. 414; 91 N. W. 713 644
Storey v. Kerr, 2 Neb. Unof. 568; 89 N. W. 601 615
Strowbridge v. Miller, 4 Neb. Unof. 449; 94 N. W. 825 673
Stuart v. Burcham, 62 Neb. 84; 86 N. W. 898; 89 Am. St. Rep. 739 .. 432
Stull v. Stull, 1 Neb. Unof. 389; 96 N. W. 196 561
Sturdevant Bros. and Co. v. Farmers & Merchants Bank of Rushville,
    62 Neb. 472; 87 N. W. 156 438

Taylor v. Reis, 2 Neb. Unof. 533; 89 N. W. 374 613
The Thomas F. Bayard, American and British Claims Arbitration, Re-
    port of F. K. Nielson, p. 573 689
Thomsen, in the Matter of, 1 Neb. Unof. 751; 95 N. W. 805 580
Thurman v. City of Omaha, 64 Neb. 490; 90 N. W. 253 463
Tidball v. Chalburg Bros., 67 Neb. 524; 93 N. W. 679 507
Topping v. Jeanette, 64 Neb. 834; 90 N. W. 911 468

Ulrich v. McConaughey, 63 Neb. 10; 88 N. W. 150 441
Union Pacific R. R. Co. v. Stanwood, 71 Neb. 150; 98 N. W. 656 .. 549
Union Pacific R. R. Co. v. Stanwood, 3 Neb. Unof. 123 633
Union State Bank v. Hutton, 1 Neb. Unof. 795; 95 N. W. 1061 586
Union Stock Yard National Bank v. Haskell, 2 Neb. Unof. 839; 90
    N. W. 233 626
United Air Lines Transport Corp. Hearing. Civil Aeronautics Author-
    ity. Docket No. 270 697
United States National Bank v. Hanson, 1 Neb. Unof. 87; 95 N. W.
    364 553
Ure v. Bunn, 3 Neb. Unof. 61; 90 N. W. 904 630

ITEM
NO.

Van Every *v.* Sanders, 69 Neb. 509; 95 N. W. 870 534
Village of Atkinson *v.* Fisher, 4 Neb. Unof. 21; 93 N. W. 211 658
Village of Holstein *v.* Klein, 4 Neb. Unof. 33; 93 N. W. 214 659
Voorheis, Miller & Co. *v.* Leisure, 1 Neb. Unof. 601; 95 N. W. 676 576

Walsh *v.* Walsh, 1 Neb. Unof. 719; 95 N. W. 1024 579
Walsh *v.* Walsh, 4 Neb. Unof. 683; 95 N. W. 1025 678
Warren *v.* Wales, 1 Neb. Unof. 446; 95 N. W. 610 564
Webster *v.* Citizens Bank of Omaha, 2 Neb. Unof. 353; 96 N. W. 118 600
Weilage *v.* Abbott, 3 Neb. Unof. 157; 90 N. W. 1128 635
Welch *v.* Tippery, 66 Neb. 604; 92 N. W. 582 497
Western Mattress Co. *v.* Potter, 1 Neb. Unof. 631; 95 N. W. 841 578
Weston *v.* Herdmann, 64 Neb. 24; 89 N. W. 384 454
Wiley *v.* Wiley, 1 Neb. Unof. 350; 95 N. W. 702 560
William Webster, American and British Claims Arbitration, Report of
  F. K. Nielson, p. 537 695
Williams *v.* Fuller, 68 Neb. 354, 97 N. W. 246 516
Williams *v.* Miles, 68 Neb. 463; 94 N. W. 705; 62 L. R. A. 383; 110
  Am. St. Rep. 431; 68 Neb. 479, 96 N. W. 151 517
Williams *v.* Turner, 63 Neb. 575; 88 N. W. 668 449
Winterringer *v.* Warder, Bushnell & Glessner Co., 1 Neb. Unof. 414;
  95 N. W. 619 562
Wright *v.* Patrick, 2 Neb. Unof. 695; 89 N. W. 746 620

Youngson *v.* Bond, 69 Neb. 356; 95 N. W. 700 529

The Zafiro, American and British Claims Arbitration, Report of F. K.
  Nielson, p. 578 692

INDEX

INDEX

(Numbers given are item numbers)

Abdication of Reason, 761
Absolutism: Administrative, 240; The Humanities or, 409; Judicial Councils vs., 241; The Recrudescence of, 236; The Revival of, 410
Acacia, The, 731, 732
Accession, Literary Application of Doctrine, 267
Actions on Penal Statutes, 2
Actorum Academiae Universalis Iurisprudentiae Comparativae, 163, 194, 195
Actual, The Ideal and the, in Law, 193
Addresses: at Annual Dinner of the American Bar Association, 366; at Dinner of Associated Harvard Clubs, 346; at Dinner to Mr. Justice Stone, 344; at Dinner to the American Bar Association in the Middle Temple Hall, 332; Dedicatory, 127; of Acceptance of a Portrait of James Brown Scott, 371; of Welcome to the Members of the American Association of Law Libraries, 399; on the Occasion of the Visit of the Bars from Across the Sea, 367; opening the Campaign to Raise Funds for the Harvard Law School, 347; upon the Occasion of the Acceptance of a Portrait of Mr. Justice Oliver Wendell Holmes, 365. [*See also titles of individual addresses.*]
Administration and Procedure, German Movement for Reform in, 27
Administration, United States Court of Appeals for, Statement on, 405
Administration of Justice: Causes of Popular Dissatisfaction with, 20; in the Modern City, 57; Preliminary Report on Efficiency in the, 424; Punitive, Inherent and Acquired Difficulties in, 30
Administrative Absolutism, 240
Administrative Application of Legal Standards, 96
Administrative Justice, Growth of, 117
Administrative Law: General Summary, 248; Modern, 251; Report of the Special Committee on, 430
Administrative Reorganization in the Harvard Law School and Aims in Legal Education, 357
Advocate (Philippine), The, 404
Agropyron, Confused Species of, 724
Aims in Legal Education, 357
Algae, Fungi and Lichens, 699
Allegheny County Bar Association. Publications, 51
Allgemeine Botanische Zeitschrift, 716
America: Criminal Justice in, 172; Criminal Justice in Nineteenth-Century, 146; Influence of Civil Law in, 1, 233; Influence of French Law in, 31; Judicial Office in, 167; Philosophy of Law in, 59
American Academy of Arts and Sciences. Proceedings, 402, 413
American and British Claims Arbitration. [*See individual claims in Table of Cases.*]
American and English Legal Ideals, 332
American Appellate Court, Work of the, 147

(Numbers given are item numbers)

American Association of Law Libraries, Address of Welcome to, 399
American Attitude toward the Trial Judge, 155
American Bar Association — The Detroit Meeting, 277
American Bar Association. Comparative Law Bureau. Bulletin, 27
American Bar Association Journal, 79, 82, 124, 132, 134, 139, 140, 147, 149,
    162, 170, 171, 185, 197, 205, 212, 219, 222, 226, 238, 239, 242, 332, 348,
    358, A 53, A 58, A 59
American Bar Association. Publications. Law Series I, 192; Law Series II,
    210
American Bar Association Report, 20, 24, 50, 96, 124, 139, 147, 162, 212,
    222, 366, 419–423, 429, 430
American City: Criminal Justice in the, 106; Criminal Justice in the — a
    Summary, 110
American Common Law, Comparative Law in the Formation of, 163
American Constitution in the Light of Today, 203
American Historical Review, A 53
American Institute of Criminal Law and Criminology, 278
American Institute of Mining and Metallurgical Engineers. Transactions, 217
American Journal of International Law, 126
American Journal of Psychiatry, 161
American Journal of Sociology, 49, 58, 84
American Judicature Society. Bulletin, 56
American Judicial Decision, Ideal Element in, 180
American Juristic Thinking in the Twentieth Century, 246
American Law: Comparative Law in the Formation of, 163; Crisis in, 136;
    Formative Era of, 234; Hundred Years of, 230; Introduction to, 97;
    Législation dans la Période de Formation du Droit Américain, 235; Place
    of Judge Story in Making of, 62; Prospect for, 225; Unsettled Problems
    in, 150
American Law and Procedure, 45
American Law Institute, 368
American Law Institute. Proceedings, 120; Publication, 120
American Law Register, 22
American Law Review, 20, 34, 42, 62, 151
American Law School Curriculum, Place of Comparative Law in, 200
American Law School Review, 50, 121, 148, 197, 199, 213
American Lawyer, 20
American Lawyer, Task of, 137
American Legal History, New Possibilities of Old Materials of, 202
American Legal News, 33, 85
American Life, Place of Higher Learning in, 772
American Magazine, A 37
American Microscopical Society. Transactions, 729
American Naturalist, 698–705, 708, 709, 712, 715, 716, 718, 721, A 45
American Political Science Association. Proceedings, 30, 63
American Political Science Review, 53, 271, A 51–A 53, A 56
American Prison Association. Proceedings, 102
American Psychiatric Association, Address before, 161
American Review of Reviews, A 32

(Numbers given are item numbers)

American Society of International Law. Proceedings, 250
American Sociological Society. Papers and Proceedings, 58, 108
American University, Prospects of the, 756
Ames, James Barr, 90
Amos, Sir Maurice Sheldon, K.C., A 12
Anachronisms in Law, 99
Analogies from History, 768
Analytical Jurisprudence: 1914–1927, the Progress of the Law, 154; Outlines of Lectures on Jurisprudence Chiefly from the Analytical Standpoint, 13
Anderson, Nels (Book review), A 56
Annals, 83, 159
Annual Review of Legal Education, 221
Anonymous, A 22–A 26, A 28, A 30–A 32, A 34, A 38, A 41, A 43
Anson, William Reynell, 370
Arbitration, American and British Claims. [*See separate cases in Table of Cases.*]
Archiv für Rechts- und Wirtschaftsphilosophie, 59, A 1, A 46, A 47
Arkansas, Bar Association of. Proceedings, 89
Articles in Foreign Languages:
    French: La Législation dans la Période de Formation du Droit Américain, 235
    German: Soziologische Jurisprudenz in Amerika, 135
    Italian: La Filosofia nel Diritto Costituzionale Americano, 109
Association of American Law Schools, 50, 121, 148, 166, 201, 202, 220; Handbook, 199
Association of American Universities. Journal of 33d Annual Conference, 181
Association of Grand Jurors, 201
Association of the Bar of the City of New York: Address at, 193; Lectures on Legal Topics, 113; unpublished addresses, 190
Atmosphere of Study of Law and Institute of Criminal Law of the Harvard Law School, 363
Auld, F. C. (Book review), A 58
Authorities, Citation of, 700

Baldwin, S. E. (Book review), A 51, A 53
Bar: Examinations in Retrospect and Prospect, 213; Training for the, 192, Training for the, in the United States, 412
Bar Briefs (North Dakota), 151
Bar Bulletin (Boston), The, 240, 367, 406
Bar Examiner, 192, 213
Baralt, José López (Translator), 43
Barnwell Bulletin, The, 773
Bartholdy, A. Mendelssohn, 35
Bassett, J. C. (Book review), A 59
Better Practitioners Needed, 378
Bibliography: Flora of Nebraska, 710; Modern Juristic Thought and Its Significance for America, 81; Organization of Courts, 83; Procedural Reform, Including Organization of Courts, 83
Bibliotheca Visseriana Dissertationvm Ivs Internationale Illvstrantivm, 119

(Numbers given are item numbers)

Bigelow Association of Masters of Law. Address before, 167
Bill of Rights, Virginia, Sesquicentennial of, 138
Black, F. R. (Book review), A 56
Blackard, W. R. (Book review), A 59
Bond Club of New Jersey. Address before, 410, 411
Book Reviews (By Pound):

    Brown, Underlying Principles of Modern Legislation. 291
    Buckland, Elementary Principles of the Roman Private Law. 297
    Buckland, Text Book of Roman Law from Augustus to Justinian. 317
    Carpenter, Judicial Tenure in the United States. 310
    Carter, Law; Its Origin, Growth and Function. 276
    Clark, Handbook of the Law of Code Pleading. 354
    Cook, Cases and Other Authorities on Equity, vol. 1. 329
    Del Vecchio, Il Concetto della Natura e il Principio del Diritto. 274
    Goadby, Introduction to the Study of Law. 288
    Goodhart, Precedent in English and Continental Law. 395
    Goudy, Trichotomy in Roman Law. 283
    Halsbury, Laws of England, vol. 2. 262
    Jenks, New Jurisprudence. 388
    Jung, Das Problem des Natürlichen Rechts. 294
    Kocourek and Wigmore, Evolution of Law. 301
    Korkunov, General Theory of Law. 279
    Kuntze, Revisio Generum Plantarum Vascularium omnium et Cellularium multarum secundum Leges Nomenclaturae Internationales cum Enumeratione Plantarum in Itinere Mundi Collectarum — Mit Erlaeuterungen. 705
    MacMillan, Observations on the Distribution of Plants along Shore at Lake of the Woods. 721
    Mikell, Cases on Criminal Law. 273
    Oliver and Williams, Willis and Oliver's Roman Law Examination Guide for Bar and University (Questions and Answers), 3rd ed. 284
    Oppenheimer, Rationale of Punishment. 296
    Osborn, Problem of Proof. 327
    Parmelee, Principles of Anthropology and Sociology in Their Relation to Criminal Procedure. 271
    Pollock, For My Grandson; Remembrances of an Ancient Victorian, 389
    Roguin, Science Juridique Pure. 331
    Salvioli, Storia del Diritto Italiano. 320
    Swain, Conservation of Water by Storage. 299
    Taylor, Science of Jurisprudence. 263
    Vinogradoff, Outlines of Historical Jurisprudence, vol. 1. 319
    Walton, Historical Introduction to the Roman Law. 290
    Wiel, Water Rights in the Western States. 289
    Wigmore, A Pocket Code of the Rules of Evidence on Trials at Law. 280
    Williston, Law Governing Sales of Goods at Common Law and under the Uniform Sales Act. 275
    Willoughby, Distinctions and Anomalies Arising out of the Equitable Doctrine of the Legal Estate. 293

(Numbers given are item numbers)

Winfield, History of Conspiracy and Abuse of Legal Procedure. 324
Works, Juridical Reform. 312
Wright, American Interpretations of Natural Law. 383
Wu, Art of Law and Other Essays, Juridical and Literary. 401
Wyman, Special Law Governing Public Service Corporations and All
    Others Engaged in Public Employment. 285
Booklist, A 51, A 56
Books, A 56, A 59
Borchard, E. M. (Book review), A 51
Boston Central Labor Union, Outline of a Course at, 97
Boston Globe, 333
Boston Herald, 336, 341, 757, 760
Boston Post, 325, 343
Boston Transcript, 65, 341, A 56, A 59
Boston University. Commencement Address, 769
Boston University Law Review, 167, A 14, A 59, A 61
Bostonia, 769
Botanical Gazette, 714, 719, 723, 724, A 22, A 23, A 44, A 45
Botanical Latin, 704
Botanical Survey of Nebraska, 706, 707, 710, 717, 727, 728; Progress of the,
    726
Botany, Brief Outline of the History of, 730
Bowdoin College, Institute of Social Science. Address, 763
Bowman, H. M. (Book review), A 59
Bradley, Phillips (Book review), A 51
Brooklyn Law School, St. Lawrence University. Dedicatory Address, 165
Brown University. Colver Lectures, 172
Brown University Papers, 772
Bryn Mawr Alumnae Bulletin, 767
Bryn Mawr College. Commencement Address, 767
Buck, W. H. (Book review), A 53
Builder, The, 732, 733, 735–738, 741–746
Bulletin de la Société de Législation Comparée, 31
Bureau of Personnel Administration. Publications, 360
Business Management, Fundamental Objectives of, — Justice, 360

C. C. H. Legal Periodical Digest, 20, 56, 151–154, 159, 162, 166, 170, 171,
    176, 178, 180, 186, 191, 193–197, 199–201, 206, 212, 218, 220, 223, 224,
    226, 227, 231–233, 237, 239, 244, 252
Calderon, Joseph (Book review), A 59
California Law Review, A 29, A 51–A 54
California, State Bar of: Alexander F. Morrison Foundation Lecture, 171;
    Proceedings, 86–88, 171
California, University of, Chronicle, 766
Call for a Realist Jurisprudence, 178
Callen, Charles Lane, A 37
Cambridge Historical Society. Publications, 62
Cambridge Law Journal, 324, A 53, A 54
Cambridge, University of, Trinity College. Lectures, 118

(Numbers given are item numbers)

Canadian Bar Review, 113, A 54, A 57, A 58
Canons of Procedural Reform, 139
Cardozo, Benjamin N. (Book review), A 53
Carr, C. T. (Book review), A 53
Case and Comment, 47, 113, 116, 138, A 18, A 33, A 55
Case Books:
    Cases on Equitable Protection of Personality and of Social and Political Relations, 75
    Cases on Equitable Relief against Defamation and Injuries to Personality, 75
    Cases on Equitable Relief against Defamation and Other Injuries by Writing or Speaking, 75
    Cases on Practice; Select Cases and Other Authorities on Procedure in Civil Causes with References to the Code and Decisions of Nebraska, vol. 1, 15
    Selection of Cases on the Law of Torts, 90
Cassidy, Lewis C., A 7
Catholic University of America, School of Law. Jubilee Law Lectures, 247
Catholic World, A 51
Central Law Journal, 2, 5, 38, 44, 48, 51, 53, 72, 282, 292
Chafee, Zechariah, Jr. (Book review), A 51
Chattanooga News, 771
Chattanooga Times, 771
Chattanooga, University of: Address, 771; Institute of Justice, 186
Chicago Bar Association, 137, 150, 226
Chicago Law Club, 35
Chicago Legal News, 34, 36, 37
Chicago, University of, Law Review, 223
Chicago, University of, Magazine, 37
Child Labor, Letter on, 350
Child Offender in the Federal System of Justice, Report on, 428
China Weekly Review, A 40
Christian Code, Law and the, 144
Christian Register, 769
Christian Science Monitor, 362
Church in Legal History, 247
Cincinnati, University of, Law Review, 196, 253
Citation of Authorities, 700
Citizenship, Place of the University in Training for, 754
Civil Law: Influence of, in America, 1, 233; Readings in Roman Law and the Civil Law and Modern Codes as Developments Thereof, 21
Civil Procedure, Revision of Code of, in Kansas, 270
Civilization, Relation of Masonry to, 733
Civilization, University and, 755
Classification of Law: Classification of Law, 121, 122; Preliminary Report on, 120
Cleveland Bar Association, Institute of. Lectures, 198
Code of Civil Procedure, The Revision of the, in Kansas, 270
Code Pleading: Outline and Practical Exercise, 16

(Numbers given are item numbers)

Codes, Modern, as Developments of Roman Law and the Civil Law. Readings, 21

Codification: Codification, 69; Codification of the Law of Nations, 164

Cohen, Morris Raphael, A 13, A 20, A 27; Book Review, A 51, A 52, A 54

College of the City of New York Chapter of Phi Beta Kappa, 377

Colorado Bar Association. Report, 61

Columbia Law Review, 11, 18, 23, 29, 60, 102, 279, A 46, A 51–A 54, A 57, A 61

Commerce: and Legal Progress, 85; Interstate, under the Constitution, 143

Commercial Law Journal, 170

Commercial Law League of America. Bulletin, 85

Commercial Law, Uniformity of, on American Continent, 33

Common Law: and Legislation, 25; the Common Law, 129, 182, 295; Comparative Law in the Formation of American, 163; Democracy and the, 47; Future of the, 160, 196; History and System of the, 249; History and System of the, Readings on, 17; Law School and the, 103; Masonic — Part I, 744; Masonic — Part II, 745; Our Lady, the, 86; Outline of a Course on the History and System of the, 97; Pioneers and the, 100; Procedure in, 87; Puritanism and the, 42; Response by Professor Pound, 295; Socialization of the, 65; Spirit of the, 19, 107; Unification through the, 205; What is the, 223, A 41

Commonweal, A 59

Comparative Law: in the Formation of American Common Law, 163; Place of, in the American Law School Curriculum, 200; Revival of, 176; What May We Expect from, 219

Conference on Criminal Law and Criminology, 281

Conference on Legal and Social Philosophy. Proceedings, 59

Congreso Científico (1° Pan Americano). Trabajos, 33

Congress, Supreme Court or Supreme, 362

Congressional Record, 138, 364

Connor, J. T. (Book review), A 61

Consideration in Equity, 95

Constitution: American, in the Light of Today, 203; in This Day and in Respect to Social and Legislative Trends, 214; Interstate Commerce under the, 143; Its Development, Adaptability and Future, 226; Recurring Attacks upon the, 384

Constitutional Law: Aspects of the Oil Problem, 217; Filosofia nel Diritto Costituzionale Americano, 109

Constructive Service, Note on, 260

Contemporary Juristic Theory, 255

Contract: Legal Doctrine and History, 183; Liberty of, 32; Note on, 259

Cook, W. W. (Book review), A 51

Cooperation in Enforcement of Law, 171

Corbin, A. L. (Book review), A 51

Corbin, J. (Book review), A 51, A 52, A 54

Cornell Law Quarterly, 237, 373, A 51, A 53, A 59

Cornil, Paul (Translator), 141

Corporations: Uniformity of Laws Governing, in the American Republics, 77; Visitatorial Jurisdiction over, in Equity, 218

(Numbers given are item numbers)

Correspondence Circle Bulletin, 740

Court Organization: Principles and Outline of Modern Unified, 254; Reform in, 94

Courts: and Legislation, 53; Bibliography of Procedural Reform, Including Organization of, 83; Federal, Law and Equity in, 44; Federal, Progress Report on the Study of, 428; New Deal in the, 204; Organization of, 56, 256, 425; Poor Man, Rich Man in, 325; Proposed Act in Relation to, 264; Reforming Procedure by Rules of, 292; Regulating Procedural Details by Rules of, 149; Rule-Making Power of the, 140; Social Problems and, 49; Vesting in, Power to Make Rules Relating to Pleading and Practice, 79; Work of American Appellate, 147

Cowles, Henry C. (Book review), A 44, A 45

Crime: and the Foreign Born, Report on, 428; and the Law, 179; Legal Interrogation of Persons Accused or Suspected of, 201; on the Causes of, Report, 428; on the Cost of, Report, 428

Crime Problem, Harvard Dean Warns of Hasty Action on, 336

"Crime Wave"; Dean Pound, Harvard Law School, Discusses, 343

Criminal Justice: Improvement of, in the United States, 394; in America, 172; in Nineteenth-Century America, 146; in the American City, 106; in the American City — a Summary, 110; Problem of, 141; What Can Law Schools Do for, 148; Why It Fails, 345

Criminal Law: Future of, 102; Institute of, Atmosphere of Study of Law and, 363; Projet for a Professorship of, 112; Toward a Better, 212

Criminal Law and Criminology: Address at the First National Conference on, 281; American Institute of, 278

Criminal Procedure: Needed Reforms in, 210; on Criminal Procedure, Report, 428; Practical Advantages of Rules of Court for, 242

Criminal Statistics, Report on, 428

Criminology: Criminological Research, Public Provision for, 265

Crisis in American Law, 136

Cult of the Irrational, 764

Culture and Population, 759

Current Legal Thought, 91, 206, 218, 227, 252

Curriculum: and the Tasks of a Law School, 376; Comparative Law in the American Law School, 200; of the Harvard Law School, 381, 393

Cyclopedia of American Government, 69

Dahl, Frantz, 413

Dakota Law Review, 151, 155, A 56

Dartmouth Alumni Lectures. Gurnsey Center Moore Foundation, 107

Dean's Reports (See Harvard Law School: Annual Report of the Dean)

Decadence of Equity, 11

Defamation: and Injuries to Personality, Equitable Relief against, 80; and Injuries to Personality, Equitable Relief against, Cases on, 75; and Other Injuries by Writing or Speaking, Cases on Equitable Relief against, 75

Delay and Unnecessary Cost in Litigation, Report of the Special Committee to Suggest Remedies and Formulate Proposed Laws to Prevent, 419–423

Democracy and the Common Law, 47

Department of Justice, Report upon Illegal Practices of, 427

(Numbers given are item numbers)
Deportation Laws of the United States, Report on the Enforcement of, 428
De Sloovere, F. J. (Book review), A 54
Deutsches Recht, A 38
Dewey, John (Book review), A 54
Dial, A 51
Dicta, 187
Difficulties, Inherent and Acquired, in the Administration of Punitive Justice, 30
Distinguished Achievement Medal, Remarks on Receiving, 751
District and County Reports, 211
Dobie, A. M. (Book review), A 54
Doctrines, End of Law as Developed in Legal Rules and, 64
Docket, The, 150
Dodd, W. F. (Book review), A 53, A 55
Dogs and the Law, 3
Domestic Relations, Individual Interests in the, 78
Duffus, R. L. (Book review), A 56
Duke University. Centennial Celebration Lectures, 246

Economic Interpretation and the Law of Torts, 252
Economic Interpretations of Jurisprudence, Political and, 63
Economic Problems of the Law, Social and, 159
Education: Abdication of Reason, 761; and the Legal Order, 184; Culture and Population, 759; Fight for Intellectual Freedom, 409; Information and Learning, 767; Masonry in its Relation to, 735; Organized, Ousting Organized Religion, 760; Place of Higher Learning in American Life, 772; Place of the University in Training for Citizenship, 754; Prospects of the American University, 756; Rejection of Liberalism, 766; Stresses Need of High Level of, 771; Task of, 770; What Can We Do through, 765; What We Can Do through, 765
Education Digest, 772
Ehrlich, Eugen, Appreciation of, 321
Eighteenth Amendment: Driving the Country to Repeal, 382; Enforcement of Prohibition Laws of the United States, Report on, 428; Repeal of the, 387
Emory University: Baccalaureate address, 765; Bulletin of, 765
Encyclopaedia Britannica, 322, 361
Encyclopaedia of Pleading and Practice, 418
Encyclopaedia of Social Sciences, 182, 183, 188, 189, 208, 368, 370, 385, 391
End of Law: as Developed in Juristic Thought, 66; as Developed in Legal Rules and Doctrines, 64; Twentieth Century Ideas as to the, 209
Endowment of Professorships in the Harvard Law School, 335
Enforcement of Law: Cooperation in, 171; Enforcement of Law, 28, 142; Reports of the National Commission on Law Observance and, 428
English Historical Review, A 53
English Legal Ideals, American and, 332
Entomophthoraceae of Nebraska, the Synchytria, Mucoraceae and, 713
Equitable Protection of Personality and of Social and Political Relations, Cases on, 75

(Numbers given are item numbers)

Equitable Relief: against Defamation and Injuries to Personality, 80; against Defamation and Injuries to Personality, Cases on, 75; against Defamation and Other Injuries by Writing or Speaking, Cases on, 75

Equity: Consideration in, 95; Decadence of, 11; Law and, in Federal Courts, 44; Maxims of, 105; On Certain Maxims of, 145; Progress of the Law, 1918–1919, 98; Recent Developments in the Law of, of Interest to Practicing Lawyers, 198; Visitatorial Jurisdiction over Corporations in, 218

Ernst, M. L. (Book review), A 57

Ethics, Professional, Proposed Codification (American Bar Association), 258

Etiquette of Justice, 40

Evans, Lawrence B., A 33

Every Man an Officer, 407

Evidence, Professor Thayer on the Law of, 8

Evil, a Note upon Legal Entanglement as a Division of, 323

Executive Justice, 22

Exsiccati, the Treatment of, in the Herbarium, 703

Farnum, George R., A 14

Fashions in Juristic Thinking, 228

Fashions in Thinking, 773

Federal Bar Association, Washington, D. C., Address, 364

Federal Courts, Law and Equity in, 44

Federal Courts, Progress Report on the Study of, 428

Federal Practice, Senator Walsh on Rule-making Power on the Law Side of, 348

Feudal Principle in Modern Law, 68

Feudal System, New, 170

Feudalism, New, 170

Finding Law, Making Law and, 72

Flora, Additions to the Reported, 727

Flora of Nebraska, 713

Flora of Nebraska, Bibliography of the, 710

Flora of the Sand Hill Region of Sheridan and Cherry Counties, 707

Florida Bar Association. Proceedings, 129

Florida, University of. Commencement address, 770

Fordham Law Review, 231, A 21

Foreign Born, Report on Crime and the, 428

Formative Era of American Law, 234; Législation dans la période de formation du droit américain, 235

Founding of the Harvard Law School, 414

Frank, Jerome, A 9, A 10

Frankfurter, Felix, 110, 425, 426, A 1, A 46, A 47

Freedom, the Fight for Intellectual, 409

Freemasonry: Lectures on the Philosophy of, 739; Transplantation of, to the United States, 731

French Law, Influence of, in America, 31

Fuller, L. L. (Book review), A 59

Fundamental Law in the Society of Today, 206

(Numbers given are item numbers)

Fungi: The Algae, and Lichens, 699; New Species, 728; of Nebraska, 717
Future: of Law, 227; of Legal Education, 101; of the Common Law, 160, 196; of the Criminal Law, 102

George Washington Law Review, 193
George Washington University Bulletin, 127
Georgetown Law Journal, A 54
Georgia Bar Association Report, 89
German Movement for Reform in Legal Administration and Procedure, 27
Ginsbourg, Anna, A 40
Goodhart, A. L. (Book review), A 54, A 59
Gould, Robert Freke, 738
Government: Balanced, 750; Revival of Personal, 89; Why Absolute Government Fails, 411
Gown, Wig and, 6
Graduate Instruction and Research with Especial Reference to the Harvard Law School, 353
Grand Lodge Bulletin, 750
Green Bag, 3, 19, 24, 28, 36, 38, 65, A 24
Grossman, William L., A 16
Grotius in the Science of Law, 126

Haines, C. G. (Book review), A 53
Haldane, Richard Burdon, 402
Hall, J. (Book review), A 56, A 59
Hardman, T. P. (Book review), A 51, A 52
Harper's Monthly Magazine, 136
Hart, James (Book review), A 52
Harvard Alumni Bulletin, 112, 125, 328, 346, 347, 365, 371, 754, A 25, A 26
Harvard Graduates Magazine, A 31
Harvard Law Review, 25, 43, 57, 64, 66, 71, 80, 91, 98, 104, 105, 113, 122, 154, 178, 180, 195, 218, 224, 252, 283–285, 288–291, 293, 294, 296–301, 310, 312, 317, 319, 320, 321, 327, 329, 331, 356, 383, 388, 389, 395, 401, A 1, A 11, A 39, A 46–A 54, A 56–A 59
Harvard Law School: Administrative Reorganization of, 357; Atmosphere of Study of Law of, 363; Curriculum of the, 381, 393; Dean's Annual Reports, 1915/16–1934/35, 304, 306, 309, 314, 316, 318, 326, 330, 335, 342, 349, 353, 357, 363, 372, 376, 381, 386, 393, 398; Endowment of Professorships in the, 335; Founding of the, 414; Graduate Instruction and Research with Especial Reference to the Harvard Law School, 353; Harvard Law School, 313; Harvard Legal Aid Bureau, 398; Institute of Criminal Law of, 363; Its History, Its Development, Its Needs, 337; Letter on, 328; One Hundred Years of, 304; Progress of Research in, 381; Some Considerations as to Legal Education in, 386; 1817–1929, 174
Harvard Law School Year Book, 174, 414
Harvard Legal Aid Bureau, 398
Harvard Teachers Record, 184
Hazeltine, H. D. (Book review), A 58
Herbarium Notes — an Alphabetical Arrangement, 698

(Numbers given are item numbers)

Hierarchy of Sources and Forms in Different Systems of Law, 194
Higher Learning in American Life, Place of, 772
Hilkey, C. J. (Book review), A 59
History: Our Times before the Tribunal of, 769; Some Analogies from, 768
History and System of the Common Law: History and System of the Common Law, 249; Outline of a Course in, 97; Readings on the, 17
History of Botany, Brief Outline of the, 730
Holdsworth, W. S. (Book review), A 58, A 59
Holdsworth Club of the University of Birmingham. Publications, 228
Holly, W. H. (Book review), A 56
Holmes', Judge, Contributions to the Science of Law, 104
Hough, C. M. (Book review), A 51
Howe, M. De W. (Book review), A 59
Huang, Ch'ü (Translator), 118
Hughes, Charles Evans — "A Great Lawyer," 358
Human Ear, an Addition to the Parasites of the, 729
Humanities or Absolutism, 409
Husik, I. (Book review), A 54
Huston, C. A. (Book review), A 50
Hyphomycetes, a Re-Arrangement of the North American, 720

Idea of Law in International Relations, 250
Ideal: Ideal and the Actual in Law — Forty Years After, 193; Ideal Element in American Judicial Decision, 180; Ideal Element in Law, 187; Ideals of Law, Comparison of, 195
Illegal Practices of the United States Department of Justice, Report upon, 427
Illinois Law Review, 26, 31, 35, 74, 83, 95, 137, 257–270, 272, 273, 275, 277, 278, 280, A 3, A 56, A 58, A 59
Illinois State Bar Association. Proceedings, 28, 36, 39
Indiana Conference on Social Work, Address before, 153
Indiana Law Journal, 153, A 55, A 56
Indiana University: Centennial Memorial Volume, 101; Commencement Address, 756
Indiana University Alumni Quarterly, 756
Indiana University Bulletin, 101
Individual Interests in the Domestic Relations, 78
Individual, Society and the, 753
Individualism and Development of a "Relational" Society, the End of, 377
Individualization of Justice, 173, 231
Information and Learning, 767
Institute of Criminal Law, 363
Institute of Justice, University of Chattanooga. Paper, 186
Instruction, Oral, to Juries, 272
Insurance, 418
Intellectual Freedom, Fight for, 409
Interests: Individual, in the Domestic Relations, 78; of Personality, 71; Theory of Social, 108
International Congress of Comparative Law, Report to, 194

(Numbers given are item numbers)

International Congress of Philosophy, Sixth. Proceedings, 157
International Journal of Ethics, 59, 68, 73, 82, A 53, A 54
International Law: Part of Philosophy in, 157; Philosophical Theory and, 119
International Relations, Idea of Law in, 250
Interpretation: Economic, and the Law of Torts, 252; of Legal History, 118;
  Political and Economic, of Jurisprudence, 63; Spurious, 23
Interrogation, Legal, of Persons Accused of Crime, 201
Interstate Commerce under the Constitution, 143
Introductions, Introductory Notes, Forewords, Prefaces:
  Ashcraft. How To Find the Law, vol. 1, 379
  Ballentine. Law Dictionary with Pronunciations, 369
  Cairns. Law and the Social Sciences, 396
  Calhoun and Delamere. Working Bibliography of Greek Law, 352
  De Sloovere. Cases on the Interpretation of Statutes, 374
  Ehrlich. Fundamental Principles of the Sociology of Law, 400
  Ewart. Waiver Distributed among the Departments Election, Estoppel,
    Contract, Release, 305
  Fowler. New Philosophies of Law, 298
  Gareis. Introduction to the Science of Law, 287
  Gay. Open Mind; Elmer Ernest Southard, 408
  Glueck, S. & E. T. Five Hundred Delinquent Women, 300
  Glueck, S. & E. T. Predictability in the Administration of Justice, 356
  Green. Inns of Court and Early English Drama, 375
  Matthews. Valuation of Property in the Roman Law, 315
  National Consumers' League. Supreme Court and Minimum Wage
    Legislation, 339
  National Law Library, 415
  Orfield. Criminal Appeals in America, 416
  Pollard. Mr. Justice Cardozo; a Liberal Mind in Action, 397
  Saleilles. Individualization of Punishment, 286
  Sayre. Selection of Cases on Criminal Law, 351
  Selected Essays on the Law of Torts, 334
  Shelton. Spirit of the Courts, 307
  Stevens. Magna Carta; A Pageant, 162
  Wenger. Institutes of the Roman Law of Civil Procedure, 417
  Winfield. Chief Sources of English Legal History, 338
  Young. Social Treatment in Probation and Delinquency, 403
Investment Bankers Association of America, Address before, 232
Iowa Law Bulletin, A 51
Iowa Law Review, 148, 166, A 17, A 56, A 57, A 59
Iowa State Bar Association. Proceedings, 70, 187, 295, 380
Irish Law Times, 3
Irrational, Cult of the, 764
Irrigation Law, 45
Irrigation, Outline of a Course in, 41
Irvine, Frank, 373
Isaacs, Nathan (Book review), A 52, A 53
It Isn't Done, 340
Iwata, Shin (Translator), 123

(Numbers given are item numbers)

Jahrbuch für Soziologie, 135
Jewish Law, Study of, 245
Joint Stock Companies, Uniformity of Laws Governing, in American Republics, 77
Journal de Botanique, 716
Journal of the American Institute of Criminal Law and Criminology, 201
Journal of the American Judicature Society, 20, 56, 99, 136, 140, 240, 254
Journal of Comparative Legislation, A 53
Journal of Criminal Law and Criminology, 282
Journal of Roman Studies, 317
Journal of Social Forces, 114
Journal of the Society of Public Teachers of Law, 229
Judgments, Are They Quasi-negotiable, 5
Judicial Councils: Function and Prospects of, 240; vs. Absolutism, 241; Work of a, 243
Judicial Decision: Ideal Element in American, 180; Theory of, 113
Judicial Justice, 61
Judicial Office: in America, 167; in the United States, 70; Political Nominations for, 268; Today, 238
Judicial Organization, 92
Judicial Procedure: Defective, 426; Regulation of, by Rules of Court, 74
Judicial Statistics, What Use Can Be Made of, 191
Judicial Writings. See Table of Cases.
Jurisdiction: to Probate Will of Non-resident (Note on), 261; Visitatorial, over Corporations in Equity, 218
Jurisprudence: Analytical, 1914–1927, Progress of the Law, 154; Call for a Realist, 178; Data of Masonic, 742; Fifty Years of, 224, 229; Jurisprudence, 130, 168, 188; Landmarks [of Masonic], 743; Lectures on Masonic, 748; Masonic, Data of, 742; Masonic, Lectures on, 748; [Masonic] Landmarks, 743; Mechanical, 29; Need of a Sociological, 24; Opportunities for Developing Research in, 181; Outlines of Lectures on, 13; Outlines of Lectures on, Chiefly from the Analytical Standpoint, 13; Political and Economic Interpretations of, 63; Realist, Call for a, 178; Science or Superstition, 185; Scope and Purpose of Sociological, 43; Sociological, Need of a, 24; Sociological, Scope and Purpose of, 43; Soziologische Jurisprudenz in Amerika, 135; Taylor's Science of, 267
Juristic Problems of National Progress, 84
Juristic Science and Law, 91
Juristic Theory, Contemporary, 255
Juristic Thinking: American, in the Twentieth Century, 246; Fashions in, 228
Juristic Thought: Bibliography and Readings on Modern, 81; End of Law as Developed in, 66; How Far Are We Attaining a New Measure of Values in Twentieth-Century, 220; Property Rights and Liberty, 239; Recent, the Law of Property and, 239
Jurists, a New School of, 14
Jury: England and the United States, 189; Oral Instructions to, 272
Justice: According to Law, 60; Causes of Popular Dissatisfaction with Administration of, 20; Changing Ideal of, New Deal in the Courts, 204;

(Numbers given are item numbers)

Child Offender in the Federal System of, Report on, 428; Etiquette of, 40; Executive, 22; Fundamental Objectives of Business Management, 360; Growth of Administrative, 117; Individualization of, 173, 231; Judicial, 61; Legal, Social Justice and, 51; New Conceptions of, Being Formed, 204; New Deal in the Courts, a Changing Ideal of, 204; Preventive, and Social Work, 115; Preventive, Letter on, 355; Punitive, Inherent and Acquired Difficulties in the Administration of, 30; Social, and Legal Justice, 51

    Criminal: Improvement of, in the United States, 394; in America, 172; in Nineteenth-Century America, 146; in the American City, 106; in the American City — a Summary, 110; Justice in America, 172; Problem of, 141; What Can Law Schools Do For, 148; Why It Fails, 345

Justice of the Peace, A 52, A 53, A 54

Kansas, Bar Association of the State of. Proceedings, 42, 132, 134
Keane, V. J. (Book review), A 56
Kearney, J. J. (Book review), A 61
Keeton, W. P. (Book review), A 59
Kennedy, Walter B., A 4
Kenny, C. (Book review), A 53
Kentucky Law Journal, 170, A 54, A 56
Kentucky State Bar Association. Proceedings, 170
Key Reporter, The, 407, 409
Kidd, A. M. (Book review), A 53, A 54
King Alfred in Legal History, 10
Konvitz, M. R. (Book review), A 59
Krause, Karl Christian Friedrich. Oration, 732
Kreilkamp, K., A 21
Kuntze's, Dr., "Nomenclatur-Studien," 715

Laboulbeniaceae, Thaxter's Studies of the, 712
Lackawanna Bar Association. Publications, 142
Lambert, Jacques (Translator), 235
Land, Law of the, 151
Landmarks, 743
Laski, H. J. (Book review), A 49
Latin, Botanical, 704
Law: Address on the, 125; Anachronisms in, 99; and Equity in Federal Courts — Abolishing the Distinction and Other Reforms, 44; and Laws, 152; and Laws in the Twentieth Century, 215; and Morals, 76, 114, 123; and Order, Prospect of, 341; and Social Work, 153; and the Christian Code, 144; and the People, 37; and the Science of Law in Recent Theories, 199; Classification of, 121, 122; Classification of, Preliminary Report on, 120; Crime and the, 179; Different Systems of, Hierarchy of Sources and Forms in, 194; Dogs and the, 3; End of, as Developed in Juristic Thought, 66; End of, as Developed in Legal Rules and Doctrines, 64; End of, Twentieth-Century Ideas as to the, 209; Enforcement of, 28, 142; Enforcement of, Cooperation in, 171; Fundamental, in Society of Today, 206; Future of the, 227; Idea of, in International Relations, 250; Ideal and

(Numbers given are item numbers)

Actual in, 193; Ideal Element in, 187; Ideals of, Comparison of, 195; in Action, Law in Books and, 34; in Books and Law in Action, 34; International, Part of Philosophy in, 157; Introduction to Study of, 54; Juristic Science and, 91; Justice According to, 60; Law, 131; Legal Profession and the, 133; Making, and Finding Law, 72; Masonry in Its Relation to Morals and, 732; More about the Nature of, 216; of Nations, Codification of, 164; of Property, 239; of the Land, 151; Philosophical Theory and International, 119; Philosophy of, Do we Need a, 18; Philosophy of, in America, 59; Philosophy of, Introduction to the, 111; Pioneers and, 359; Politics, and Religion, 156; Pound Traces the, 169; Problem of the, 134; Progress of, Analytical Jurisprudence, 1914–1927, 154; Progress of, Equity, 1918–1919, 98; Rule of, 208; School of, 177; Science of, Grotius in the, 126; Science of, Judge Holmes' Contribution to, 104; Social and Economic Problems of the, 159; Sociology and, 158; Study of, Atmosphere of, 363; Study of, Introduction to, 54; Taught Law, 50; Theories of, 52; Theory of, and Legislation, Outline of Course on, 55; Unification of, 205
Law and Religion, 254a
Law Books and Publications, Report of the Special Committee to Consider and Report as to the Duplication of, 429
Law Journal, 332
Law Library Journal, 399
Law Making, Masonic, 746
Law Observances and Enforcement, Reports of the National Commission on, 428
Law of Nations, on the Codification of the, 164
Law of Priority, A Question Regarding the Application of the, 701
Law Quarterly Review, A 2, A 35, A 52, A 53, A 54
Law Review Case Notes: Contracts — Offer under Seal — Options — "Mutuality," 259; Constructive Service — Name — Error in the Initials of a Middle Name, 260; Wills — Probate — Jurisdiction to Probate Will of a Non-Resident, 261
Law School: and the Common Law, 103; and the Professional Tradition, 128; Need of Standards for, 406; School of Law, 177; Task for the University, 165; Tasks of a, Curriculum and, 376; Tasks of a National, 349; Work of the American, 116
Law Teaching, A Generation of, 244
Law Times, 28, 140, 151
Lawlessness in Law Enforcement, Report on, 428
Laws: Law and, 152; Law and, in the Twentieth Century, 215
Lawyer: Lay Idea of, 93; Lay Tradition as to, 67; Lay Tradition of, 132; Problem of, 134; Task of American, 137
Lawyers Club of New York City. Publications, 143
Lawyers Club, University of Michigan, Law School. Dedicatory Address, 128
Lawyers' Journal (Philippines), 20, 212, A 42
Lay Idea of the Lawyer, 93
Lay Tradition: as to the Lawyer, 67; of the Lawyer, 132
Learning: Higher, Place in American Life, 772; Information and, 767
Lectures on Legal Topics, 113

(Numbers given are item numbers)

Legacies on Impossible or Illegal Conditions Precedent, 26

Legal Action, Limits of Effective, 82

Legal Administration, German Movement for Reform in, 27

Legal Development, New Lines of, One Hundred Years of the Harvard Law School and, 304

Legal Doctrine and History, Contract, 183

Legal Education: Aims in Legal Education, 35; Evolution of, 12; Future of, 101; in the United States, 361; Legal Education, 9; Next Step in, 342; Present Tendencies in, 221; Some Considerations as to, and Progress of Research in the Harvard Law School, 386; What is a Good, 197

Legal Entanglement as a Division of Evil, A Note upon, 323

Legal History: American, New Possibilities of Old Materials of, 202; Church in, 247; Contract — Legal Doctrine and, 183; History and System of the Common Law, 249; History and System of the Common Law, Outline of a Course on the, 97; History and System of the Common Law, Readings on the, 17; Interpretations of, 118; King Alfred in, 10; Some Parallels from, 124

Legal Ideals, American and English, 332

Legal Institute on Modern Federal Administrative Law, 248, 251

Legal Intelligencer, 56, 211

Legal Interrogation of Persons Accused or Suspected of Crime, 201

Legal Justice, Social Justice and, 51

Legal Order, Education and, 184

Legal Periodical, Types of, 166

Legal Philosophy, Trends of Current, 211

Legal Position of Women in the United States, 322

Legal Procedure, Science and, 161

Legal Profession and the Law, 133

Legal Progress, Commerce and, 85

Legal Rights, 73

Legal Rules and Doctrines, End of Law as Developed in, 64

Legal Standards, Administrative Application of, 96

Legislation: as a Social Function, 58; Common Law and, 25; Courts and, 53; Législation dans la période de formation du droit américain, 235; Legislative Trends, Constitution in This Day and in Respect to Social and, 214; Outlines of a Course on, 207; Some Implications of Recent, 232; Theory of Law and, Outlines of a Course on, 55

Lei, Peh Hung (Translator), 54

Leiden, University of. Lecture, 119

Leonhard, Rudolph (Book review), A 46, A 47

Letter from Dean Pound, A 36

Letter of Greeting to the 1937 Class, Philippine Law School, 404

Liability, 385

Liberalism, Rejection of, 766

Liberty of Contract, 32

Liberty, Property Rights and, 239

Library of American Law and Practice, 54

Library, State, in Modern Society, 758

Lichens, The Algae, Fungi and, 699

(Numbers given are item numbers)

Limits of Effective Legal Action, 82
Literary Application of Doctrine of Accession, 267
Literary Review, A 51, A 53
Litigation, Report of the Special Committee to Suggest Remedies and For-
    mulate Proposed Laws to Prevent Delay and Unnecessary Cost, 419–423
Llewellyn, Karl N., A 11; (Book review), A 54
Lloyd, W. H. (Book review), A 53
Long, J. R. (Book review), A 57
Los Angeles Daily Journal, 171
Los Angeles Institute of Public Affairs. Lectures, 141, 146
Louisiana Law Review, 233, A 59, A 61
Louisiana State Bar Association. Report, 176
Louisiana State University Law School. Paper at Dedicatory Exercises, 233
Lowell, A. Lawrence, A 19, A 39
Lowell Institute of Boston. Lectures, 65
Lu, Ting-K'ueh (Translator), 43
Lummus, Henry T., A 18; (Book review), A 59
Lyon, Hastings (Book review), A 56

Mc Bain, H. L. (Book review), A 56
MacMahon, H. B. (Book review), A 54
McMasters, W. H. (Book review), A 56
McMurray, Orrin Kip, A 29
Maebara, Mitsuo (Translator), 123
Magna Carta, Foreword to the Pageant of, 162
Making Law and Finding Law, 72
Marquette Law Review, A 4, A 54
Maryland State Bar Association. Report, 34
Masonic Common Law I, 744; II, 745
Masonic Jurisprudence: Data of, 742; Landmarks, 743; Lectures on, 748
Masonic Lawmaking, 746
Masonic Philosophy, a Twentieth-Century, 733
Masonic Symbolism, A Preface to, 747
Masonry: Relation of, to Civilization, 733; Relation of, to Education, 735;
    Relation of, to Metaphysics and the Problem of Reality, 737; Relation of,
    to Morals and Law, 732; Relation of, to Religion, 736
Massachusetts Bankers Association. Address, 341
Massachusetts Law Quarterly, 62, 83, 140, A 30
Massachusetts, Most Worshipful Grand Lodge of Ancient Free and Accepted
    Masons. Proceedings, 732–737, 740–747
Maxims of Equity: Maxims of Equity, 105; On Certain, 145
Meaning of Tree Life, Comment on, 714
Mechanical Jurisprudence, 29
Mechem, F. R. (Book review), A 52
Medical Times *and* Long Island Medical Journal, 179
Men and Rules, 190
Menorah Journal, 245
Metaphysics and the Problem of Reality, Masonry in Its Relation to, 737
Michigan Law Review, 33, 67, 78, 128, 244, A 28, A 51–A 54

(Numbers given are item numbers)

Michigan, University of: Address, 754; Law School. Dedicatory Exercises, 215; Lawyers' Club Dedication Papers, 128

Middlesex (Mass.), Bar Association of County of. Publications, 67

Mining Law, Outline of a Course on, 46

Minnesota Botanical Studies, 711, 720, 722

Minnesota Geological and Natural History Survey. Bulletin, 711, 720, 722

Minnesota Law Review, A 55, A 57

Minnesota State Bar Association. Proceedings, 56

Missouri Bar Association. Proceedings, 51, 155

Missouri, University of, Bulletin, 152

Modern Administrative Law, 251

Modern Juristic Thought and Its Significance for America, Bibliography and Readings on, 81

Modern Law, Feudal Principle in, 68

Modern Life, Social Order and, 762

Modern Society, The State Library in, 758

Moley, R. (Book review), A 56

Montague, G. H. (Book review), A 53

Morals: and Law, Masonry in Its Relation to, 732; Law and, 76, 114, 123

Morse, C. (Book review), A 54

Morse, W. L. (Book review), A 56

Mucoraceae: and Entomophthoraceae of Nebraska, the Synchytria, 713; a Revision of the, with Especial Reference to Species Reported from North America, 711

Mutualism, Symbiosis and, 708

Names, Generic and Specific, Too Nearly Alike, 702

National Advisory Council on Radio in Education, Inc. Lecture, 192, 210

National Civic Federation, New York City, 311

National Civic Federation, Women's Department, Massachusetts Section, 333

National Commission on Law Observance and Enforcement, Reports of, 428

National Conference of Bar Examiners. Address, 213

National Conference of Charities and Correction, 49

National Conference of Judicial Councils. Address, 205, 240

National Conference of Social Work. Proceedings, 115, 175, 753

National Conference on Criminal Law and Criminology. Proceedings, 281

National Consumers League, New York City. Letter, 350

National Economic League of Boston. Publications, 424

National Law Library. Volume 1, 415

National Popular Government League, Washington, D. C. Publications, 427

National Probation Association. Official Bulletin, 355; Yearbook, 173

Nation's Business, 411

Nature of Law, More about the, 216

Nebraska Academy of Sciences, 726

Nebraska, Grand Lodge of Ancient Free and Accepted Masons. Proceedings, 732, 733

Nebraska Law Bulletin, 160, 221, 225

Nebraska Legal News, 1, 4, 6–10

Nebraska State Bar Association. Proceedings, 11, 19, 40, 89, 160, 225

(Numbers given are item numbers)

Nebraska State Journal, 752
Nebraska, University of, Botanical Seminar, 708, 715; Law School, 12, 14
Neumann, Franz L. (Book review), A 61
New Age Magazine, 750
New Deal in the Courts: a Changing Ideal of Justice, 204
New Demands on Law Teachers and New Demands upon Law Schools, 372
New Feudal System, 170
New Feudalism, 170
New Hampshire, Bar Association of the State of. Proceedings, 89
New Jersey State Bar Association. Yearbook, 76
New Republic, 425, 426, A 27, A 51, A 56
New School of Jurists, 14
New York County Lawyers' Association. Yearbook, 129, 344
New York, Grand Lodge of Free and Accepted Masons. Proceedings, 751
New York Herald-Tribune, 384
New York Law Journal, 193
New York Law Review, A 36
New York Masonic Outlook, 749
New York State Bar Association. Bulletin, 169, 378, 392
New York Times, 204, 336, 345, 350, 377, A 54, A 56, A 60
New York University Law Quarterly Review, A 7, A 59
New Zealand Law Journal, 412
Newark Evening News, 410
Nineteenth-Century America, Criminal Justice in, 146
Nomenclatur-Studien, Dr. Kuntze's, 715
Nomenclature, Some Recent Papers on, 719
Nomiyama, On (Translator), 119
Non-Christian Candidates, 741
North Carolina Bar Association. Proceedings, 100
North Carolina, University of. John Calvin McNair Lectures, 1923, 123
North Dakota Bar Association. Proceedings, 29
Northwestern University: Honors Convocation Address, 765; Publications, 765
Notre Dame Lawyer, A 61

Oberlin Alumni Magazine, 761
Oberlin College. Commencement Address, 761
Officer, Every Man an, 407
O'Grady, D. C. (Book review), A 61
Ohio Commission to Investigate the Causes of Delay and Expense in the Administration of Justice in Civil and Criminal Actions in the Courts of Ohio (1914), 74
Ohio Law Bulletin, 72, 82
Ohio Law Reporter, 72
Ohio State Bar Association. Proceedings, 72
Oil Problem, Some Constitutional Aspects of the, 217
Oklahoma State Bar Association. Proceedings, 133, 340
Oliver, 736
Omaha Sunday World-Herald, 359

(Numbers given are item numbers)

Onandaga Lawyers Hear Dean Pound Talk, 392

One Hundred Years of the Harvard Law School and New Lines of Legal Development, 304

Only One Earth and All of Us Want It, 333

Order, Prospect of Law and, 341

Ordered Society, Problem of an, 186

Oregon Law Review, 162, 191, A 56

O'Reilly, J. D., Jr. (Book review), A 59, A 61

Organization: Judicial, 92; Modern, and an Old Profession, 222; of Courts, 56, 256, 425; of Courts, a Bibliography of Procedural Reform, 83; Reform in the Court, 94

Organized Education Ousting Organized Religion, 760

Osawa, Sho (Translator), 119

Our Lady, the Common Law, 86

Our Thucydides, 738

Our Times before the Tribunal of History, 769

Outlines: Code Pleading, Outline and Practical Exercises, 16; History and System of the Common Law, Outline of a Course, 97; Law of Irrigation, Outline of a Course, 41; Lectures on Jurisprudence, 13; Lectures on Jurisprudence Chiefly from the Analytical Standpoint, 13; Legislation, Outlines of a Course on, 207; Mining Law, Outline of a Course on, 46; Theory of Law and Legislation, Outline of a Course on, 55

Outlook, A 56

Page, W. H. (Book review), A 52

Pan-American Financial Conference, Report to, 77

Panel, The, 201

Parasites of the Human Ear, Addition to the, 729

Parker, J. J. (Book review), A 56

Parole, Report on Penal Institutions, Probation and, 428

Pasadena, Address at, 171

Patterson, E. W. (Book review), A 51

Penal Institutions, Probation and Parole, Report on, 428

Penal Statutes, Action on, 2

Pennsylvania Bar Association. Report, 82

Pennsylvania, University of, Law Review, A 53, A 54

People, The Law and the, 37

Periodical, Types of Legal, 166

Perkins, R. M. (Book review), A 56

Personal Government, Revival of, 89

Personality: Equitable Protection of, and of Social and Political Relations, Cases on, 75; Equitable Relief against Defamation and Injuries to, 80; Equitable Relief against Defamation and Injuries to, Cases on, 75; Interests of, 71

Phi Beta Kappa, 377, 407, 409

Phi Delta Phi, 83, 237

Philadelphia, Law Academy of. Address, 211

Philadelphia, Law Association of. Publications, 56

Philippine Law School. Letter of Greeting to the 1937 Class, 404

(Numbers given are item numbers)

Phillips Brooks House Association, Harvard University. Lectures, 156

Philosophy: Part of, in International Law, 157; Philosophical Theory and International Law, 119

Philosophy of Freemasonry: Lectures on the, 739; Twentieth-Century Masonic, 733

Philosophy of Law: Do We Need a, 18; Filosofia nel Diritto Costituzionale Americano, 109; in America, 59; Introduction to the, 111; Trends of Current Legal, 211

Phytogeography of Nebraska, I, 725

Pike, 737

Pioneers: and Law, 359; and the Common Law, 100

Pittsburgh Legal Journal, 201, 203, 204, 238

Pittsburgh Monthly Bulletin, A 56

Pittsburgh, University of: Bulletin, 759; Commencement Address, 759

Plant-Geography of Germany, 718

Pleading: Code, Outline and Practical Exercises in, 16; Rules Relating to, Vesting in Courts Power to Make, 79

Police, Report on, 428

Political and Economic Interpretations of Jurisprudence, 63

Political Genius, Must Again Exert, 757

Political Nominations for Judicial Office, 268

Political Relations, Social and, Cases on Equitable Protection of, 75

Political Science Quarterly, 274, 276

Politics, and Religion, Law, 156

Pollak, Walter, A 8

Pollock, Frederick, A 2, A 35; (Book review), A 53, A 54

Poor Man Has Not Equal Chance with Rich Man in Our Courts of Law, 325

Population, Culture and, 759

Portland Evening News, 763

Portrait of Dean Ezra Ripley Thayer. Address of Acceptance, 303

Portrait of James Brown Scott, Esq. Address of Acceptance, 371

Portrait of Mr. Justice Oliver Wendell Holmes. Address of Acceptance, 365

Powell, T. R., A 51

Practice: Pleading and, Vesting in the Courts the Power to Make Rules Relating to, 79; Reform, Principles of, 38; Remarks on Report of Special Section on Reformation of Practice, 88

Practitioners, Better, Needed, 378

Preliminary Report: on Classification of the Law, 120; on Efficiency in the Administration of Justice, 424

Preston, William, 735

Preventive Justice: and Social Work, 115; Letter on, 355

Priority, Law of, Question Regarding Application of, 701

Private Law, Public Law and, 237

Probate, Note on, 261

Probation, 355

Probation and Parole, Report on Penal Institutions, 428

Problem: of an Ordered Society, 186, 763; of Reality, Masonry in Its Relation to, 737; of the Law, 134; of the Lawyer, 134

(Numbers given are item numbers)

Problems: Social and Economic, of the Law, 159

Procedure: Civil, The Revision of the Code of, in Kansas, 270; Criminal, Needed Reforms in, 210; Criminal, Practical Advantages of Rules of Court for, 242; Details, Regulating by Rules of Court, 149; in Common Law, 87; Judicial, Defective, 426; Judicial, Regulation by Rules of Court, 74; Legal, Science and, 161; New Technicalities and Old Principles, 266
    Reform: Bibliography of, 83; by Rules of Court, 292; Canons of, 139; Cardinal Principles to be Observed in, 48; Legal Administration and, German Movement for, 27; Letter on, 282; Practical Program of, 36, 39; Proposals of the Judges for, 269; Roscoe Pound on, 282; Some Principles of, 35

Profession, Modern Organization and an Old, 222

Professional Ethics, Proposed Codification by the American Bar Association, 258

Professional Tradition, Law School and the, 128

Progress: Commerce and Legal, 85; Juristic Problems of National, 84

Progress of the Law: Analytical Jurisprudence, 1914–1927, 154; Equity, 1918–1919, 98

Progress of Research in the Harvard Law School, Some Considerations as to Legal Education and, 381, 386

Prohibition Laws of the United States, Progress Report on, 428

Property Rights and Liberty; the Law of Property and Recent Juristic Thought, 239

Prosecution, On, 428

Public Law and Private Law, 237

Public Opinion and Social Control, 175

Punitive Justice, Inherent and Acquired Difficulties in the Administration of, 30

Puritanism and the Common Law, 42

Radin, Max (Book review), A 51, A 52, A 54

Readings: in Jurisprudence, 108, 122, 154, 180, 194; in Roman Law, 21; on the History and System of the Common Law, 17

Realist Jurisprudence, Call for a, 178

Reason, Abdication of, 761

Recent Developments in the Law of Equity of Interest to Practicing Lawyers, 198

Recent Theories, Law and the Science of Law in, 199

Recrudescence of Absolutism, 236

Reform: Court Organization, 94; Criminal Procedure, Needed Reforms in, 210; Law and Equity in Federal Courts, 44; Practice, Principles of, 38
    Procedure: Bibliography of, 83; by Rules of Court, 292; Canons of, 139; Cardinal Principles to be Observed in, 48; German Movement for, in Legal Administration and Procedure, 27; Legal Administration and, 27; Letter on, 282; Practical Program of, 36, 39; Proposals of the Judges for, 269; Roscoe Pound on, 282; Some Principles of, 35

Reformation of Practice, Remarks on Report of Special Section on, 88

Regulation of Judicial Procedure by Rules of Court, 74

Rejection of Liberalism, 766

(Numbers given are item numbers)

Religion: Law and, 254a; Law, Politics, and, 156; Masonry in Its Relation to, 736; Organized Education Ousting Organized, 760

Repeal: Driving the Country to, 382; of the Eighteenth Amendment, 387

Reports: of the National Commission on Law Observance and Enforcement, 428; of the Special Committee on Administrative Law, 430; of the Special Committee to Consider and Report as to the Duplication of Law Books and Publications, 429; of the Special Committee to Suggest Remedies and Formulate Proposed Laws to Prevent Delay and Unnecessary Cost in Litigation, 419–423; on Crime and the Foreign Born, 428; on Criminal Procedure, 428; on Criminal Statistics, 428; on Lawlessness in Law Enforcement, 428; on Penal Institutions, Probation and Parole, 428; on Police, 428; on Prosecution, 428; on the Causes of Crime, 428; on the Child Offender in the Federal System of Justice, 428; on the Cost of Crime, 428; on the Enforcement of Prohibition Laws of the United States, 428; on the Enforcement of the Deportation Laws of the United States, 428; Preliminary Report on Efficiency in the Administration of Justice, 424; Progress, on the Study of the Federal Courts, 428; upon the Illegal Practices of the United States Department of Justice, 427

Reporters, Something about, 7

Research: Graduate Instruction and, 353; in the Field of Jurisprudence, The Opportunities for Developing, 181; Progress of, in the Harvard Law School, 381

Response by Professor Pound, 295

Reuschlein, Harold G., A 15

Review of Reviews *and* World's Work, 382, A 51

Revista Juridica de la Universidad de Puerto Rico, 43

Revival of Absolutism, 410

Revival of Comparative Law, 176

Revival of Personal Government, 89

Revue de Droit Pénal et de Criminologie, 141

Rheinische Zeitschrift für Zivil- und Prozess-Recht, 35

Rhode Island Bar Association. Report, 67

Rice Institute. Commencement Address, 768

Rice Institute Pamphlet, 254a, 768

Rights, Legal, 73

Ritchey, C. J. (Book review), A 54

Ritual, Causes of Divergence in, 740

Rivista Internazionale di Filosofia del Diritto, 109

Roberts, W. L. (Book review), A 54

Robinson, J. J. (Book review), A 56

Rogers, J. G. (Book review), A 58

Rohrlich, Chester (Book review), A 60

Roman Law: Readings in, 21; Study of, 4

Rule of Law, 208

Rule of *Stare Decisis*, Conference on the Status of the, Survey of, 253

Rule-Making Power: of the Courts, 140; on the Law Side of Federal Practice, Senator Walsh on, 348; Rules Relating to Pleading and Practice, Vesting in the Courts the Power to Make, 79

Rules: Legal, and Doctrines, End of Law as Developed in, 64; Men and,

(Numbers given are item numbers)

190; Relating to Pleading and Practice, Vesting in the Courts the Power to Make, 79

Rules of Court: for Criminal Procedure, Practical Advantages of, 242; Reforming Procedure by, 292; Regulating Procedural Details by, 149; Regulation of Judicial Procedure by, 74

Russell, Colton (Book review), A 45

Saint John the Evangelist, On the Feast of, 734

St. John's Law Review, A 56

St. Louis Law Review, 755

St. Louis Magazine, A 56

Salander (Book review), A 54

Sand, Ada (Translator), 141

Saturday Review, A 51, A 53

Sayre, P. L. (Book review), A 55, A 56

School and Society, 754, 756, 761, 772

School of Law, 177

Schutzner, Dr. Joseph, A 6; (Translator), 130

Science and Legal Procedure, 161

Science of Jurisprudence, Taylor's, 267

Science of Law: Grotius in the, 126; in Recent Theories, Law and the, 199; Judge Holmes' Contributions to the, 104

Science or Superstition, Jurisprudence, 185

Scott, Austin W., 425, 426

Secondary Species, a Method of Determining the Abundance of, 722

Selected Essays on Constitutional Law, 32, 60, 96, 170

Selected Essays on Torts, 71, 334

Sesquicentennial of the [Virginia] Bill of Rights, 138

Sewanee Review, 236

Shattuck, Judge Charles E., Remarks on, 308

Smith, Jeremiah, 90

Smith, S. (Book review), A 57

Social and Economic Problems of the Law, 159

Social and Legislative Trends, Constitution in This Day and in Respect to, 214

Social and Political Relations, Cases on Equitable Protection of Personality and, 75

Social Control, Public Opinion and, 175

Social Function, Legislation as a, 58

Social Interests, Theory of, 108

Social Justice and Legal Justice, 51

Social Order and Modern Life, 762

Social Problems and the Courts, 49

Social Work: Law and, 153; Preventive Justice and, 115

Socialization of the Common Law, 65

Society: and the Individual, 753; of Today, Fundamental Law in, 206; Problem of an Ordered, 763; "Relational," End of Individual and Development of, 377; State Library in Modern, 758

Society of Medical Jurisprudence. Publications, 179

Society of Public Teachers of Law. Paper, 229

(Numbers given are item numbers)

Sociological Jurisprudence: Need of a, 24; Scope and Purpose of, 43; Soziologische Jurisprudenz in Amerika, 135
Sociology and Law, 158
Solicitors' Journal, A 52
South African Law Journal, A 8
South Carolina Bar Association. Transactions, 61
South Dakota Bar Association. Report, 155
South Dakota Bar Journal, A 41
Special Libraries, 758
Spectator, A 53
Speech (before the Iowa State Bar Association), 380
Spirit of the Common Law, 19, 107
Springfield Republican, A 51, A 54
Standards: Administrative Application of Legal, 96; for Law Schools, Need of, 406
Stare Decisis, Rule of, 253
State Bar Journal (California), 149, 205, 362
State Library in Modern Society, 758
Statement on United States Court of Appeals for Administration, 405
Statistics, Judicial, What Use Can Be Made of, 191
Stone, Julius, A 17
Stone, Mr. Justice, Remarks at Dinner to, 344
Story, Joseph, 391; Story, Judge, Place in the Making of American Law, 62
Study of Federal Courts, Progress Report on, 428
Study of Law: Atmosphere of, 363; Introduction to, 54
Summons, The, 171, 766
Superstition, Jurisprudence: Science or, 185
Supreme Court or Supreme Congress, 362
Survey, 106, A 56
Swan, T. W. (Book review), A 51
Symbiosis and Mutualism, 708
Symbolism, Preface to Masonic, 747
Synchytria, the Mucoraceae and Entomophthoraceae of Nebraska, 713
Systems of Law: Hierarchy of Sources and Forms in Different, 194

Takayanagi, Kenzo, A 5; (Translator), 118, 123, 227
Task: for the University Law School, 165; of Education, 770; of the American Lawyer, 137
Tasks: of a Law School, 376; of a National Law School, 349
Taught Law, 50
Taylor's Science of Jurisprudence, 267
Teacher Oath, Pound Scores, 771
Tennessee Bar Association. Proceedings, 53
Tennessee Law Review, 151, 186, 206, 210, A 59
Texas Bar Association. Proceedings, 92–94
Texas Bar Journal, 241, A 43
Texas Law Review, 243, A 53, A 59
Thaxter's Studies of the Laboulbeniaceae, 712
Thayer, Ezra Ripley: Address of Acceptance of Portrait of, 303; Ezra Ripley Thayer, 300; Remarks on, 302

(Numbers given are item numbers)
Thayer, Professor, on the Law of Evidence, 8
Theories of Law, 52
Theory: of Judicial Decision, 113; of Law and Legislation, Outline of a
    Course on, 55; of Social Interests, 108; Philosophical, and International
    Law, 119
Thilly, F. (Book review), A 53
Thinking, Fashions in, 773
Thucydides, Our, 738
Times [London] Literary Supplement, The, A 53
Tokyo Imperial University. Publications, 227
Toronto, University of, Law Journal, A 59
Torts: A Selection of Cases on the Law of, 90; Law of, Economic Interpre-
    tation and, 252
Tradition: Lay, as to the Lawyer, 67; Lay, of Lawyer, 132; Professional,
    Law School and, 128
Training for the Bar, 192
Training for the Bar in the United States, 412
Translations by Pound:
    Laws of France, 1919, Town Planning and Reparation of Damages
        Caused by Events of World War, 311
    Number of Plants, 709
Translations of Pound's Works:
    Chinese:
        Interpretations of Legal History (Fa-lü shih kuan), 118
        Introduction to Study of Law (Fa hsüeh i-yen), 54
        Jurisprudence (Fa hsüeh shih), 168
        Scope and Purpose of Sociological Jurisprudence (She-hui fa di-
            hsüeh lun lüch), 43
    Czechoslovakian:
        Jurisprudence (Právní Věda Našeho Času Ve Svých Význačných
            Rysech A Problémech), 130, A 6
    French:
        Hierarchy of Sources and Forms in Different Systems of Law
            (Rapport Général de M. Roscoe Pound), 194
        Influence of French Law in America (Étude sur l'Influence du
            Droit Français en Amérique), 31
        Problem of Criminal Justice (Le Problème de la Justice Criminelle),
            141
        The Vienna Propositions (Les Propositions Viennoises de Nomen-
            clature), 716
    German:
        Some Principles of Procedural Reform (Grundsätze der Prozess-
            reform), 35
        The Vienna Propositions (Die Wiener Nomen-clatur Vorschläge),
            716
    Japanese:
        Future of Law (Hô no Shirai), 227
        Interpretations of Legal History (Hôritsu shi kan), 118
        Law and Morals (Hô to dôtoku), 123
        Law and Morals (Hôritsu to dôtoku), 123

(Numbers given are item numbers)

Philosophical Theory and International Law (Tetsugaku-teki riron to kokusai hô), 119

Spirit of the Common Law (Ei-Bei hô no seishin), 107

Spanish:

Scope and Purpose of Sociological Jurisprudence (La Extension y Propósito de la Escuela Sociológica de Jurisprudencia), 43

Uniformity of Commercial Law on the American Continent (Uniformidad de las Leyes en Todo el Continente Americano), 33

Tree Life, Meaning of, 714

Trial Judge, American Attitude toward, 155

Tribunal of History, Our Times before, 769

Trusts and Estates, 239

Tufts, J. H. (Book review), A 53

Tulane Law Review, 176, 194, 200, A 18, A 59, A 61

Tulane University, Law School of. Edward Livingston Centennial Lectures, 234

Twentieth Century: American Juristic Thinking in, 246; Ideas as to the End of Law, 209; Juristic Thought, How Far Are We Attaining a New Measure of Values in, 220; Law and Laws in the, 215; Masonic Philosophy, 733

Umbreit, K. B. (Book review), A 59

Unification: of Law, 205; through the Common Law, 205

Uniformity of Commercial Law on American Continent, 33

Uniformity of Laws Governing the Establishment and Regulation of Corporations and Joint Stock Companies in the American Republics, Report upon, 77

United Air Lines Transport Corporation Hearing, 697

United States: Court of Appeals for Administration, Statement on, 405; Department of Justice, Report upon the Illegal Practices of the, 427; Improvement of Criminal Justice in, 394; Judicial Office in, 70; Legal Education in, 361; Legal Position of Women in the, 322; Training for the Bar in the, 412

United States Federation of Justice. Address, 231

United States Investor, 232

United States Law Review, 20, 203

University: and Civilization, 755; Law School, Task for the, 165; Place of the, in Training for Citizenship, 754; Prospects of the American, 756

University Record (Florida), 770

University Studies (Nebraska), 14

Updegraff, C. M. (Book review), A 57

Utah, State Bar Association of. Proceedings, 151

Valery, Jules (Translator), 31

Values in Twentieth-Century Juristic Thought, How Far Are We Attaining a New Measure of, 220

Vegetation Regions of the Prairie Province, 723

Vermont Bar Association. Report, 129

Vienna Propositions, 716

(Numbers given are item numbers)

Villaluz, Sisenando, A 42
Vinogradoff, Paul, A 53
Virginia Bill of Rights, Sesquicentennial of, 138
Virginia Law Review, A 51–A 54, A 56, A 59
Virginia State Bar Association. Proceedings, 167, 248, 251
Visitatorial Jurisdiction over Corporations in Equity, 218
Visseriana, Bibliotheca, Dissertationvm Ivs Internationale Illvstrantivm, 119
Vital Speeches of the Day, 232, 409

Waite, J. B. (Book review), A 56
Walsh, Senator, on Rule-making Power on Law Side of Federal Practice, 348
Warren, Edward H. (Book review), A 48
Washington University. Commencement Address, 755
Washington University Law Quarterly, A 59
Washington's Birthday Memorial, 364
Wellesley Alumnae Magazine, 764
Wellesley College. Commencement Address, 764
West Virginia Bar Association. Proceedings, 76
West Virginia Law Quarterly *and* The Bar, 100, 116, 202, 220, 232, A 51, A 52
Western New York, Federation of Bar Associations of. Report, 214
What Came We Here to Know, 749
Wheat, Price of, 752
Wheaton College, Norton, Mass. Address, 760
Why Absolute Government Fails, 411
Wig and Gown, 6
Wilde, Norman (Book review), A 54
Williams, T. (Book review), A 59
Wills, Note on, 261
Wilson, L. P. (Book review), A 51
Wisconsin Law Review, 117
Wisconsin State Bar Association. Proceedings, 117
Women: the United States, Legal Position of, 322
Worcester County (Mass.) Bar Association. Publications, 70
World Today, The, 387, 394
World Tomorrow, A 56
Wu, John C. H., A 3

Yale Law Journal, 32, 52, 199, 227, 354, A 16, A 51, A 52, A 54, A 55
Yale Review, A 51
Yale University. William L. Storrs Lecture Series, 111
Yamaguchi, Takazo (Translator), 107
Yntema, H. E. (Book review), A 53

Zeitschrift für Völkerpsychologie und Soziologie, A 54